THE
MAKING
OF A
DREAM

THE
MAKING
OF A
DREAM

════════

*How a Group of Young Undocumented
Immigrants Helped Change What It
Means to Be American*

════════

LAURA WIDES-MUÑOZ

HARPER

An Imprint of HarperCollinsPublishers

HarperCollins books may be purchased for educational, business, or sales promotional use. For information, please email the Special Markets Department at SPsales@harpercollins.com.

All photographs courtesy of the author unless otherwise noted.

FIRST EDITION

Library of Congress Cataloging-in-Publication Data has been applied for.

ISBN 978-0-06-256012-4

18 19 20 21 22   LSC   10 9 8 7 6 5 4 3 2 1

FOR JOAQUIN AND CIBELLE

CONTENTS

CAST OF CHARACTERS

The following is a list of the significant players in this book. It is in no way meant as an exhaustive list of all those who have contributed to the immigration reform effort in the United States, nor even all those who are leading the undocumented immigrant youth movement.

MAIN CHARACTERS

HARETH ANDRADE-AYALA, came to the United States from Bolivia at age eight in 2001.

BETTY AYALA, Hareth's mother.

MARIO ANDRADE, Hareth's father, husband of Betty Ayala.

ELIANA ANDRADE, Hareth's aunt and Mario Andrade's sister.

HAZIEL ANDRADE-AYALA, Mario and Betty's second daughter, came to United States with Hareth at three.

CLAUDIA ANDRADE-AYALA, Mario and Betty's youngest daughter, the only one born in the United States.

DARIO GUERRERO MENESES, came to the United States from Mexico with his parents at age two in 1995.

DARIO GUERRERO SR., Dario's father.

ROCIO MENESES, Dario's mother and wife of Dario Guerrero Sr.

FERNANDO GUERRERO MENESES, Dario's younger brother, born in the United States.

ANDREA GUERRERO MENESES, Dario's younger sister, born in the United States and the baby of the family.

ALEX C. BOOTA, Dario's freshman roommate.

FELIPE SOUSA-RODRIGUEZ (FELIPE MATOS SOUSA), came to the United States from Brazil at age fourteen in 2001.

ISABEL SOUSA-RODRIGUEZ, Felipe's spouse, came to the United States from Colombia at age six.

FRANCISCA SOUSA MATOS, Felipe's mother.

CAROLINA SOUSA, Felipe's older sister.*

JUAN RODRIGUEZ SR., Isabel's father.

MARIE (GONZALEZ) DEEL, came to the United States from Costa Rica at age five with her parents in 1991.

MARINA MORALES MORENO, Marie's mother.

MARVIN GONZALEZ, Marie's father, married to Marina Morales Moreno.

CHAPIN DEEL, Marie's husband.

ARACELI DEEL, Marie's first daughter.

LORENA DEEL, Marie's youngest daughter.

"ALEX" ALDANA, came to the United States from Mexico with his family at age sixteen in 2003.

LAURA MORALES, Alex's mother.

CARLOS ALDANA, Alex's older brother.

YOUNG IMMIGRANT LEADERS

MOHAMMAD ABDOLLAHI, early member of United We Dream, split off to found the National Immigrant Youth Alliance, also with Dream Activist.

ERIKA ANDIOLA, Our Revolution political director, worked on Senator Bernie Sanders's presidential campaign and for United We Dream, Arizona activist.

WALTER BARRIENTOS, lead organizer at Make the Road New York and political director for MTRNY Action Fund, early United We Dream leader.

---

* Name changed to protect her privacy.

JULIETA GARIBAY, founding member and United We Dream Texas director.

JU HONG, former Los Angeles–based leader of the National Asian American and Pacific Islander DACA Collaborative.

GREISA MARTINEZ, advocacy director for United We Dream, based in Washington, DC.

CRISTINA JIMÉNEZ MORETA, cofounder, executive director of United We Dream.

MARIA GABRIELA "GABY" PACHECO, program director at thedream .us, former political director for United We Dream. She walked the "Trail of Dreams" from Miami to Washington with Felipe, based in Miami.

CARLOS A. ROA JR., immigrant youth activist turned aspiring Chicago architect, also walked the "Trail of Dreams."

CARLOS SAAVEDRA, cofounder of United We Dream, Boston activist, went on to work at the immigrant rights group Movimiento Cosecha.

ASTRID SILVA, cofounder of Nevada-based immigrant advocacy group DREAM Big Vegas, spoke in prime time at Democratic National Convention in 2016.

TANIA UNZUETA, legal and policy director for Mijente, Chicago-based early immigrant youth leader.

KEY LAWMAKERS

Senate

RICHARD "DICK" DURBIN, D-Illinois

WILLIAM "BILL" FRIST, R-Tennessee (Senate Majority Leader, 2003– 2007)

LINDSEY GRAHAM, R-South Carolina

ORRIN HATCH, R-Utah

EDWARD "TED" KENNEDY, D-Massachusetts

JOHN McCAIN, R-Arizona

HARRY REID, D-Nevada, (Senate Majority Leader, 2007–2015)

JEFF SESSIONS, R-Alabama (current Attorney General of the United States)

House
HOWARD BERMAN, D-California
JOHN BOEHNER, R-Ohio (Speaker of the House, 2011–2015)
CHRIS CANNON, R-Utah
LINCOLN DÍAZ-BALART, R-Florida
MARIO DÍAZ-BALART, R-Florida, younger brother of Lincoln
LUIS GUTIÉRREZ, D-Illinois
JAMES "JIM" KOLBE, R-Arizona
NANCY PELOSI, D-California (Speaker of the House, 2007–2011)
ILEANA ROS-LEHTINEN, R-Florida

ORGANIZATIONS

AMERICAN FEDERATION OF LABOR AND CONGRESS OF INDUSTRIAL ORGANIZATIONS, AFL-CIO, nation's largest labor union, with more than 12 million members.

AMERICANS FOR IMMIGRANT JUSTICE (FLORIDA IMMIGRANT ADVOCACY CENTER, FIAC), immigrant advocacy, litigation, and legal service organization.

AMERICA'S VOICE, unofficial communications arm of the immigrant rights and reform movement.

CENTER FOR COMMUNITY CHANGE, CCC, founded in 1968 to carry on the legacy of Robert F. Kennedy and to develop community organization and change.

COALITION FOR HUMANE IMMIGRANT RIGHTS, CHIRLA, California-based immigrant advocacy group.

DREAMACTIVIST, originally an online site to connect immigrant youth, later served as a springboard for anti-deportation and other activist campaigns.

FLORIDA IMMIGRANT COALITION, FLIC, statewide alliance of more than sixty-five immigrant advocacy groups, created by Florida Immigrant Advocacy Center.

MAKE THE ROAD NEW YORK, seeks to strengthen Latino and working-class communities through organizing and policy innovation, education, and survival services.

MIJENTE, a national "Latinx" and "Chicanx" civil rights group founded in 2015 that focuses on issues facing low-income communities, including, but not limited to, immigration.

MINUTEMAN PROJECT, founded in 2004, sought to independently monitor the border in response to what it viewed as lack of action by the Department of Homeland Security.

MOVIEMIENTO COSECHA, decentralized immigrant rights group founded in 2015, focused on peaceful, "non-cooperation" techniques like work-stoppages to highlight national reliance on immigrant labor.

NATIONAL IMMIGRATION FORUM, national immigration policy group that in recent years has focused on reaching out to business, law enforcement, and religious groups.

NATIONAL IMMIGRATION LAW CENTER, NILC, defends the rights of immigrants with low incomes.

NATIONAL YOUTH IMMIGRANT ALLIANCE, NIYA, immigrant youth-led organization that splintered off from United We Dream and reached its peak in 2012–2013 with mass actions at the border.

SERVICE EMPLOYEES INTERNATIONAL UNION, SEIU, represents some 2 million service workers.

STUDENTS WORKING FOR EQUAL RIGHTS, SWER, Florida immigrant youth-led social justice group supported by FLIC.

UNIDOSUS (NATIONAL COUNCIL OF LA RAZA, NCLR), one of the largest Latino advocacy groups in the United States.

UNITED WE DREAM, UWD, largest immigrant youth-led network in the nation, with affiliates in twenty-six states.

ADVOCATES

JOSH BERNSTEIN, attorney for SEIU, formerly NILC.

DEEPAK BHARGAVA, head of the CCC.

IRA KURZBAN, Miami immigration attorney, authored one of the nation's top immigration law sourcebooks.

CHERYL LITTLE, founded Americans for Immigrant Justice, formerly FIAC.

JOSE LUIS MARANTES, worked at FLIC, the CCC, and UWD, early mentor to Felipe.

CECILIA MUÑOZ, NCLR policy advocate, later served as adviser to former president Barack Obama.

ALI NOORANI, head of the National Immigration Forum.

ESTHER OLAVARRIA, worked at FIAC, later served as legislative aide to Senator Ted Kennedy and as policy adviser for DHS.

MARIA RODRIGUEZ, head of FLIC.

ANGELICA SALAS, head of CHIRLA.

FRANK SHARRY, head of America's Voice, previously led the National Immigration Forum.

AUTHOR'S NOTE

I spent nearly a decade interviewing some of the main characters in this book, particularly Felipe and Isabel Sousa-Rodriguez. I spent the last five years regularly interviewing most of the others, fact-checking all of their accounts with those who know them, and with available public and private records and recordings, as well as speaking to dozens more sources named and unnamed. Any direct and unsourced quotes in this book come from these interviews. In some cases, I've used italics to depict the main characters' thoughts or to depict dialogue when I was unable to confirm the exact language with a primary or secondary source. All secondary sources, including the articles I wrote for the Associated Press, are attributed.

THE
MAKING
OF A
DREAM

1

IN THE BEGINNING

Sign posted during an undocumented "coming out" event at Harvard University, Cambridge, Massachusetts, April 2013.

I t would only be a few weeks.

That's what Hareth Andrade-Ayala's parents told her when they planned the trip to Washington, DC. Eight-year-old Hareth and her little sister would travel from La Paz, Bolivia, with their grandmother and grandfather. Their parents would join the girls later.

Hareth's grandparents had lived with the family as long as she could remember, always game for her bits of theater, jokes, and dances, all the stuff her parents were too tired to sit through. She'd traveled to visit relatives with them before. This would be another one of those adventures.

The night before they left, Hareth's mother tucked her elder daughter's favorite books into the suitcase. Betty Ayala had bought the books on layaway with money from her accountant work at city hall. One book was filled with jokes, another with tongue twisters. The last book was titled *Why Is This So?*

Betty paused on that one. "*¿Por qué es así?*" was one of Hareth's favorite phrases. Already it was tough for Betty to answer all her daughter's questions. Her own mind twirled around the biggest "whys": Why leave? Why risk everything?

Hareth's father, Mario Andrade, had a few classes left before he finished his architecture degree at the university and was already helping build a multiple-story commercial building in La Paz. Betty, who had left her job at the municipality after Hareth's younger sister Haziel was born, kept the books for Mario's projects. Compared with many in Bolivia, they were doing okay.

At first the idea really was just a vacation. Mario's parents regularly visited his sister, Eliana, who'd moved to the United States in 1994, had obtained citizenship, and now lived in Maryland. They could take the girls with them this time, let Hareth and Haziel practice their English. Mario and Betty applied for their daughters' visas. The request was easily granted.

But even then, Betty was forming a backup plan. Famous for its jagged Andes and Quechua people in bowler hats and flounced skirts, Bolivia also held the distinction of being South America's poorest country. Social unrest had been creeping like a stubborn vine across the mountains in recent years, and now it was spreading its tendrils from the remote hills down to the streets.

The government's efforts to eradicate coca farming in the late 1980s and 1990s, with help from the US government, had left thousands of small farmers desperate and without any alternative sources of income. Then came the water wars. In 2000, mass protests swept Cochabamba, the nation's third largest city, after the government gave a private international consortium control of its water service.[1] Bolivians were outraged that a foreign company had come to control what they viewed as a basic public good. When price hikes quickly followed,[2] it was too much. The protests multiplied and the unrest spread,[3] leading to food shortages in other cities.

By the spring of 2001, the unrest found its way to Betty and Mario in La Paz. Activists began demonstrating in the streets against similar water privatization. Thousands of miners planted themselves in the heart of the city, demanding the government help revive their industry. They set off explosions at a courthouse and marched toward the Congress.[4]

Mario and Betty lay awake at night. If they waited until total chaos hit, they would be among thousands seeking to escape. They could try to get a US residency visa by entering the American government lottery, which allotted each nation a set number of visas annually, but fewer than a hundred such visas were usually granted to Bolivians each year.[5] They could ask Eliana to sponsor Mario on a sibling visa, but that would likely take at least a decade. No, they would apply for tourist visas just like their daughters. They would send Hareth and three-year-old Haziel ahead. They would stay behind, sell their belongings, and pack up the house. In a month or so, they would join their daughters. And if things went well, they would stay and eventually seek permanent US residency. It was a risk giving up Mario's budding professional career, saying a permanent good-bye to many friends and family, and likely having to wait years to receive legal permanent immigration status in the United States, but those were risks they were willing to take. Waiting to see if things got worse was scarier.

"Be good," Hareth's parents told her at the airport. They would see each other soon. Hareth frowned, puzzled by her mother's serious expression. Of course they would see each other soon. At security, Betty stopped and buried her face in the girls' hair. Mario pulled them in to his broad chest, his hands big enough to clasp each daughter's head as he gently bestowed kisses on them.

They let go, and Hareth held tight to her grandmother's hand, while her grandfather carried Haziel in his arms. Then the excitement of a plane ride wrapped around her and skipped her feet down the airport corridor. On that August day, as Hareth pressed her small face against the plane window, her heart thumped against her ribs. Her grandmother gave her a spoonful of cold medicine to help her sleep through the seven-hour flight, and Hareth nestled against her grandfather. The plane lifted off over the rust-colored homes, stacked against one another on the hillsides of La Paz. Behind them, the snowcapped Andes offered a silent good-bye.

They landed first in Miami. A summer storm had delayed their next flight, and they would have to spend the night there before the final leg of their journey to Maryland where "La Tía Eli," as Hareth called her, lived, so they set off in search of a nearby hotel. Hareth's grandmother took the girls to the bathroom.

It was only a few moments before Hareth looked around and didn't see her sister. "Haziel?" she called. "Haziel?!!!" One minute Haziel was there. The next, she had vanished. Hareth's breath caught in her throat.

Hareth couldn't speak English, nor could her grandparents, but they had landed in Miami, where that wasn't a prerequisite. They scanned the faces of the travelers striding past them, wondering whom they could approach for help. Her grandparents hesitated.

Hareth did not. She approached a man in uniform. *Please*, she said, looking up at him. *We've lost my sister. Can you help?* They went from one official to another. Hareth and her grandmother were in tears. How could she have disappeared so quickly? Their minds jumped to the possibilities: a little girl lost in a vast airport, or worse. They searched up and down the cavernous corridors until at last they found

Haziel, happily playing with airport security guards, who had found her.

As they boarded their flight the next day, Hareth clutched her sister's hand tightly in hers. More unsettling than Haziel's disappearance was her grandparents' reaction—how uncertain they'd seemed in the midst of the emergency. Hareth silently swore she would never again lose Haziel. She would take charge of her family from now on.

It was a relief to see their aunt waiting for them at Baltimore-Washington International Airport. On the way to her house, the girls spotted a McDonald's. They knew little about this new country, but they recognized the golden arches. "McDonald's!" they screamed. Eliana dutifully pulled into the parking lot. Inside the restaurant, Hareth demanded her aunt translate every menu option, every detail of the kids' meal, before making her selection. But her throat closed when she tasted the hamburger with its strange pickles and onions. All she really wanted was the plastic toy. Afterward, the girls marveled at the restaurant bathrooms, which didn't even smell.

At Eliana's, they settled into a routine. Hareth and Haziel shared a room with their aunt, and they moved from Maryland to Virginia, where Eliana enrolled Hareth in an elementary school. The school was near the dry cleaner's where Eliana worked in Washington's wealthy Woodley Park neighborhood, up the street from the National Zoo. Hareth practiced her English watching *Sesame Street* and *Full House* at home or at the cleaners while her aunt sorted suits and silk blouses. Occasionally they watched Spanish-language news together, but mostly Hareth paid little attention to the political debates quietly brewing over what the country should do about immigrants like her. She missed her parents, but her grandparents and her aunt assured her that they would come soon.

Looking back later, Hareth would struggle to reconcile that first uneventful dinner at McDonald's and those early months at school as she awaited her parents, with the radical changes that would follow in her life, eventually leading her onto the national stage. Hareth would grow up part of a generation of young immigrants often collectively known as the DREAMers: kids raised in a country whose language and culture they identified with, whose pledge of allegiance they recited every morning in school—and yet a country that sought to render them akin to ghosts the moment they became adults, making it impossible for most to seek a college education, work legally, or have any official say in the political system. But these teens refused to become ghosts, to hide as their elders had. And ultimately, despite their immigration status, or in part because of it, many have become among the nation's most politically engaged young citizens—in all but name.

Some, like Hareth, have fought for change overtly, sharing their stories with countless other youths and lawmakers, advocating for immigration reform. Others have taken a stand through the simple act of demanding to be recognized for their contributions to the country. Some have worked within the system, and some have pushed up against it. No one person has led the fight, nor have these young immigrants done it alone. But over the course of two decades, they have effectively shaped the debate over who should be considered an American, forcing the United States to recognize the millions of people working in the shadows to keep this country's economic engine humming. They have demanded difficult conversations be had about the future of our country, and they have faced opposition in the nation's most powerful Washington corridors. In truth, it remains to be seen how their story will end and how many will be forced to leave their adopted country before it does, but in many ways, the millennium is where their story begins.

HARETH AND HER GRANDPARENTS arrived in the United States just as the government began toughening sanctions against those who entered the country illegally or overstayed their visas. Soon it would become nearly impossible for most undocumented immigrants in the country to legalize their status. Even those who could apply to become permanent residents often had to go back to their home country, where, in a Catch-22, they generally faced a ten-year ban on returning. Hundreds of thousands of people, if not millions, who in the past might have had another option to adjust their status, now faced the permanent threat of deportation.

In the fall of 2000, nearly a year before the Andrades arrived, Josh Bernstein sat tensely through a panel in a drab classroom at the Catholic University of America in Washington, DC, listening to lawyers describe the upswing in immigration cases. The Catholic Church had been helping children who had come to the United States unaccompanied, as well as immigrant children who'd been abandoned, neglected, or were fleeing abuse. If the children could document their cases, they were allowed to stay. The problem was the growing number who couldn't provide evidence, who didn't have witnesses lined up or police reports from their home countries. The speakers described children, many from war-torn Central America, who had been allowed to remain in the United States as their cases wound through the courts, only to turn eighteen, lose legal protection as minors, and likely face deportation back to countries they barely knew.

Josh ran a one-man shop in the nation's capital for the Los Angeles–based National Immigration Law Center, a nonprofit group dedicated to helping low-income immigrants. The son of liberal Jewish parents who'd met on a picket line during the civil rights movement,[6] Josh couldn't help finding parallels between that struggle and the challenges facing undocumented immigrants in Los Angeles. Josh's personal and political life had further intertwined in the 1980s, when he fell in love and married an undocumented woman from Mexico whom he had met at a local café.

In the last year, he'd been flooded with requests for help from desperate immigrants facing deportation. In addition to the unaccompanied-minor cases he received, there were calls from teachers and social workers about children whose families were intact but who were now coming of age and discovering that despite growing up in the United States, they had no legal status and could be picked up and deported at any moment.

Those kids who managed to fly under the radar through high school graduation found themselves unable to work legally, ineligible for in-state college tuition, and unable to afford the tuition otherwise. In many states, they couldn't even fill out the college application because they lacked the proper legal documents. Any work had to be paid under the table. It was as if, upon graduation, they reverted to being phantasms.

As the law center's chief policy analyst, Josh worked to enlist the support of sympathetic lawmakers. With his round face, pale blue eyes, wire-rimmed glasses, and soft Valley-accented voice that seemed to turn every statement into a question, he seemed more suburban rabbi than immigrant champion, but his unassuming nature dis-armed the lawmakers to whom he appealed.

There were certain things senators and congresswomen and -men could do: private bills they could file, simple phone calls they could make that could tip the scales for one specific child or another. But there were only so many of those favors to go around; it was like asking someone to inflate a thousand inner tubes with just his own breath. And as the case list grew, Josh found his contacts running out of air.

THINGS WERE GETTING BAD in Mexico. Land reform had enabled agri-businesses to buy up huge tracts of farms, sending many smaller growers to the cities or al Norte for work. The 1994 North American Free Trade Agreement had enabled US corn producers to flood the Mexican market, providing increasingly tough competition for the remaining small farmers. Then came more blows—the devaluation of the peso and massive inflation—culminating in basic economic meltdown. Mexicans increasingly decided to seek their fortunes in the United States.

Among those headed north was Dario Guerrero. He and his wife, Rocio, grew up in merchant families in Guadalajara, where Dario's parents owned a furniture store and Rocio's parents sold construction materials. As an adult, Dario ran a small offshoot of the family busi-ness. Rocio managed a clothing shop up the block, taking their new baby, Dario Jr., to work with her during the day. Next door, her brother sold bathroom interiors. They tried to make it work even after the peso dropped in half and inflation jumped 50 percent.

But when the assaults began, Dario began to rethink things. First, they came to Rocio's store and held a knife to her stomach as they grabbed her cash. Soon after, the girl in her brother's shop next door was assaulted as she worked. Rocio heard the cries from the other side of the wall. Too terrified to react, she cowered in her own shop, praying she wasn't next. The police were little help, arriving only if her husband took them a bottle of wine. As the economy grew worse, and people grew more desperate, nightly newscasts were increasingly filled with reports of kidnappings, once a hazard only for the wealthy. The financial crisis had set off a historic leap in crime.

In the spring of 1995, friends in Los Angeles invited Dario and Rocio to their wedding. Dario took that as a sign from the heavens. *I don't want to go back*, he said. Maybe he was bluffing, but she couldn't imagine life without him back in Guadalajara. *Okay*, she finally told him, *I'll stay with you*. It was still relatively easy at the time to come and go across the border, and even more for young women, who didn't fit the single-male-in-search-of-work profile. Rocio agreed to go back with little Dario and sell their belongings, then return once and for all.

In California, they quickly found a tiny apartment to rent right under a flight path of Los Angeles International Airport, just a bathroom and a living room. They slept on the living room couch. At night they cried quietly on the thin mattress, wondering if they had been fools to leave. They had spent their savings on the move, left a middle-class life, family, and friends. As much as they wanted to, they had no money to go home and were too proud to return with nothing to show for it.

But Rocio and Dario were lucky in one sense: they arrived shortly before the 1996[7] passage of the pivotal immigration law that would make it more difficult to adjust immigration status—that official move from being an "illegal alien" in the eyes of the US government to a "permanent resident." When they arrived, it was still possible to apply for Social Security numbers and obtain driver's licenses. Dario wasn't supposed to use the number to work, but, like many other immigrants, he did. He found work in construction, waking most days before dawn, kissing his wife and son good-bye as they lay in bed still asleep. Dario didn't worry about life at home; Rocio took care of it all. He took extra work on nights and weekends to make ends meet. Sometimes he fell asleep at the dinner table. But before long, he had earned the trust of his employers and was managing some of the other workers.

By 2000, the couple had welcomed another baby, Fernando, and moved to downtown Los Angeles. Rocio had her hands full. Little Dario walked at nine months and was talking in fluent sentences at two and a half. *You must put him in special enrichment classes*, a friend said. *He is moving so fast.* But for that they needed more money. The family spent their few free hours together at the beach or the park, Dario Sr. often with a video camera capturing brief scenes of their lives. He meant to send them back as proof to his family in Mexico that all was well.

Instead, the tapes became his and Rocio's family memories, preserving their life for posterity—just in case. The anxiety gnawed at him that one day their number would come up, that life was too short, that just by walking down the street with his wife and children, he was putting himself in danger of deportation. But he relaxed behind the camera; his worries about their future disappeared as he aimed the lens at the world around him.

One summer afternoon the family strolled through Elysian Park north of downtown Los Angeles. Dario brought his camera, and as they walked through the grass, he filmed the other families picnicking on the playground and on the nearby lawn. There was something comforting about so many familiar-looking strangers. As he filmed, Dario spun the camera around at the parents, children, grandparents, aunts, and uncles, chattering in a mix of Spanish and English.

"You are all afraid they are going to deport us," he joked to his family back in Mexico, as he recorded. "[But look,] they'd have to deport the whole city."[8]

JOSH WAS HARDLY ALONE in looking for a solution to the onslaught of immigration cases. In late 2000, advocates at the nonprofit National Council of La Raza, which would eventually become UNIDOS.US, and other advocacy groups were working on bills to provide in-state tuition to undocumented immigrants living in places like Texas and California, where it made the most sense for state lawmakers to protect educational—and economic—opportunity for so many of their de facto residents. It was a campaign rooted in part in the 1985 legal case of an undocumented girl known in court filings as Leticia A.[9] She had won the right to pay in-state tuition to attend a California state university. Although her victory was reversed a few years later in state court, it had planted the idea of a special status that would better enable undocumented teens to pay for and graduate from college.

In Washington, Josh began to think maybe the federal government could step in. *If they could just pass one bill for all the kids . . .* he told a friend one afternoon. *If the kids have been here five years, they could stay and go to college.* He was half joking. The idea seemed so impossible. Yet as soon as the words left his mouth, they took on a power of their own.

He asked around and learned California Democratic senator Dianne Feinstein was possibly interested in such a bill. Maybe she would be his champion.

Between Christmas and New Year's, Josh hunkered down in his cramped office along Washington's H Street NW corridor, surviving on Coca-Cola and Chinese takeout, furiously writing and researching legal precedent along with fellow advocates. Feinstein passed on the proposal. But now Josh had a written draft, and he wasn't about to let it go. He got word that Illinois Democratic senator Dick Durbin was interested in such a bill. Earlier in 2000, Durbin had been approached about the case of another undocumented immigrant student, a musical prodigy named Tereza Lee.[10] Born in Brazil to post–Korean War refugees, Tereza had grown up in Chicago and was living in the country illegally. She had no legal status in the United States. Brazil had never granted the family citizenship, and Tereza had never even been to Korea. She was essentially a girl without a country. Durbin, whose own mother had immigrated to the United States from Lithuania at around the same age as Tereza,[11] had been so moved by the girl's case that he was eager to help. He was quickly earning a reputation as one of the Washington lawmakers most sympathetic to this burgeoning group of students. His staff began refining Josh's initial proposal and working to get it onto the Senate floor.

For educators and immigrant activists, the Children's Adjustment, Relief, and Education (CARE) Act,[12] as Durbin's bill was officially known, was in part about basic math. If the federal, state, and local governments combined invested roughly $130,000 in sixteen years of public schooling for each student,[13] they might as well invest in another two or four years so the student could earn enough to pay taxes and help create a few jobs.

The advocates knew the immigrant education bill had to be bipartisan from the start to succeed. Utah Republican senator Orrin Hatch, moved by the story of undocumented students in his state who could not attend college, was also working on a version of the legislation. Days after Durbin unveiled his bill, Hatch proposed a similar one: the "Development, Relief, and Education for Alien Minors Act." Soon the two senators combined forces, and the result quickly and forever became known as the DREAM Act,[14] eventually spawning the moniker "DREAMers" for the young immigrants eligible for its protections. Josh and others sought out Representative Chris Cannon, a moderate Republican from Utah, to sponsor a version in the House, along with California Democratic representative Howard Berman.

For immigrant advocates, the bill was also about finding a winnable battle. The last half-decade had felt like one loss after another. In August 1996, as part of Republican House Speaker Newt Gingrich's

"Contract with America," Congress had cut health care and other benefits for legal immigrants, including pregnant women and children, through the Personal Responsibility and Work Opportunity Reconciliation Act. A month after that, lawmakers approved the Illegal Immigration Reform and Immigrant Responsibility Act, which also limited many protections even for those in the country legally.

There had been a few small victories. Advocates had managed to block in the courts a 1994 California measure known as Proposition 187, which prohibited illegal immigrants from accessing public services, including public school. More broadly, they'd won back some benefits for Americans and legal residents under the Work Opportunity Act.

Still, they needed to show their colleagues that fighting *for* something (rather than simply staving off another catastrophe) was more than a "pie in the sky" strategy.

The inauguration of President George W. Bush seemed in many ways like the answer to the prayers of immigrants and their champions. The new president's brother was married to a Mexican immigrant, and a month after taking office in 2001, Bush announced plans to visit Mexican president Vicente Fox. By July, Bush's administration floated the idea of a new amnesty program for Mexicans[15] and an expanded guest worker program for those harvesting the nation's crops, tapping Secretary of State Colin Powell and Attorney General John Ashcroft to look into legalizing 3 million to 4 million Mexican immigrants,[16] and possibly millions from other countries as well.

Yet the broader reform still faced many hurdles. *Amnesty* was becoming a dirty word with many Americans, who were seeing more jobs outsourced, and many labor unions feared expanding the US guest worker program would further decimate wages. Josh figured a small win for the students could lead to bigger gains and a way to build back confidence after the 1996 law that had made life tougher for many undocumented immigrants, even as the demand for their labor continued to grow. Such a win might even embolden immigrants to claim more basic protections (a theory that did not go unnoticed by conservatives, even those who were sympathetic to the kids). He pushed on for the DREAM Act.

WHEN FOURTEEN-YEAR-OLD Felipe Matos Sousa arrived in Miami on a plane from Rio de Janeiro in the winter of 2001, he wasn't thinking about college, let alone how to pay for it—not yet. He had come to help care for his older sister Carolina's toddler. It would be an extended vacation, his mother told him.

He wasn't sure he wanted an extended vacation. But as Carolina drove him from the airport, he looked out the window, stunned by all the green. He couldn't remember ever seeing so many lush leaves in a city—not outside the apartment where he was born near the Rio favelas, nor in the town where he and his mother moved when he was in elementary school. Even the industrial parts of Miami looked like the Emerald City.

Felipe had been eight when Carolina left for the United States, desperate to avoid the life of their mother, who worked as a cleaning lady, scrubbing toilets in private homes and at a local clinic. With an absent father, his older sisters often cared for him or he played alone. His grandmother's death left his mother enough money to buy a little plot of land in Duque de Caxias, a small city bordered by Rio de Janeiro to the south. Slowly they built their new home, living for months with plastic tarps over the windows and door. They had no electricity and no running water much of that first year. Francisca Sousa Matos refused to let her young son feel sorry for what they didn't have. One morning, as the two of them walked home from the bakery, she ordered him to give the baguette they'd bought to a boy begging in the street.

Why? Felipe protested. *We are hungry, too.*

Because the boy is hungrier, she replied. *If you want to change the world, you have to work till your hands bleed and then work some more.*

To help his mother, Felipe lied about his age and got a job distributing political campaign flyers during election season, his first brief foray into politics.

LIFE GOT EASIER once Carolina found cleaning jobs in the United States and started to send money. They finished the roof, added windows and a door and later two bedrooms. They finally had running water. But Felipe still saw much he wanted to change. Each morning he dressed in his government-issued school uniform: blue pants and a white shirt with blue stripes and a gold sun. The sun was supposed to be a symbol of bright power and potential, but for Felipe it was a bright, burning symbol of poverty—an announcement to all the world that he couldn't afford even his own clothes.

To get to school, Felipe rode his bike along the open sewage ditch at the edge of the road. During the rainy season, the water rose and the sewage washed over the streets. As he biked, he often thought of his mother's brother. Tío José had organized against the Brazilian dictatorship in the 1970s and had attained a level of respect and prestige in that movement that even now was a source of pride for Felipe. He tried to imagine what his uncle would do about the sewers. He was a man people would listen to. *One day I will be, too,* Felipe vowed.

When he heard that the mayor would make a campaign stop at his school, he decided it was time to take action. As the mayor came to shake hands, twelve-year-old Felipe handed him a list of demands for the neighborhood: sewers, streetlamps, medicine for the hospital, paved streets, a playground. The mayor took the paper. He would see what he could do. Felipe never heard back, and in the following months, nothing changed. But later, after Felipe left, his mother informed him that the municipality had begun to pave the streets and a playground was built. The hospital improved. *Maybe I had something to do with it,* he thought to himself, even if he could never be sure.

Eventually, Felipe's sister suggested he come to Florida. Their mother's back was in great pain, and she needed to rest. He could help Carolina care for her young daughter while she worked. Felipe agreed to go. He told the immigration agent at the consulate how much he wanted to visit Disney World.

Carolina made Felipe promise to stick it out for the year. And it only later occurred to him that perhaps that had been the plan all along, enough time that he wouldn't want to return.

In Florida, there was so much to get used to. At home, milk had been a luxury. Felipe would often just stand in the milk aisle of the grocery store, staring at the row upon row of cartons, wondering how he was supposed to choose.

By the summer of 2001, Felipe could chat easily in English with his friends. All arms and legs, with thick brown hair and golden brown eyes to match, he missed his mother. At night, away from the world, he thought of her, of his friends back home, and tears slipped down his pillow. But his life was now in Miami. He threw himself into school, where he excelled. He thought less about becoming like his uncle. More and more, he wanted to become a teacher. He wasn't quite sure of the path, but in a country where you could find a dozen different kinds of milk in the supermarket aisle, he figured there had to be a way.

And that summer, across the country in Washington, congressional staffers were looking for one, spending long days writing and rewriting a bill to create a lawful pathway for students like Felipe to stay in the United States. They researched the legal justifications and lined up expert testimony for the DREAM Act. Durbin's office arranged for Tereza, the music prodigy, to fly to Washington to testify and possibly play the piano for the lawmakers, as well as for another undocumented Chicago teen, Tania Unzueta, whom Durbin had helped in Chicago, to tell her story. Josh hadn't felt this confident about a piece of legislation in years. He could barely sleep in the run-up to the bill's first big hearing, set for September 12, 2001.

Then, one day before the hearing, Hareth in Virginia, Felipe in Miami, and Dario and Rocio with their sons in Los Angeles watched on TV the smoke and crumbling steel and concrete—the tiny dark spots plummeting from the burning towers—trying to comprehend what they were seeing. How could this happen in the United States of America? Who would want to do this to us?

AFTER THE SEPTEMBER 11 ATTACKS, few in Washington wanted to talk about how to keep the kids, or anyone else, in; they wanted to talk about how to keep dangerous people out. Within weeks, massive concrete barriers appeared outside the US Capitol to deter suicide car bombers. The USA PATRIOT Act passed on October 26, expanding government surveillance and allowing for indefinite, and sometimes secret, detention of immigrants suspected of having terrorism ties. Congress also passed a bill to step up border security and improve the exchange of criminal and visa information across agencies.

Embassies around the world canceled visa interviews as the nation struggled to assess the damage, including Betty Ayala and Mario Andrade's September 15 appointment at the US Embassy in La Paz. They would have to wait till December to make their case for the tourist visas they hoped would reunite them with their daughters. Each night, as she slept, Betty dreamed her girls were next to her, their small legs and arms strewn across her body. And each morning she awoke to the empty space. They would be reunited soon, Mario assured her, but in December, their visas were denied. They put out their Christmas presents for Hareth and Haziel anyway, and Betty spent the evening staring at the brightly wrapped gifts. They would try again in the new year, Mario promised, but again they were denied visas in 2002.

Americans felt vulnerable in a way they never had before. Across the nation, the fear opened new space for the expression of long-simmering resentment of some Americans about the increasing number of Latino, Middle Eastern, and Asian immigrants, who brought with them new traditions and whose arrival had coincided with the increasing number of blue-collar jobs lost to both global outsourcing and automation.

Even in the heart of the country, far away from the terrorists' intended targets, the winds had changed for immigrants. Recent immigrants were no longer predominantly staying in the port of entry cities where they arrived, such as New York, El Paso, Los Angeles, and Miami. Increasingly, they began to follow the demand for work into the American heartland and along the southeastern coast. In Missouri, for example, Latinos made up only 2 percent of the population, yet their numbers had nearly doubled from 1990 to 2000.[17] Missourians were beginning to take notice.

It was in this new climate that fifteen-year-old Costa Rican native Marie Gonzalez and her parents, Marvin and Marina, found themselves in the crosshairs of the war on terror and the burgeoning backlash against the state's growing undocumented population. A month after the September 11, 2001, attacks, Marvin, a government mail clerk, was sorting packages for Missouri governor Bob Holden when he came across a package addressed to the governor that included an unmarked envelope and a book about Osama bin Laden.[18] Frightened but remaining calm, he alerted his superiors. The nation was on the lookout for another terrorist attack, after a series of anthrax incidents had killed five people, sickened more than a dozen,[19] and left the country once more on edge. State investigators later determined the package did not contain anything hazardous, but the government took anything that looked like the deadly white powder seriously, and the FBI came to Jefferson City, Missouri, to interview Marvin. He and others in the mail room began wearing protective gloves and masks when they handled the mail and were moved out of the capitol building. Marvin kept his head down and hoped that was the end of it.

But in December, as Marvin opened another letter addressed to the governor postmarked from a nearby prison, white powder spilled out onto his leg. He was terrified. The FBI visited again. He called his wife. *Don't get scared, but a powder spilled on me when I was opening mail, and I don't know if I'm going to be all right.* They quarantined Marvin for the day and ran tests. For a week he waited for the lab results. A few days after the incident, the left side of Marvin's face swelled up, and he developed a rash, but officials told him the powder had tested negative for any biohazard. Marie accompanied her father to the doctor and translated the diagnosis for him. The doctor suggested the rash was from something he ate. Marvin and Marina didn't know what to believe. Now Marvin began to dread going to work. He couldn't sleep, but for Marie, he tried to pretend everything was okay.

Marvin became something of a hero after that, but it was attention he didn't want. Marvin had brought his family to the United States a decade before on a tourist visa, and, like Dario and Rocio Guerrero, they'd stayed long past the legal limit. The last thing he needed was people looking into his life and realizing that the governor's trusted mail clerk lacked legal authorization to be in the country.

Marvin had sold his seafood restaurant in Costa Rica back in 1991 after a cholera epidemic[20] crashed the local tourism industry. He and Marina packed up as much of their lives as they could into suitcases and flew with then five-year-old Marie to Southern California in late November. Los Angeles seemed the place to be, and Marvin looked for work once more in the restaurant industry.

Five months later, Los Angeles erupted in flames. A mostly white jury had acquitted four white police officers on charges of brutally beating an unarmed black man named Rodney King. African Americans across the city took to the streets in a massive release of anger, grief, and frustration at a system that seemed to place so little value on their lives.

Marvin and Marina were already frightened of the big city and understood little of the history behind the fires. When a friend from Costa Rica mentioned a restaurant opportunity in Missouri, the Gonzalezes eagerly picked up once again, eventually landing in Jefferson City. Marvin took over the American Wok, a popular downtown restaurant started by Nicaraguan immigrants that catered to the government worker lunch crowd. Then Missouri governor John Ashcroft, who would soon be appointed US attorney general by George W. Bush, was among those to stop by and leave a signed photo. They moved in upstairs. And eventually Marvin and Marina saved up enough money to buy the restaurant. During the afternoons, Marie did her homework at a table and in the evening played by herself in a side room her parents closed off, the smells of sizzling ginger and garlic wafting in from the kitchen.

When she wasn't at the restaurant, Marie would hang out at the library across the street. She spent so much time there that the librarians sometimes had her test out new educational software. She took the job seriously, her green eyes scanning the screen, tight black curls bouncing ever so slightly as she read. Eventually, her parents saved enough money, along with the help of a scholarship, to enroll her in a nearby Catholic school. Marie loved school and took up tennis and track, deftly avoiding the dreaded label of nerd.

Watching her father crunch numbers at his desk in the back, she learned early not to complain about being alone or about her parents' having to work at the restaurant instead of attending her tennis games. She knew the difference between telling her parents she wanted something and telling them she needed it. And she prided herself at being her parents' helper, their translator, and their adviser.

Marvin and Marina took out a small business loan for the restaurant and diligently repaid it, but the restaurant hours took their toll, and business was fickle. In January 2001, the father of one of Marie's schoolmates told Marvin about the $20,000-a-year mail room messenger job with the governor. Finally he and Marina would have good medical insurance and a steady income. They bought a house on a quiet residential street, a one-floor brick home with an elm tree in the front yard. It never occurred to Marvin or his family that his connection to the state's highest-ranking official would prove his undoing, nor that it would lead his daughter to help ignite a national movement.

By high school, Marie no longer spent her afternoons alone. Increasingly, she was busy with the track and tennis teams, attending church on Sundays with her parents. The governor even sent Marie a handwritten letter congratulating her on her academic achievements. Life was good, at least until her father began opening the letters with the powder inside. He wasn't the same after that. He became more anxious, distracted. At the time, Marie thought it was just because of the threat of the attacks.

In April 2002, when Marie turned sixteen, she, like her friends, made a beeline with her mother to the Department of Motor Vehicles to obtain that piece of plastic signifying freedom for teenagers across the United States. But the DMV wouldn't accept her identification. She had come in on a child's passport, one that needed to be renewed every five years. And her parents had never renewed it. They hadn't thought about traveling anywhere, and it seemed an unnecessary expense. Her US visa had also expired. She had no proof of identity. At work, colleagues joked with Marvin about Marie's not getting her license and offered to help. The governor's chief of staff accompanied Marie and her mother to get the coveted card, but again they were rebuffed. Now Marie was worried. What did it mean that she didn't have the right papers to get her license? *It will all get sorted out*, she told herself. *These kind of things always do.*

It wasn't for lack of trying that Marvin and Marina remained in the country without legal status. When they'd lived in Los Angeles, they'd forked over thousands of dollars to immigration lawyers to get on the right side of the law. The lawyers had told them if they worked hard, paid taxes, bought a home, and stayed out of trouble, after five years they would have a good shot at applying for a green card. And the lawyers had been right. Back then, to avoid deportation, immigrants had to show the "extreme hardship" they might face if they were sent back to their home country. But in practice, one often had to show simply the likelihood of more routine hardship, including separation from children, with the US government taking into account the person's age, his or her time in the United States, the financial strain of deportation, lost educational opportunities, and family connections. After five years, Mario and Marina were told the wait had now stretched to seven years. But then the law changed in 1996, and the wait became ten years. The Gonzalezes moved to Missouri, where finding a lawyer who spoke Spanish was no small task. They briefly looked for one, but just paying the bills on the restaurant, and later the house, took up most of their money and energy.

Soon after the license fiasco, Governor Holden spoke at an event where Marie was honored for her academic success and again at a ceremony recognizing the state's growing Latino community. The governor gave a shout-out to Marie and her father's patriotism. Once again Marvin winced at all the attention.

In early June of 2002, his fears came true. The governor's office alerted Marvin that it had received an anonymous tip: Holden's trusted messenger and mail room clerk was in the country illegally and had been for years, the caller said. Someone should look into it. Marvin had presented a Social Security number and a valid driver's license when he applied for the job. Like Dario Guerrero, he'd been issued the Social Security number when he arrived, and he'd gotten his driver's license with it. And back then, that was enough to get hired as a state employee. The governor's staff didn't need to see a work permit.

Federal agents came to Marvin's office and interviewed him for two hours. This time, no one treated him like a hero. He phoned Marina to warn her that the agents might come to the house. Someone leaked the investigation to the media, and by the evening, the family made the local news. The following day the story had gone national. Holden's staffers weren't willing to stick their necks out for an undocumented immigrant who appeared to have duped them.

Marie wondered who had called in the tip. A jealous staffer? A friend? Someone seeking to damage the governor? She no longer knew whom she could trust. Terrified of what people would think, she began calling everyone she knew—teachers at school, friends from church—trying to explain they were not criminals.

Their friends at church didn't understand how the family they knew could be "illegals." Marie had gone to school with their children; her mother had worked as a teacher's aide; her father had even been a government employee. These kinds of cases didn't happen in Jefferson City, at least not to people they knew. Sure, they didn't want drug dealers and gangbangers sneaking across the border. But this was different. The community rallied around the Gonzalezes. A group of friends began calling themselves the "Gonzalez Group" and reached out to every lawmaker, every political contact they knew.

But others were wary of being associated with Marie and her family. After so much recognition from the governor's office, Marvin was quickly cast out. And now that his case had made the headlines, no one would hire him. Fortunately, Marina was allowed to continue working at her school as a volunteer, receiving donations and gift cards in lieu of pay. Now she was the main breadwinner.

At night, Marie watched the stories on CNN and Univision of people being deported. *Oh, my God,* she thought. *That could be us.*

But the immigration agents didn't come, not at first. There weren't any in Jefferson City back then. Governor Holden's office recommended an attorney, and Marie's parents drove all the way to St. Louis to meet her, but she barely gave them the time of day. And she was expensive. Through friends, they found a pro bono lawyer, Ben Mook. He wasn't even an immigration lawyer, but he was local and eager to help. It wasn't until the summer of 2003 that the agents finally arrived. Marie was at a Christian youth camp in Asheville, North Carolina. She called home, and her mom sounded curt. "What's wrong?" Marie asked.

"Ask your father," Marina answered, and handed him the phone.

An agent from the newly created Department of Homeland Security had come to the home and interviewed Marvin and Marina. That first interview was simple. The officer was cordial enough and warned the couple that it could have been much worse. He could have come in a show of force, with several vehicles, and taken them into custody.

Later other agents would return to interview the couple separately about a small-business loan they'd taken out years before and paid off, seeking, it seemed to Marie, to catch them in some misstatement, some illegal act. As the officers watched, Marvin and Marina carefully pulled out years of records establishing their ties to the country: ownership of the American Wok, the loan, their home mortgage, the years Marina had spent as a teacher, the background checks they'd undergone for their jobs in government and at the school. They were, in fact, anything but undocumented.

The family had their first hearing in December 2003, driving two and a half hours to Kansas City, the nearest immigration court. Theirs was the only case on the docket that day, and Ben had told them the judge wouldn't even be there but would instead talk to them via teleconference. They would likely get a postponement and would have more time to map out their case. When they arrived, Marina was shocked to see a group of immigrants sitting in chairs, handcuffed. They didn't look like criminals to Marina. But now she wondered whether that was how others saw her. Then, to their surprise, the judge walked into the courtroom and quickly made things clear: they had no claim to stay in the United States and now were officially in deportation proceedings. But the judge did agree to allow Marie to finish out her school year. The family walked out hearts in hand. Together they vowed to appeal the decision.

At night, Marie tried to put it all together, going over the events of the last year and a half. She had known they weren't citizens, but she'd always assumed they were in some sort of protected gray area. If only she hadn't been so set on getting her driver's license, maybe no red flags would have been set off. *Stupid, stupid!* she thought. But maybe she'd never know what had triggered the anonymous call about her father and the media leak. It was so bewildering. Through it all, one thought came back to Marie: *I should have protected him.*

2

SEEDS PLANTED

Marie Gonzalez speaks at a DREAM Act rally, on the Capitol grounds in Washington, DC, April 20, 2004. (COURTESY OF JOSHUA BERNSTEIN)

Hareth stopped counting the days till her parents would come as the protective shell in which she had arrived in the United States began to crack. In 2003, Hareth's grandfather became ill. When he died, her grandmother returned to Bolivia to grieve. Then Eliana lost the lease on an apartment, and for a few months they moved in with other relatives until they could once more find a place to live. School remained the constant. One year, Hareth's teacher had the class memorize the Gettysburg Address. Hareth loved the drama of the speech. She imagined herself one day standing before a crowd, issuing declarations that would make people stop and listen. At night she lay in bed, rolling the words over her tongue:

Fourscore and seven years ago our fathers brought forth upon this continent, a new nation, conceived in Liberty, and dedicated to the proposition that all men are created equal.

Now we are engaged in a great civil war, testing whether that nation, or any nation so conceived and so dedicated, can long endure.

Her parents still called every night. But sometimes she would avoid the phone. The sound of her mother's voice over the line cut into her chest like the glass shards scattered outside their apartment. There was too much to fill in about daily life, too many questions to answer. She didn't even try to explain about the Gettysburg Address—the power of Lincoln's simple words: a "government of the people, by the people, for the people."

But Betty couldn't wait much longer. She was pregnant. She hadn't planned to have another baby, not while her other two were so far away. And now she was terrified that if she waited too long, she wouldn't be able to travel at all. Friends suggested that if they couldn't get visas from Bolivia, maybe they needed to arrive from somewhere else, a wealthier country, like Argentina, where they would face less scrutiny. In June 2004, with Betty nearly eight months pregnant, they decided once more to try to reach the United States. They planned to split up. Mario tested the path first. He traveled to Buenos Aires and spent a few days with a cousin. From Argentina, he used an altered passport with his brother's information to reach the United States.

He was terrified walking past the security in Buenos Aires. *Don't let anyone see. They are watching, watching from the windows, from places you don't even see*, he reminded himself. *Breathe. Everyone is watching.* He hated feeling like a criminal with something to hide. He smiled broadly at the agents as he passed. No one flagged him. As he leaned back into his seat on the plane, Mario thought about what he was leaving behind: the weight of his degree, his reputation, his friends, his extended family. He knew it would not be easy. No one would hand them anything. They would have to start over. He forced himself to push aside those worries, refusing to allow himself to imagine failure. Instead, he thought only about his daughters' big black eyes and small round faces. As he stepped off the plane at Washington Dulles International Airport, outside Washington, he prayed the men in military gear with sniffer dogs wouldn't stop him.

No one told Hareth or Haziel he was coming, just in case he didn't make it. The girls scampered through the airport, excited to see whichever distant relative had arrived. Hareth, already a tween and two heads taller than when she'd left home three years before, was stunned to hear her father call her name. She froze, barely recognizing him. But Haziel knew him from recent pictures and ran to greet Mario.

"Papi!"

That night the girls slept on either side of their father, huddled all together.

Mario wanted to learn everything about his daughters' lives. That first week he borrowed Eliana's car and dropped Hareth off at her school. As he pulled up along the narrow, hilly street, another parent opened the door of a parked SUV, and smacked into Eliana's car. Mario froze. *Unbelievable*, he thought. Already an accident. Now he would be blamed. And what would he tell Eliana? The other parent got out as a school traffic officer approached, and Mario took a deep breath, shifting into park. Hareth wondered if she should intervene, as she had with her grandparents when they had lost Haziel.

Mario calmed Hareth. He would handle it.

Hareth leaned back in the car, relieved.

The other driver approached Mario's side and stuck out his hand. He hadn't been looking. It was his fault. He was sorry. By now the officer had reached them and waved the two men along, directing them to take their kids inside first and exchange information later. Mario exhaled as he dropped Hareth at the school gate. He would have to be much more careful driving in the United States. The last thing he needed was to be on the radar of the police and have them ask about his plans in the country. As he had on the plane, Mario once more swept those fears to the back of his mind. Landing too long on those what-ifs could drive a person crazy.

A month later, Betty made the same trip. The stress had kept her from gaining much weight during her pregnancy. She wore a baggy sweatshirt and sweatpants so no one would notice her swollen belly. She worried officials might think she was too pregnant to travel or, worse, that they would stop her out of fear she was trying to have an anchor baby. But she was determined that nothing would stand in the way of reuniting with the babies she already had. Much to her surprise, no one in Customs asked about her pregnancy.

This time Hareth was prepared. As they waited at the airport, she scanned the gate, searching for her mother. Finally Betty appeared, smaller than she remembered, more fragile. Hareth burst away from her sister and father and tore to the spot where her mother stood. In an instant, she was in Betty's arms, her face enveloped in her mother's thick black hair, her chin fitting perfectly into the crook of her neck, the warm melody of Betty's voice dancing softly in her ears.

I'm here now. I'm here.

With the family back together, Betty began sleeping through the night again for the first time in years. During her last months of pregnancy, she quickly put on the weight she'd never gained in Bolivia. Mario had already begun to put his architectural background to use in the construction boom, as the Washington Beltway corridor expanded out through Virginia and Maryland. Now he stepped up his efforts and began specializing in electrical jobs where he could make more money. Betty began to pick up English from neighbors as she waited for the baby to arrive.

Claudia was born in August. They couldn't find a Virginia hospital willing to take them without insurance, but in Washington, DC, they did. A hospital administrator patiently explained to Betty about the city-run Women, Infants, and Children program, funded by the federal government, which would provide supplemental milk and other basic food for Claudia until she was five. Three months later, Betty took an overnight job caring for an elderly woman so she could be home with the girls in the afternoon. She worked five nights a week and barely slept. Betty moved Hareth to the neighborhood school, where Hareth found herself back in English-learner classes. Much to her chagrin, the school had deemed her reading insufficient for the general track. Hareth was furious over the switch and the remedial lessons. Once again it felt as though she were restarting her life. Worse, her parents did not seem to know even the most basic rules. They had no idea how to be the kind of "American" parents Hareth was used to watching on TV or eating dinner with at friends' houses. Betty and Mario hadn't had a big television in Bolivia, and there wasn't much to watch, so it didn't occur to them to take Hareth's TV privileges away if she didn't listen to them. They didn't do "time-outs" in Bolivia. And they didn't know what to do about the constant phone calls Hareth received. How could a kid talk so much to friends she'd seen only an hour or two before and would see again less than twenty-four hours later?

Betty was shocked at her daughter's liberal use of American slang. ¡Que lenga! What a mouth! She pushed Hareth to study more, to transition as quickly as possible. Go read! Betty ordered her daughter, remembering how much Hareth loved books as a small child. But Hareth didn't want to go read, and no one was going to tell her what to do. She'd been on her own for three years, and she knew how to take care of herself. And besides, she wasn't used to speaking so much Spanish again. How long would it take for her parents to learn English anyway?

In fits and starts the Andrades began to rebuild their family. Eliana found a new place, so the Andrades had the two-bedroom apartment to themselves. Hareth picked Haziel up from the bus stop after school and cared for her sister while doing her homework in the afternoons. Betty made dinner before going to her night shift job, or Hareth did, and Mario ate with the girls. Eventually, their grandmother returned to help, and Eliana still chipped in. They attended Baptist church on Sunday. The apartment was full. Sometimes it seemed like there were too many parents now, but secretly Hareth didn't mind. If she arrived later than she said she would, she lost telephone privileges. If she sassed her parents, she lost TV privileges. Hareth soon transferred back into the general classes at her new school. On the weekends, she and her mother cleaned house, swapping stories from work and classes, Hareth practicing her Spanish, Betty her English, as they fell into a new rhythm.

DISCUSSIONS ABOUT BROAD IMMIGRATION reform became less frequent in the United States in the years immediately following September 11 but never really went away, even as the country marched into war with Iraq. They couldn't because undocumented immigrants were so interwoven into the fabric of America that their presence sneaked in even to discussions of military strategy and troops in Iraq. The second US casualty in the war turned out to be a young man from Guatemala who had crossed the California border illegally. An orphan who had fled his own war-torn country, Lance Corporal Jose Gutierrez[1] had lied about his age so he would appear to be a minor and could more easily stay in the United States, where he eventually enlisted in the marines to fight on behalf of his adopted country.

By the time Mario and Betty arrived, Congress had passed enough border security legislation that the immigrant rights movement began to stand up and dust itself off. And in 2003, two bills began making their way through the Senate that would help immigrants rather than merely penalize them. One, backed by the Senate's longtime liberal champion, Massachusetts's Ted Kennedy, aimed to provide a pathway to citizenship for undocumented farmworkers. The other was the DREAM Act, Republican Orrin Hatch and Democrat Dick Durbin's effort to provide a path to citizenship for those who had come to the country as children. In the House, Republican Chris Cannon and Democrat Howard Berman again offered a similar proposal. Under the bill, anyone aged twenty-one and under who had arrived before his or her sixteenth birthday, had no criminal record, and had lived in the United States for five years could attend college, the military, or a trade school and generally get on track for legal permanent residency.

Immigrant advocates knew they needed outside help, and they saw an opening. In 2003, a seismic shift in US labor politics was under way that would help reframe the entire immigration debate and breathe new life into the movement. Since their inception, labor unions had been wary of immigrants taking American jobs and providing a cheaper, more docile alternative to the titans of industry. American Federation of Labor president Samuel Gompers had written back in the 1920s that the US labor movement, "does not declare that America is for Americans alone, but it does insist that there should be and must be some restriction of immigration that will prevent disintegration of American economic standards."[2]

Yet union numbers were plummeting, and states were increasingly passing union-busting regulations. Union leaders needed the new immigrants to build back their movements' numbers and hoped legalizing them would reduce unfair competition from those willing to take less because they were afraid to argue for more. Welcoming these new members wouldn't stop the march toward automation or even the outsourcing of jobs overseas, but it might level the playing field at home. The AFL-CIO had endorsed a path to citizenship for those in the country illegally for the first time in its 2000 national platform, but the policy shift hadn't trickled down to the rank-and-file members.

Now, immigrant advocates, together with union leaders, sought ways to make more visible the connection between union members' working conditions and those of immigrants. Josh's group, the National Immigration Law Center, along with the National Immigration Forum in Washington, DC, headed by immigrant advocate Frank Sharry, came up with the idea for a caravan of buses full of immigrant tomato pickers, hotel maids, and construction workers to travel from California to the nation's capital, teaming up along the way with union members from across the country. They called it the Immigrant Workers Freedom Ride, harkening back to the civil rights–era bus rides that sought to end segregation across the South.

Reverend James Lawson Jr., who participated in the 1961 freedom ride from Montgomery, Alabama, to Jackson, Mississippi, spoke in Los Angeles as thousands gathered for the kickoff in late September. The Service Employees International Union, whose workers often included immigrants, helped fund and promote the effort.* Garment workers in Southern California came out to support them as well, as did other big players, like the Coalition for Humane Immigrant Rights of Los Angeles, known as CHIRLA, and the National Korean American Service and Education Consortium, NAKASEC.

A brash Spanish-language radio host, Renán Almendárez Coello, known as "El Cucuy de la Mañana," spoke at the Los Angeles kickoff. Only blocks away from where they gathered, immigrant garment workers labored long hours, at times without drinking water, toilet paper, or air-conditioning, and little if any overtime, he shouted to the crowd.[3] Some 900 immigrants and advocates made their way across the country, drawing their biggest crowd of 100,000 at a New York City rally. The caravan didn't immediately move the needle in Congress, not with comprehensive reform and not for the DREAM Act. But it became a coming-out of sorts for the immigrant rights movement, which had been so demoralized by the 1996 immigration and welfare laws, and then by the nation's emphasis on national security following 9/11. Immigrant advocates inhaled a renewed

---

* The AFL-CIO, whose rank-and-file members were still warier of immigrants potentially taking their jobs, was less enthusiastic but lent its official support.

sense of urgency, even as their efforts brought new and more critical scrutiny.*

The DREAM Act's supporters felt the momentum. Josh looked for young students to bring to Washington and testify before Congress. It wasn't hard to find the kids, but few wanted to call attention to their plight lest they trigger an immigration raid. The bill went to markup in the Senate Judiciary Committee Subcommittee on Immigration in October, and Alabama Republican senator Jeff Sessions was among the few committee members to flat-out oppose it. During one marathon late-night committee hearing, Sessions, who would become the US attorney general under President Donald Trump, offered roughly two-dozen amendments designed to kill the bill. He didn't succeed. The DREAM Act staggered on, and eventually it sailed out of the Senate Judiciary Committee with strong support.

Josh found a young Haitian woman, Majan Jean, from Connecticut, whose family had lost its asylum case and who was willing to speak out because she was already facing deportation. Eventually, lawmakers from Connecticut would help Majan get a reprieve through a private bill.

Marie's lawyer, Ben Mook, had been researching her case, looking for similar congressional help. Like Majan, Marie and her family were already in deportation proceedings. Unlike Majan, Marie's representatives didn't appear interested in helping her. The two senators from Missouri had refused to introduce a private bill on her behalf, as Durbin had done for Tereza Lee and others. (It likely didn't help that they were both conservative Republicans, while her father had worked for a Democrat.) One lawmaker did try to help get her into the military, only to realize she couldn't qualify because she was un-

---

* David Ray of the Federation for American Immigration Reform complained on an October 4 CNN morning news show, "Here we have a group of people who, first of all, thumb their nose at U.S. immigration laws, and then ride around the country trying to blanket themselves in a status of victimhood. I mean, this is a joke." ("Interview with David Ray, Maria Elena Durazo," *Saturday Morning News*, CNN, October 4, 2003. http://transcripts.cnn.com/TRANSCRIPTS/0310/04/smn.11.html.)

documented. Ben came across a press release with Josh's name on it. He got in touch. Josh was elated. Marie's case might fit perfectly. Josh called her in early 2004. Marie had little left to lose. This was their opportunity, he told her.

Marie was terrified. Speak in front of a group of adults in Washington? Lawmakers? Talk about her family's situation? *No way.*

People were living in fear. *You could be their voice*, he argued.

Josh's quiet insistence instilled a confidence Marie hadn't felt in months. She could actually do something instead of waiting in dread. She flew to Washington that spring, using her school ID, terrified she would be detained at any minute. Staffers from the nonprofit Center for Community Change picked her up at the airport. The group, which had been founded in 1968 to honor the memory of Robert F. Kennedy's work on civil rights, would soon prove instrumental. Before she knew it, Marie was at the offices of an NPR affiliate, doing her first major interview. Her voice trembled. She wondered why anyone would want to listen to her. As the interviewer focused on Marie and other students like her, a hard knot tightened in her stomach. *Don't forget my parents*, she wanted, but was afraid, to say.

Later, Josh sat her down. She needed to tell her story again, but with more emotion.

If she needed to cry while telling it, she should cry, he and others gently suggested, because if she wanted to convince US senators, she would have to touch their hearts. Then Marie did cry, in anger and frustration. Why did she need to show those officials weakness? Josh probably saw her as some petulant teen, she figured. But when she allowed herself to imagine losing her country, her friends, her life, her heart started beating so fast she could barely breathe. Reciting what was happening to her family as if it were happening to a stranger was the only way she could get through it. That's why she did it in such a flat matter-of-fact tone. That's why she forced herself to sound more like a robot than a high school senior.

That night Marie couldn't sleep as she wondered how on earth she would get up the next day and speak in front of hundreds of people.

Later, after practicing with Josh, more interviews and a speech to immigrant advocates, she donned a royal blue cap and gown she planned to wear at her high school graduation the following month and spoke at a mock version of graduation as the honorary "valedictorian." It was all part of an action Josh had helped the Center for Community Change organize on the US Capitol grounds.[4] There she met other burgeoning leaders, like Walter Barrientos, a young Guatemalan from New York, who was already recognized among the small group of young, undocumented activists in cities like Austin, Chicago, Los Angeles, and New York. She was amazed to meet teens from Bangladesh and Trinidad, even Germany, all without immigration status. They sang the national anthem. One student read Langston Hughes's poem "Harlem," whose opening lines seemed prescient more than fifty years after he penned them.

But few apart from Marie were willing to give their names or speak about their own cases. They were still mostly flying under the federal radar, wanting to participate but terrified of the backlash they might draw against themselves and their families.

Josh helped write her speech. "Like any normal kid, I went through the daily routine of school and extracurricular activities. . . . I've worked hard to become the person I am, with good grades, athletics, Christian service, and other community involvement. . . . I was even honored by being named to the homecoming court of 2003," she told the crowd of reporters. "What makes me angry is that our nation's immigration laws don't take any of that into account. The DREAM Act would change that. It would give 65,000 young people like me the opportunity to prove we can give back to our communities, communities like mine that have been incredibly supportive."[5]

Even as Marie begged the audience to recognize her ties to Missouri, she felt torn, adding "Even if the DREAM Act passes in time for me to stay, I am faced with the difficult fact that my parents would have to leave. They have been my support through my whole life."

The older advocates kept emphasizing that she and the others had come to the United States through no fault of their own. But that clearly laid blame on someone else: her parents. She thought of the long hours her parents had put in at the restaurant and her father's terror at opening the envelope of white powder while working for the governor. She thought of how frustrated he now was at home, unable to find work because of his notoriety. It was true: she wouldn't even be in Missouri if it weren't for them, wouldn't have her friends, wouldn't have lived in the small brick house on the leafy street that always seemed to her out of a picture book. How could she fault them or even insinuate they were guilty of some crime?

She could because that was what was needed to win reprieve from deportation. She was a "Show Me State" girl, and she wanted to remain one. And if she could convince officials to exercise discretion in her case, she could set a precedent for thousands of other teens. Still, she felt as though she was betraying those she loved most.

On that trip and subsequent ones, Marie told her story again and again. At one such meeting, a senator suggested, perhaps only half joking, that she was already sixteen and ought to marry to get her green card.

Marie looked the man in the eye. "Do you have a daughter, sir?" she asked.

Another senator threatened to call immigration officials and have Marie deported from his office, not realizing that it was precisely because the government had already requested her deportation that she was brave enough to be there.

Marie returned from Washington with a newfound understanding that she was not alone. There were thousands of teens like her. That helped somewhat as she watched her friends go off to college in the fall while she devoted her time to her family's deportation case. And despite everything, Marie was in awe. If Uncle Sam didn't throw her out, she vowed, someday she'd return to Washington, not to defend her family but to work for the US government, which simultaneously terrified and captivated her.

IT TOOK MONTHS for staffers to resolve the details of the DREAM Act bill. Lawmakers received hundreds of calls from well-organized opposition for every one call of support for the bill. Even immigrant advocates were split: if they helped only the DREAMers or the field workers, what about everyone else?

By the time the bill's supporters reached an agreement on the wording around barring students from receiving federal financial aid, opponents had built enough opposition that Republican Senate majority leader Bill Frist of Tennessee refused to bring the bill to the floor. Even if he had, it would have had an even tougher road through the Republican-led House. The DREAM Act wouldn't make it out of committee again as a stand-alone bill for the rest of the decade.

With the failure of the DREAM Act, Marie refocused her efforts in Missouri and doubled down on her own case. By now she had come to the attention of many of the nation's top immigrant advocates. Marie embodied everything they were looking for: positive energy, academic achievement, a churchgoing family, and a willingness to speak up in that soft midwestern twang that somehow seemed to make lawmakers in Washington stop and listen.

Immigrant rights leaders came up with a national campaign: "We Are Marie." In the pre–social media age, local groups created a listserv around her case, one of the first real national immigrant advocacy online media campaigns. And they encouraged Marie to keep a public blog, a precursor of the Facebook posts that would later transmit the DREAMers' stories nationwide.

THE FIGHT TO SAVE MARIE from deportation heralded a quiet revolution among advocates. It was beginning to dawn on them what they had in their corner: young, American-raised immigrants like Marie, whom the rest of the country could more easily relate to than their less assimilated relatives. But it was also becoming clearer what they lacked. They needed more than caravans, big demonstrations, and marches. They needed sustained pressure from outside Washington. Yet, unlike the 1960s civil rights movement, which had relied on historic institutions such as black churches as bases for organizing across the South, or labor groups, which had union halls, undocumented immigrants had few central hubs where they could meet. The very nature of their immigration status made many of them wary of, or ineligible to join, established organizations and fearful of publicly associating with any group particularly dedicated to their issues. They needed a safe physical space before they could create a political one. They needed a ground game.

Strong immigrant rights coalitions existed in the big cities, but Cecilia Muñoz, an outspoken policy advocate for the National Council of La Raza, began to push other Washington advocates to bring in the community organizers. Yes, it was messy, but it was essential.

Cecilia, who would later serve in the Obama White House,* and others realized that the parts of the country where grassroots immigrant networks were most needed were precisely where such coalitions were weakest. Los Angeles immigrant groups were important in mobilizing and fighting for reform, for example. Yet to get anything passed in Congress, they would need grassroots pressure in states with burgeoning immigrant hubs and in swing states, such as Wisconsin and Tennessee, and Florida. As Cecilia pushed her fellow immigration advocates to look beyond Washington, Deepak Bhargava, the head of the Center for Community Change, began reaching out to nonprofits in those areas, helping provide training to young immigrants to organize around local issues like college tuition.† Marie's case to remain in the United States became one of its first national immigration campaigns.

---

* Muñoz became the director of the White House Domestic Policy Council.

† The CCC had established an immigrant-organizing committee in 2000. Now it took on a bigger role under the new title of the Fair Immigration Reform Movement.

The Center's support was important for the development of the immigrant rights movement, but so many members of this new immigrant network's local members were scrappy local advocacy groups
barely getting by just attending to the daily needs of their clients.
There simply weren't enough hours in the day or enough money for
the big-picture work. Into this void stepped New York philanthropists
Taryn Higashi and Geri Mannion, who in 2003 had begun to sow the
financial seeds for what would eventually become a national youth-
led immigrant network. Taryn worked in the Ford Foundation's human rights division, which oversaw its immigration grants. Following
the September 11, 2001, terror attacks, the foundation had provided
money to groups defending due process for immigrants, particularly
Muslims and Arabs at risk of being rounded up and deported as potential terrorism suspects. Geri worked at the Carnegie Foundation,
which had a long history of backing efforts to integrate immigrants
into American ways of life.

The two women saw how the 9/11 attacks had silenced even those
immigrants living in the country legally. But the big foundations
weren't set up to reach down to small grassroots organizations and
help them develop a base willing to speak out. They needed inter-
mediaries. Taryn and Geri set up the Four Freedoms Fund, a grant-
making conduit, which carefully chose a handful of regional groups
around the country to seed. The foundations had started in traditional
immigrant hubs like New York, Chicago, Detroit, Los Angeles, Miami,
and later Boston, and they added newer immigrant communities in
states such as Tennessee, Oregon, Washington, and Nebraska. These
nonprofits in turn could funnel the money to even smaller initiatives,
spreading the roots of the modern immigration rights movement.

It was out of these roots that the Florida Immigrant Coalition
sprouted as one of the crucial DREAMer incubators. Founded in 1998
and officially incorporated six years later, the statewide coalition was
the brainchild of Miami-based immigration attorney Cheryl Little.
She had opened a local legal advocacy center in 1996 that was now
occupied morning to night with Haitians, Cubans, Central and South

Americans, some legal, some not, all in need. The Four Freedoms Fund provided start-up money for a spin-off organizing group while the CCC lent training. And in 2004, the Florida Immigrant Coalition stepped out for its first big fight: in-state tuition for undocumented students. California and Texas had been charging their high school graduates matriculating at state universities the same tuition, regardless of immigration status, since 2001. Half a dozen more states had since passed similar legislation. It seemed natural that Florida, another immigrant-heavy state, would join them. A young dynamic Cuban American state lawmaker from South Florida named Marco Rubio championed the bill in the Tallahassee legislature. Rubio's mentor, Governor Jeb Bush, threw his support behind the effort as well. The fledgling Florida Immigrant Coalition sent university students to the state capital to offer personal testimonials.

In the end, Florida's Northern lawmakers balked, and the bill didn't pass. But the Florida Immigrant Coalition marked the in-state campaign as a breakthrough. Although the coalition hadn't won, the students had left an impression and an opening. And Cheryl and the other advocates had glimpsed what Josh Bernstein and grassroots groups around the country were beginning to see as well: the moral authority these young immigrant students wielded before lawmakers was unmatched.

AT THE TIME of the first in-state tuition debate in Florida, Felipe was a junior in high school and just beginning to think about college. It didn't occur to him that he might have to pay roughly triple the tuition rate of his classmates because of his immigration status. Felipe and his sister's family lived in a blue-and-white apartment complex, just over the line north of Miami in Broward County. Carolina was helping with her husband's business selling computer parts to Brazil and across Latin America. The family was doing better financially, but at night the couple increasingly argued. Felipe felt responsible, that his presence had placed undue stress on the union.

One morning, as he walked to school, a classmate from a neighboring apartment drove past and offered him a ride. Her name was Laura Figueroa. She was the daughter of immigrants, and her mother worked long hours. Like Felipe, she was often on her own. They quickly became confidants. Laura began to spend the weekends with Felipe's family while her mother worked, her presence a welcome distraction from the tensions at home.

Both teens found escape at Laura's church, an evangelical congregation and a far cry from the formal Catholic services Felipe had attended as a kid. The G12, as the church was known, was built around a constantly expanding set of twelve-person "cells," all connecting back to its founders, the Columbian couple Cesar and Claudia Castellanos, whose daughter Lorena led the church's Christian indie pop band, Soulfire Revolution. The G12 sermons were almost terrifying at times, with lights and video projections. It was almost like attending a rave. It was unlike anything Felipe had experienced before, and he loved it. Best of all was Lorena, bouncing up and down onstage, black boots, jeans, and a tank top, long blond hair swaying to stadium pop melodies as she sang.

Through the church, Felipe learned to proselytize, to listen to strangers, to find out what mattered to them, and to earn their confidence. He learned how to inspire Latin American immigrants in Miami to raise money for children seeking education in war-torn Uganda. He led three Bible study groups in three different parts of the city. Each week was a call to concrete action, and as long as he brought in new congregants and followed church rules, he saw a clear path ahead, a place to belong.

One night, as Felipe and Laura sat in her car, the moon rising over the palm trees and stucco apartments, air-conditioning blowing on their faces, they debated what Heaven and Hell were really like and what would happen on Judgment Day. They both wanted to be pastors and mapped out ways they could help save the world with the sorts of grandiose projects they were too embarrassed to share with their other friends. But Felipe's yearlong tourist visa had run out, and despite having grades that qualified him for state college scholarships, he was ineligible for in-state tuition. He didn't even know if he could legally apply to college.

"God is going to take care of it," Laura assured him, urging him to talk with the pastors. When Felipe told them about his status, they didn't condemn him for breaking the law by overstaying his visa, as he had expected. They hugged him and prayed for him to get a green card. It was a response that stemmed from biblical scripture, Leviticus 19:34: "You shall love the alien as yourself, for you were aliens in the land of Egypt."

It was also a practical response. By the late 2000s, about 20 percent of Latinos identified with Christian faiths other than Catholicism or mainstream Protestantism.[6] As more Latino immigrants joined the politically conservative evangelical movement, the institutions naturally responded to their new congregants' needs, including support for immigration reform.

The church was less forgiving about rule breaking in other areas. The pastors frowned on secular music and on congregants' associating with those who'd left the church. Sexual love between two men or two women was intolerable. Felipe wanted to follow all the rules, but increasingly he had to admit he was failing. The thing he'd spent years trying to ignore could no longer be ignored. He found himself attracted to other young men at school, at work, even at church. It didn't matter, he told himself, because he was also attracted to girls. Yet as much as he tried to discipline himself, he couldn't will it away. Too frightened to tell Carolina or even Laura, once more Felipe turned to his church mentors. This time they did not embrace him.

Felipe had the Devil in him, they said.

Felipe panicked. "I have the Devil inside me!" He had to fix himself, to rid his body of this offense. If he could have paid for the sessions with therapists that some in the church talked about, sessions they said could cure people, he would have. But he was broke.

His church mentors told him to fast and pray. He followed their advice. At first he fasted one day, then two. It didn't help. He tried ten days and passed out. He felt like a failure. He would have to try harder. He dived further into Bible study and church meetings.

In the spring of 2005, Felipe graduated from high school. And while everyone else chattered incessantly about their future plans, Felipe saw only a dark blank path. At a career counselor's suggestion, he went to work in a warehouse at his sister's company. When high school friends asked why he wasn't going to college, he pretended that despite his 3.75 GPA, he preferred the freedom of warehouse work. "I hate school," he lied.

Another friend from church tried to lift his spirits and mentioned one afternoon that Miami Dade College had begun accepting a small number of undocumented students, thanks in large part to one woman, Maggie Aguiar. The Cuban American international student admissions counselor, whose own family had fled Fidel Castro's revolution, had a soft spot for the undocumented teens and guided them through the application process and to the limited financial aid that was available. Not long after his friend gave him the tip, Felipe applied to Miami Dade College's honors program. He could barely speak when he received a letter of acceptance months later. That fall he took a job as a server at a nightclub in the suburb of Aventura to pay the $2,500 a semester he owed.

In fact, Maggie and others like her at Miami Dade College did more than help teens like Felipe get in to school. In welcoming them to their institution, they inadvertently created a pipeline of young, well-educated activists for the Florida Immigrant Coalition. The Coalition's new director, Maria Rodriguez, had gotten her start in activism protesting apartheid at Georgetown University and was eager to work more with the students who had testified in Tallahassee for the in-state tuition bill. Among them was a vocal, young Ecuadoran native and student government leader named Maria Gabriela "Gaby" Pacheco. Soon Maria and Gaby helped establish a new offshoot of the Coalition led by the students themselves, modeled after similar groups in Los Angeles, Chicago, and Boston. They called it Students Working for Equal Rights, or SWER.

But Felipe wasn't looking for any such group when he arrived at the college. As part of his commitment to the church, he looked for ways to raise awareness about aid for Ugandan schoolchildren, framing the issue as a question of access to education. And if he couldn't participate in the US democratic process, he could at least participate on campus. He decided to run for student government, making the Ugandan children part of his platform. To his surprise, he won, and through student government quickly became friends with Gaby. They both dreamed of becoming teachers, but they had something else in common: just like Felipe, Gaby's family was living in the country illegally.

There's another group you might be interested in, Gaby told him one day. And so he found his way to SWER, an organization that would change Felipe's life and, through him, inspire thousands of others across the United States.

OUTSIDE OF SAFE HAVENS like Miami Dade College, though, the mid-2000s ushered in an even more difficult time for those in the country illegally. Whether most Americans wanted to admit it, many of the nation's largest industries—farms, hotels, restaurants, in-home health and child care, construction—increasingly thrived off the muscle of undocumented workers.

Yet because these immigrants were often paid under the table and were not officially recognized as being in the country, much of the added stress they created on the local infrastructure also could not be officially addressed, meaning the responsibility to help them integrate into American life often fell to local law enforcement and politicians, those with the fewest resources. The children of new arrivals often required language support in schools. Undocumented immigrants were less likely to go to the doctor out of a combination of fear and lack of access to insurance, but proportionately, they were more likely to end up in the emergency room.[7,8]

It was hard to see where textile jobs went overseas or how many machines were now doing the work of locksmiths and factory workers. Visible were the changing last names and the changing color of many new Americans. Between 2000 and 2010,[9] while the white US population remained steady, the percentage of Asian Americans and Latinos each grew by 43 percent.

Americans had once directed such fear and mistrust toward Italian, Jewish, Chinese, and Irish immigrants.[10] Now it was increasingly directed at those coming from Latin America. The United States had long maintained a complicated relationship with its neighbors in the south, particularly Mexico, importing Mexican laborers during times of need, particularly during both world wars, then sending them back as soon as US soldiers returned. But in fact, for most of the nation's history, fear of new immigrants focused on those coming from Europe and Asia.

Then came the 1965 Immigration and Nationality Act, which ultimately ended national visa quotas in an attempt to loosen discriminatory regulation on southern Europeans, Jews, and Chinese. It also included a new twist, "family reunification," which gave priority to relatives of those already in the United States, a move that lawmakers believed would weigh in favor of white northern European immigrants already living in the country, who would presumably bring in more relatives and balance out the newcomers from Asia, Africa, and Latin America. But as it turned out, most of the European families that wanted to migrate already had. And with the last world war more than a generation behind, their home countries had become increasingly stable. Instead, family reunification became a lifeline for Latin American and Asian immigrants seeking a new home in the United States. Four decades later, many of those who had feared the influx of immigrants, now feared what would happen if millions of these potential new citizens were allowed to petition for their spouses, parents, children, and siblings.

In 2005, more than 150 immigration enforcement bills were pro-

posed in thirty states seeking to penalize those living in the country
illegally as well as anyone who sought to help them. That same year,
the federal government passed a law requiring states to provide a national REAL ID card to more easily catch those in the country without
authorization.

Around that time, news outlets began to pick up stories about a
loose coalition of private citizens patrolling the US-Mexican border.
The previous year, a retired CPA and Marine Corps veteran named
Jim Gilchrist from Orange County, California, had founded what became known as the Minuteman Project. This group of gun-wielding
vigilantes was fed up with government inaction and promised to stop
the criminals crossing the border and protect Americans from the
"Latinization"[11] of their country. Gilchrist's cofounder, Chris Simcox,[12]
would later be convicted of sexually molesting a young girl and receive a nearly twenty-year sentence for his crime. But at the time, the
Minuteman Project served up a visual symbol of Americans' desire
for greater law and order, and the group's very existence pressured the
federal government to take more action.

President Bush condemned the Minuteman leaders' vigilante
swagger, but he urged Congress to step up enforcement and pass
some kind of immigration reform. As the former governor of Texas,
he understood the role immigrants played in his state's economy, and,
after all, his younger brother Jeb had married a woman from Mexico.
Yet the president's exhortations were too little, too late. He had spent
most of his political capital on the Iraq War, and much of what remained he'd bet on an unsuccessful push to overhaul Social Security.
Congress seemed to heed only the president's call for enforcement.
Bill Frist, a doctor turned politician, was the Senate majority leader,
and his four years at the helm coincided with a massive increase in
funding for border security and for the detention[13] of immigrants living in the country illegally.*

---

* Senator Frist wasn't in charge of who won Immigration and Customs Enforcement contracts, but during his leadership, much of the increase in detention

BACK IN MISSOURI, Marie's family story became something of a celebrity cause, reaching some of the most powerful people in the government. It wasn't just the "We Are Marie" campaign. The Jefferson City Council passed a resolution urging federal lawmakers to allow them to stay. Senator Durbin asked to meet with Marie after seeing her interviewed on TV. *Latina* magazine named her one of its top ten Women of the Year in 2005. Officials at a small liberal arts school, Westminster College, in nearby Fulton, Missouri, learned of Marie's case, and its admission officers encouraged her to apply. She received a partial private scholarship.

"If we should turn our back on someone like her," Westminster College president Fletcher Lamkin warned, "it sends a very powerful negative message that something's wrong, something's really wrong."[14]

But none of her celebrity lifted the very real threat of deportation. And as summer approached, Marie and her family waited for a last-minute reprieve. Despite fourteen years of living in the United States, despite buying a home and paying taxes every year, Marvin and Marina had little legal claim to stay. They were at the mercy of DHS's discretion, and the government was not predisposed to waive a deportation order, especially not for what had become such a high-profile case.

As evidenced by the very name of the "We Are Marie" campaign, advocates had never really banked on saving the entire family; it was Marie they set their sights on. And it was she who could set a precedent for the kind of prosecutorial discretion that might justify the broader DREAM Act.

---

money found its way to the private prison company Corrections Corporation of America (CCA), based in his home state of Tennessee (where at least two top Frist staffers would eventually land). CCA and the GEO Group engineered contracts that guaranteed them a minimum number of detainees each night, creating de facto detention quotas for law enforcement. CCA, later rebranded CoreCivic, had been on the brink of bankruptcy at the turn of the century. Detaining immigrants gave the company a new lease on life.

Marie still felt nauseous each time she told her story and framed herself as almost a victim of a crime. Yet she also knew that in the worst-case scenario, her parents could survive back in Costa Rica, while Missouri was the only home she remembered. She clung to the hope that through her own story, she could spare them all. Through the CCC, she not only kept a blog to count down their departure, but she also did a podcast to raise awareness about her case and the DREAM Act. She traveled to Wisconsin, Chicago, and Miami to do radio interviews and make speeches.

The family's deportation date was set for July 5, 2005. The three of them bought plane tickets for Costa Rica. On the afternoon of July 1, 2005, Marie received a call from her attorney: DHS had granted a last-minute reprieve from deportation.

Marie gripped the phone, shouting. She wanted to sing! The news was too good to be true!

Wait, wait, her attorney stopped her. *It's just you.* At the last minute, Durbin had reached an Immigration and Customs Enforcement (ICE) official at an Independence Day party, convincing him to sign off on Marie's waiver.

Marie tried to breathe. She had four days to say good-bye to her parents, maybe for a decade. Marvin and Marina faced a ten-year ban from the United States for overstaying their visas. If Marie were to leave to go visit them, she would be banned from returning for ten years as well.

The family spent the July Fourth holiday weekend packing. The day her parents left, they all wore T-shirts emblazoned with the words "God Bless the USA."[15] They met friends at a nearby park and prayed with fellow churchgoers. Local TV stations showed up to cover Marvin and Marina's departure. An independent filmmaker captured their last hours together.

Marie vowed to continue her fight, "and use my story so this doesn't happen to other families."

Marvin put one arm around Marina, the other around Marie. He spoke a few prepared words. "Everybody, take care of my daughter," he pleaded.[16]

Later, Marvin lifted his suitcases into the family SUV and hugged his daughter so hard he nearly crushed the reading glasses dangling around his neck. Some forty cars caravanned with them through downtown Jefferson City to say good-bye.

And then they were gone.

Marie exchanged her plane ticket to Costa Rica for one to visit relatives in California, while friends back in Missouri auctioned off most of her family's belongings to raise money for her. Marie couldn't bear to watch. That fall she attended Westminster College as an exchange student, meaning she had to sit in orientation sessions with privileged classmates from around the globe as they learned about American culture, politics, and history. Meanwhile, she moved in with a friend's family, storing the last of her family's belongings in the basement, where she slept until school started.

At Westminster, it was hard enough to focus during those first few months—her mind often distracted with her parents' resettlement—but then there were the cameras, following the famous young immigrant activist across campus. Some days, Marie wished she could simply melt away. At nineteen, she was balancing her freshman-year course load with selling her family home, maintaining grades high enough to keep her scholarships, working to pay the rest of the tuition, and sending money to her parents in Costa Rica. By the time she got her work permit (and finally her driver's license), she was a semester behind in school payments. Her reprieve was only for 365 days. Every morning as she woke up and looked around her dorm room, Marie wondered where she'd be in a year.

She didn't have much time for the freshman social scene. In the rare moments between work and school assignments, Marie hurried to the gym, as if by running in place on the treadmill she could somehow escape the panic attacks that woke her up in the middle of the night. One afternoon on her way there, a football came flying at her from across the green. Marie instinctively caught it and tossed it back to its owners. One of them, a blond, blue-eyed, corn-fed Kansas boy named Chapin Deel, introduced himself and complimented her throw. Marie recalled him from the school welcoming committee. He was a burly senior and in a fraternity. Marie could hear her mother's voice: *Stay away! Far away.*

Chapin's friends urged her to come to a party at their house. Marie demurred. After that, though, she seemed to run into Chapin everywhere. The only thing Chapin knew about immigrant visas was that his uncle had married a woman from Ukraine and easily secured her a green card. He didn't understand why Marie's parents had been deported if they'd paid taxes and bought a home. He didn't understand why Marie had been given only a year's deferment when it was clear little would change her immigration status in that time. Chapin asked Marie to tell him her story. She'd told already it so many times. Yet somehow she found the words tumbling out to Chapin. And he listened.

She spoke with her parents every day, and in time, the blue-eyed boy with the wavy wheat-colored hair found his way into their conversations. Marie wondered how she could be so happy when her heart was still cracked open, how she could dream about Chapin and also wake up sobbing for her parents. The two realities seemed to brush past one another each day and return to their separate universes. But with Chapin, she could have fun. She didn't feel like the immigrant girl on TV.

Marie began to get more emails and calls from other teens asking how to save themselves and their families from deportation. She tried to give advice, referring them to the lawyers and advocates who had been essential to her victory. But she couldn't respond to them all. There were too many. And it seemed crazy to suggest each student mount a national campaign to win a reprieve. Still, she flew back to Washington to advocate for herself and others, and when there was no money for the flight, she took the bus. She continued the blog. She tried to shield Chapin, but one afternoon, in tears, she showed him a series of online comments posted by people suggesting she be both deported and killed.

Chapin's mouth dropped open. "Don't ever read that stuff again," he told her.

In the fall of 2005, Marie was among the first to receive what would become the Center for Community Change's annual Change Champion Award. Her fellow recipients included an actress, a philanthropist, a media pioneer, and a charismatic freshman senator from Illinois named Barack Obama.

3

A WAKE-UP CRY

Hundreds of thousands of immigrants demonstrate in downtown Los Angeles, California, May 1, 2006. (DAVID S. HOLLOWAY/GETTY IMAGES)

On Monday, April 10, 2006, teachers at Thomas Jefferson Middle School in Arlington, Virginia, stood in front of nearly every exit. They had heard the rumors, seen the scattered headlines over the weekend. The demonstrations had arrived in the nation's capital, and although marches were nothing new across the Potomac River, school administrators sensed this one was different. For days, whispers floated through the teacher's lounge about students planning to cut school.

Hareth was one of those students. Now an eighth grader at Thomas Jefferson, she mingled with the offspring of K Street lobbyists and congressional staffers. Many of her classmates were also foreign born, yet Hareth knew without being told that her immigration status was different from her friends born in Argentina, Mexico, or even Bolivia whose families held permanent residency or citizenship. She and her parents did not discuss it much at home, but Hareth knew not to cause trouble, not to miss school.

This day was different. Spanish-language TV and radio had been airing news around the clock, encouraging turnout at the marches. Hareth's mother had to go to work at her nanny job, but Hareth's father planned to take her now three-year-old sister, Claudia, to the rally. Even her Tía Eli was going. Hareth and her friends planned their outfits the night before. Through the radio, they knew participants were supposed to wear white. Purity. Hope. An effort to avoid controversial slogans? Hareth wasn't sure of the meaning. She was just excited to be part of this thing bigger than herself, than her friends, than even her family.

The teachers were fast, but the kids were faster, having honed their escape skills with midday snack runs to the 7-Eleven across the street. One teacher spotted them and yelled down the hallway, but Hareth and several of her friends kept running. They found an unguarded exit and sprinted toward it, not stopping until they'd pushed open the heavy metal doors, spilled down the steps, and finally reached the bus stop across the street. Hareth's heart was still pounding when a bus finally wheezed to a stop and opened its doors. Inside, she collapsed onto the cool plastic seat. They had made it.

By the time they arrived at the National Mall an hour later, it was teeming with people yelling chants in Spanish and English, banging drums, and blowing horns to a tropical beat. From their windows and office balconies along the demonstration route, men in suits and women in starched shirts looked down at the demonstrators with a combination of surprise, awe, and shock.

"The people, united, will never be defeated!" the crowd chanted. Above the sea of white shirts floated thousands of signs. Many were homemade. Many others were professionally printed, subtle calling cards for the organizations behind the rally, like the blue "We Are America" sign from a new coalition cofounded by the Center for Community Change; "Justicia y Dignidad para Todos Los Immigrantes" (Justice and Dignity for All Immigrants); and the signs from the League of United Latin American Citizens, or LULAC, a group started nearly eighty years before by Hispanic World War I veterans.

And then there was the simple message "Today we march. Tomorrow we vote."

Senator Kennedy addressed the crowd. The veteran lawmaker had steered the 1965 immigration bill through Congress in the wake of his brother's murder as part of a package of civil rights–related laws. He still considered immigration reform more of a civil rights issue than an economic one. That day he promised those gathered a broad immigration bill with a path to citizenship. "We will never give up! We will never give in!" he thundered.[1] The crowd roared back, "*¡Sí se puede!*"

Looking up at the faraway figures standing onstage, Hareth tried to imagine herself up there one day, too. She couldn't remember ever in her life seeing so many people peacefully together, so many people who looked like her, so many people asking for something that seemed so awfully basic—not just a law, but to be seen, to be recognized.

The march in Washington was big, yet it wasn't the biggest march that spring. Across the United States millions of immigrants, many in the country illegally, came out during the spring of 2006 and shook the nation awake.[*]

---

[*] Two years before, the quirky independent film *A Day Without a Mexican* had

The same day Hareth went to the National Mall, at least 100,000 rallied in Chicago;[2] up to 500,000 had rallied the day before in Dallas, with smaller marches in cities such as Nashville, Boston, and Atlanta.[3] The marches were for the most part led by adults. Still, in a handful of cities, including Los Angeles, New York, and Boston, young leaders like Walter Barrientos, whom Marie had met at the Capitol, spoke about the DREAM Act to ensure it wasn't forgotten in the broader call for immigration reform. Walter and another rising young leader, Cristina Jiménez Moreto, helped organize buses to take students to the demonstrations in New York and good-naturedly competed with their friends in Boston to see who could get the biggest DREAM Act banners on the nightly news.

In Chicago, college senior Tania Unzueta biked twenty minutes across the city to join the demonstrators along Lake Michigan, shivering in the chilly wind but warmed by the crowd. Tania worked part-time at a community paper and radio program, and as she wove through traffic she considered the question one of her bosses had posed to her a few days before. *Are you a journalist or an activist? You have to choose.*

What was she? She was an undocumented immigrant. She was also a hard-driving honors student who'd been her high school swim team captain and had dreamed of going to college. She'd wanted to do things the right way and had voluntarily returned to her native Mexico in 2001 after graduation in the hope of obtaining a student visa. At first, she'd viewed the trip as an opportunity to see her grandparents and cousins for the first time in years. That changed after her visit to the US embassy. Years later Tania still remembered a US official not only denying her student visa request but also berating her for the thousands of dollars the federal government had spent on her elementary and secondary education. And by returning to Mexico, Tania

---

comically imagined what the country would look like without its Latino workforce (baseball rosters half empty, children without nannies, food production backed up, government bureaucrats gone, leaves blowing everywhere). Now it seemed as if the essence of the film were coming true.

had triggered the ten-year ban against reentering the United States. Senator Durbin had come to her rescue, helping her obtain humanitarian parole.* She'd been given a year and had returned to Chicago to attend the University of Illinois. But now she was once more undocumented and generally tried to keep a low profile when it came to her status. Initially, she had planned just to cover the event for the community paper. Then her father, who'd helped organize the march, suggested she speak at the rally. They needed more young, undocumented people to share their stories, he'd urged. *He's right*, Tania thought. *This march, this movement, needs more young people.*

As she parked her bike and made her way through the demonstrators, Tania felt the energy of the crowd course through her. This wasn't the path she had wished for. But if her choice were between journalist and activist, there really was no choice, not today. She stepped up onto the stage.

Most Americans who watched English-language TV coverage of the rallies nationwide were dumbfounded. Where had these masses of people come from? In Washington, Leonard Downie Jr., then the executive editor of the *Washington Post*, summoned the department heads to a meeting. Many major news outlets, including the *Post*, had missed the huge story in the run-up to the marches. He didn't intend it to happen again. Downie created new beats, making immigration a top priority; similar conversations took place in newsrooms across the country.

Had the *Post* or the rest of the country followed the Spanish-language media chatter, they wouldn't have been surprised at all about the rallies that spring. Those newscasts were covering the run-up to the marches around the clock. Some of the cameramen and field producers were the sons and daughters of undocumented immigrants or had once picked strawberries themselves.

But in 2006, an invisible wall existed between Spanish-language

---

* She had been scheduled to go to Washington, DC, along with Tereza Lee, to testify at the ill-fated September 12, 2001, DREAM Act hearing.

and mainstream English-language media. Few journalists in the mainstream media were bilingual, and even fewer considered it worthwhile to follow what was happening in Spanish. That invisible wall allowed both Democratic and Republican candidates to say one thing in Spanish to one group of constituents and a completely differ-ent thing in English to another. It was what allowed most Americans not to see the millions of people living in fear as they quietly helped keep the engine of the US economy running.

Still, pressure for reform had begun to grow on all sides. In the twilight of his presidency, George W. Bush pushed once again for comprehensive immigration reform that would resolve the situation for millions of immigrants living in the country illegally. To get busi-ness on board, the bill made it easier for companies to hire temporary workers, and it toughened enforcement policies. It was the kind of comprehensive legislation not seen since the Immigration Reform and Control Act of 1986, passed under President Ronald Reagan. It was a bill that could secure the increasingly unpopular president[4] a legacy beyond the quagmire of the Iraq War. For Democrats and Republicans in Congress, tackling immigration was good policy *and* good politics—controversial enough to energize their bases and boost turnout during the midterm elections.

Immigrants, already concerned about the stepped-up enforcement, waited nervously to see what kind of bill would prevail. The bad news arrived in time for the December holidays, with the House passage of a measure by Wisconsin Republican representative Jim Sensenbren-ner. The bill, officially titled the Border Protection, Antiterrorism, and Illegal Immigration Control Act of 2005,[5] quickly became known sim-ply as the "Sensenbrenner bill." It would make living in the United States without a valid visa no longer an administrative violation; now it would be a federal crime. Overnight, millions of people would qualify as criminals. Those who provided undocumented people with shelter or even a ride to work (or hired them as a gardener or nanny) could also face felony charges and up to three years in prison, possibly more.

Even Republican lawmakers quickly realized adding the criminal-

ization section was akin to dropping a smoldering match on Southern California's parched San Bernardino Mountains. Sensenbrenner
tried to save his bill, offering to tone down the language. But Democrats weren't having it. Anything that would give the proposal a better
chance was bad news from their perspective. The majority of Democrats voted to keep the bill as is, strategically ensuring the bill would
leave committee with a so-called poison pill, one they hoped would
doom it or at least create a significant backlash.

Then they promptly voted against the entire proposal. The bill
passed the GOP-led House anyway and, by December 2005, sailed
over to the Republican-led Senate.

The backlash outside Congress was swift. The name Sensenbrenner became a new rallying cry on the lips of immigrants, prompting
marches around the country.

DARIO GUERRERO MENESES rode with his dad to downtown Los Angeles
to join some 400,000 people for the May 1 march on International
Workers Day. Like Hareth, he was headed into eighth grade in the fall,
and a top student who'd just won a spot at a summer program sponsored by Johns Hopkins University. Dario daydreamed about becoming a physicist and rarely missed class. But when his dad suggested
they go with friends to show solidarity, he jumped at the chance.

Dario Guerrero Sr. had worked his way up from contractor to manager in his small company, now overseeing a dozen other immigrant
laborers. The work meant he had medical insurance, and it had enabled the family to leave their cramped apartment and purchase a
small two-bedroom house a few blocks from the freeway in the com-
muter town of Carson. It also meant Dario's father was rarely home,
leaving Dario's mother to oversee the day-to-day child care. Spending
a day with his father usually meant helping out at a work site. Dario
knew his dad wouldn't take the day off if this wasn't something important. Besides, Dario liked the idea of joining in with so many other
Mexican immigrants.

As they sped up the 405 freeway that morning, Dario sat packed into the back seat with several of his father's friends, listening happily as the men cursed the traffic and pretended to spot *la migra*. They parked on the outskirts of downtown, and Dario watched the undulating crowd, some carrying Mexican flags, most carrying American ones, wondering what it must be like for all those people, his father's friends, who'd crossed the border illegally and whose lives remained forever in limbo. At his magnet school, Dario was one of the few Mexican Americans in the honors program and definitely one of the few who had to commute to get there, but that was nothing compared to what some of his father's workers had to go through. After all, his parents owned a house, or at least they had a mortgage. They had come on a visa. His dad had a driver's license. And at work his dad was almost *el jefe*.

Yet as they walked under the bright sun, images Dario usually shoved to the back of his mind flitted to the forefront: multiple credit card offers and other mail he'd seen arrive for his father in different names; his parents' reluctance to talk to police; the fact that his dad and mom had never taken him to visit Mexico, the country they professed to love so much. Dario turned to his father. He looked so free, happier than Dario remembered seeing him in a long time.

Dario Sr. glanced over at his son. He wondered whether now was the time. It would be a relief to come clean, yet such a burden. His son was so smart, too smart for his own good sometimes, but still he hated to weigh the kid down. He'd tell him when he had to, not before. He grinned back at Dario.

They turned toward the thousands of people streaming past them. Staring at the humanity before him, Dario silently asked the same questions those in the English-language media were beginning to ask: Where had they all come from? What had united them all enough to come out on this day? The Sensenbrenner bill might have been the catalyst. But the Los Angeles turnout, and indeed the turnout nationwide, was the result of more than anger and frustration. It also took careful planning by immigrant advocates and an extra push from two American traditions: the Catholic Church and the morning radio DJ.

In early March, Los Angeles Catholic cardinal Roger Mahony gave an Ash Wednesday address encouraging both parishioners and clergy to defy the Sensenbrenner bill, were it to pass. It was a call to action echoed by clergy nationwide. Still, the activists needed something more, a megaphone to reach beyond their echo chamber. They found it in a pair of the nation's top Spanish-language radio hosts, better known by their on-air monikers: Tweety Bird and The Boogeyman.

Eddie "Piolín" (Tweety Bird) Sotelo had crossed the border illegally years before, working as a DJ long before a radio station manager helped him get a work permit and eventually a green card. He'd never forgotten the fear and the stigma he faced early on as he tried to keep his immigration status a secret. He had made it his personal mission to stop the Sensenbrenner bill. When he heard about the marches, he decided to pitch in, orchestrating a secret meeting with his rival DJs, including his mentor Renán "El Cucuy" (The Boogeyman) Almendárez Coello, who had spoken at the 2003 Immigrant Workers Freedom Ride. Together, the group agreed to promote the demonstrations.

"I told God that if he gave me an opportunity as a radio announcer, I was going to help my people," Sotelo told the Los Angeles Times shortly after the first LA marches.[6] In late April, he devoted several hours of his show to the bill and the march, time usually spent more on the latest celebrity sex scandals and off-color jokes. Soon the DJs' messages were picked up by the Spanish-language TV stations and unfurled across their syndicated radio broadcasts nationwide.

IN MIAMI, the showing that spring was far weaker than in other major cities. Only a few thousand people turned out. Miami was not a place where people marched. The high heat and humidity made afternoon strolls anywhere but the beach unpleasant six months of the year. For many residents, especially those from Cuba, such events also left a bad taste, too much a reminder of the "spontaneous" pro–Fidel Castro marches that were compulsory back home. For others from Latin

America, protesting in the streets had landed friends and family in jail or worse.

But that was only part of the reason. By 2006, more than half of Miami-Dade County residents had been born outside the United States.[7] The nation's two largest Spanish-language media companies had most of their studios there. Top doctors, lawyers, and city officials were bilingual. It wasn't just a badge of pride to speak two languages; it was often a requisite for doing business. Many immigrants in Miami weren't living outside the main power structure. They were part of it.*

Not all of these people were well off by any means. Many were South American immigrants who had overstayed visas after fleeing economic and political crises back home and did fear deportation. Still, they enjoyed a level of social, if not economic, support regardless of their immigration status, a security not always accorded to many recent arrivals in other parts of the country.

Puerto Ricans were also flocking to Florida, skyrocketing from roughly 100,000 in 1980 to more than 1 million by 2014.[8] Unlike other new arrivals, Puerto Ricans could speak up because they didn't have to worry about being in the country illegally. They were already citizens.

Conversely, those immigrants in South Florida who didn't have that support—and those who were black or looked more indigenous, including the Haitian and Central American tomato pickers, hotel workers, and home builders—often had even fewer resources and support networks than immigrants in places such as California and New York, where they made up a larger share of the undocumented

---

* The Cuban Adjustment Act of 1966 allows most Cubans who make a legal entry into the United States to apply for residency after a year. Cubans can also generally receive financial aid and other benefits almost immediately. And until January 2017, Cubans who made it to dry US territory were generally allowed to stay, regardless of whether or not they came with a visa. But one of the most underreported benefits that Cubans have is that there is an additional twenty thousand visas set aside for them each year. That's nearly the same number of visas given to Mexico, whose population is more than ten times that of Cuba.

community. Many couldn't risk marching. And yet in small pockets elsewhere in the state, marchers did come out en masse, with some 75,000 farmworkers and allies turning out on April 10 in Fort Myers.

But for Felipe, the thousands of protesters who did show up might as well have been a million. Living in a Portuguese-speaking home where the Univision and Telemundo networks were rarely on, he was almost as surprised as the rest of America to see so many people pouring into the streets. The TV images of flags waving past the heart of downtown Miami and past the historic Freedom Tower, where Cuban refugees had once been processed as they fled Castro's revolution, etched themselves into his brain.

Felipe joined the marchers that day, and seeing all those people together, he could feel something new breaking loose inside. The change wasn't immediate. Over the next year, he still spent most of his extracurricular energy on the church. By 2007, he began dating a young woman and proposed to her less than twelve months later. It was as if he were fighting against his own rebellion. He hoped that if he could commit to his fiancée, he could rid himself of the Devil once and for all. The two married in 2008 but separated a few months later. Felipe castigated himself. He had failed at one of the most sacred promises, failed to rid himself of the Devil, failed to listen to the voice inside that had warned him that he was making a mistake.

As he struggled with his marriage, Felipe began to struggle more with the church's rigid rules. He began to chafe at the pressure not to maintain friendships with those who'd left it. Slowly, school activities replaced the singular focus the church had held in his life. He began to frequent SWER, the immigrant student group his friend Gaby had introduced him to. After Gaby's home was raided by immigration agents and another friend was detained, Felipe grew more outspoken. He threw himself into his student government responsibilities and into SWER activities with the same energy with which he had not long before proselytized for the church. He was elected student body president. Now Felipe turned to the Florida Immigrant Coalition's director, Maria Rodriguez, for the counsel he'd once sought in the church. Unlike the pastors, Maria didn't condemn him for whom he was attracted to. For the first time, Felipe began to believe that even his sexuality might be worthy of respect in God's eyes. Still, he kept that and his immigration status to himself and to his close circle of friends.

It was in SWER's cramped campus office that Felipe met a tall, charismatic Colombian named Juan Rodriguez. Juan was in the process of legalizing his immigration status thanks to his stepmother. Unlike Felipe, he'd come to the United States as a small boy, but he had lived most of his years in South Florida as an undocumented immigrant. He had spent high school determined to win an academic scholarship, joining the creative writing club and pretty much every other nonsports extracurricular activity at school. He'd graduated with top marks. And yet like Felipe, his immigration status had relegated him to janitorial work until he, too, found his way to the honors college at Miami Dade.

Juan listened to Felipe lament the demise of his marriage and the uncertainty of his future. Juan was outspoken both politically and personally, unabashed about his attraction to both women and men. His blunt confidence was infectious. When Felipe stood next to Juan, his legal status, the arguments within his family, none of it mattered quite so much. When Juan laughed, Felipe could breathe more easily. Sometimes Felipe looked over and caught his friend staring back. Sometimes he had to look away. But at that time Juan had a girlfriend, and Felipe was still married, at least on paper, and he still feared the Devil inside.

So he focused on the political. He could feel it, something was happening. In pockets around the country, young immigrants who had quietly honed their organizing skills campaigning for college access were beginning to find one another. As with the student group in Miami, they often became active with the broader immigrant coalitions first before splitting off on their own.

Back in 2005, the National Council of La Raza had held its annual conference in Philadelphia and brought together several of these up-and-coming leaders. Julieta Garibay, a shy student at the University of Texas at Austin, was close to earning her nursing degree but had no way of finding employment in her field. Tired of lying to even her closest friends, she had sent out an email blast, sharing her predicament with them. To Julieta's surprise, her in-box was flooded with confessions like her own. Soon after, she began organizing a support group for fellow undocumented students at UT Austin and was invited to speak at NCLR's national conference. NCLR leaders suggested that she combine her talk with those of other burgeoning undocumented leaders: Walter Barrientos, the Guatemalan activist, now a graduate of Baruch College in New York; and a Peruvian from Boston named Carlos Saavedra. They shared similar stories. They promised to stay in touch. And they did, over the next few years forming a small but tight-knit network, spread out across the country.

IN THE WAKE OF THE 2006 PROTESTS, the Senate version of the Sensenbrenner bill never made it to the floor. The marchers had won, but their victory had exacted a price. They had made themselves visible and also vulnerable. Employers cracked down on those who sought to miss more work for subsequent protests. The demonstrations became smaller.

The Sensenbrenner bill may have generated the most controversy, but it was never the only proposal on immigration up for consideration during that time. Throughout much of 2006 and 2007, lawmakers and activists remained hopeful of a bipartisan compromise on comprehensive immigration reform. In the House, a Republican from Arizona, Jim Kolbe, who unlike the Milwaukee-raised Sensenbrenner had grown up along the border and now represented it, tried to pass a more balanced bill, along with a fellow Arizonan, Jeff Flake, also a Republican, and a Democrat from Illinois, Luis Gutiérrez.

Kolbe wanted to find middle ground: add security to the border, help adjust the status of those who'd been working in the United States for years, and make it easier for people to come legally and work for short periods of time. The congressional veteran had seen the immigration crisis coming for decades, and nowhere was it more evident than in his home state. He remembered as a kid watching Mexican men pull back a few barbed wires early in the morning to cross over for work. It was that easy. Kolbe was a freshman congressman when they passed the last big immigration bill in 1986. Along with a path to citizenship for those in the country illegally, it had included provisions to crack down on the demand for undocumented workers—mainly penalties for companies that relied on their cheap labor. But the sanctions had ended up as mostly a wink and a nod.

"I said at the time it's going to fail because you're going to create a one-time thing, and then you're going to get another wave that says 'When are we going to get our amnesty?'" Kolbe later recalled.

The 1996 immigration law a decade later did add sanctions. But the sanctions, coupled with tougher penalties for the immigrants who sought to reenter the United States, meant not only did fewer immigrants dare to leave, but now they saved up to bring over their spouses and children instead of returning home. The handful of men living in one apartment next to a factory morphed into immigrant families spending Sunday at the mall and enrolling their children in local schools.

"People said, 'Oh my God, what is this flood?' Well, the flood was people bringing in their families," Kolbe said. "That is the most fundamental change that has taken place."

For Kolbe, it didn't help that lawmakers in California and Texas had put up such a fuss that they were able to beef up border security in San Diego and El Paso, funneling more people across the rocky Arizona desert, where building a wall was virtually impossible. By 2006, Kolbe's own brother was giving him grief about immigration. He lived on a private tract of land within the Sierra Vista, along the San Pedro Riparian National Conservation Area, a rare desert waterway. The land, overseen by the Bureau of Land Management, was a favorite crossing spot for those coming into the United States illegally.

It had become littered with discarded backpacks, empty water jugs, and other trash left behind by the immigrants.

To make matters more complicated, when the Border Patrol apprehended immigrants who needed medical attention, first responders complained that the agents would often call them rather than transport the wounded,[9] even when the injuries were the result of a Border Patrol chase. Whichever agency transported the sick and wounded would likely be stuck with the bill. Health care providers and first responders chafed at the added burden.

Local residents were not feeling inclined to generosity toward the people they saw incurring these costs for their community. In 2006, Arizona voters had opted to end years of providing in-state college tuition to undocumented immigrants living there. Not long after that ballot initiative passed, the state legislature toughened sanctions against companies that knowingly hired those in the country illegally. In Washington, Kolbe's compromise bill never made it out of committee. During the 2006 midterm elections, he opted not to run for a third term and was replaced in the primary by a state lawmaker well known for his hard line on immigration (who promptly lost to newcomer Democrat Gabrielle Giffords).

Even so, in the Senate, Kolbe's fellow Republican Arizonans, veteran lawmakers John Kyl and John McCain, along with Ted Kennedy, pushed on for a compromise, understanding that a pure enforcement approach would never address the number of people who had already made their home in the country without legal status. To shape the bill, Kennedy tapped the staffer he trusted most on immigration: Esther Olavarria, a native of Cuba raised in Florida, who had worked with Cheryl Little at the Florida Immigrant Advocacy Center a decade before.

Esther had been waiting years for lawmakers to pay enough attention to get something passed. Both the House and Senate had flipped during the 2006 midterm elections, and Democrats, who were more likely to support the legislation, had a majority. Time was of the essence. Now was her chance.

While lawmakers sought a legislative solution, DHS had meanwhile stepped up large-scale work site raids across the country. Among the businesses raided: a factory in New Bedford, Massachusetts, Kennedy's home state, where undocumented immigrants were making backpacks for soldiers in Iraq.[10] The raids were meant to signal to Congress and the nation that the Bush administration was serious about enforcement. They also served as a warning for businesses of what they could expect going forward under the legal status quo. By December 2006, Immigration and Customs Enforcement had tripled the number of work site raids it had conducted the year before to roughly 4,400. Operation Wagon Train, as it was called, was the largest work site crackdown in the nation's history.

In the end the businesses suffered little. They mostly faced minimal fines and hired new workers. Those hit hard were the immigrants themselves.[11] In some cases, DHS agents rounded up and deported parents without giving them time to arrange care for their children.

The federal actions were soon replicated in some places at the local level, most famously in Arizona. That year, local Spanish-language radio hosts began warning undocumented residents about stepped up raids by Maricopa County sheriff Joe Arpaio, who liked to brag that he was "America's toughest sheriff." Arpaio had already garnered media attention for building an outside overflow tent city at the local jail, where prisoners stayed even during the scorching 103-degree Arizona summer nights. He boasted his dogs ate better than his inmates.

Arpaio would make his next big splash the following year by testing out a new law that prohibited businesses from knowingly hiring an "unauthorized alien." He sent his agents to raid the Arizona corporate offices of a major Maricopa employer, Golfland Entertainment Centers, which ran several water parks.[12] Rumors swirled that some 100 employees might be undocumented, and deputies collected records on about 400 of them, but ultimately fewer than a dozen of the 1,000 workers were detained. The raid was billed as a crackdown on illegal business practices, though in the end, Golfland never faced any pen-

alties since it had participated in the federal government's new, voluntary E-Verify program to check whether potential hires were eligible to
work. It was essentially off the hook for anyone who managed to slip
through the system.[13] As with the federal raids, so it often went.

IN KENNEDY'S OFFICE, Esther continued to work on refining the bipartisan, comprehensive bill, reaching across the aisle and building support among veteran immigration advocates.

During that time, the advocates increasingly turned to the young
group of "DREAMers" to promote both the DREAM Act and the
broader legislation, regularly reaching out to students such as Walter
Barrientos and Ecuadoran native Cristina Jiménez in New York; Julieta Garibay from Texas; Carlos Saavedra of Massachusetts; and Gaby
Pacheco, Juan Rodriguez, and later Felipe Matos, from Florida.

Marie Gonzalez was often called on as well. Her case had become
so well known that she was often the first person other students contacted when Immigration and Customs Enforcement agents came
knocking on their door. It was Marie whom Gaby Pacheco called when
her home was raided. The two had met at a conference, and Gaby immediately felt Marie would know what to do. She would understand.
Marie tried to help where she could. Yet the travel, combined with
the responsibilities of school and work, took its toll. She wanted to
help people like Gaby, but increasingly she demurred at the speaking
invitations. She ceded the public space to others, like twenty-four-year-
old Tam Tran, also a so-called DREAM elder. Born in Germany to
Vietnamese refugees, Tam had come to California as a young child
with her parents, who had sought asylum in the United States. But,
as in the case of Tereza Lee, the United States wouldn't take them,
nor would Germany. She'd never been to Vietnam, and her parents
refused to return. Tam, an aspiring filmmaker and recent University
of California, Los Angeles, graduate, had begun to film some of the
DREAM Act-eligible students telling their stories. In May 2007, she

flew to Washington to show one of her films at a House Judiciary Sub-committee immigration hearing, crashing at Josh Bernstein's house the night before and staying up till dawn to write her speech. In the film, she had to blur the faces of the teens who'd spoken to her.

I hope one day I can show this film without them hiding their identity, she told lawmakers.

The young leaders were in high demand. But their stars were on the rise just as the light was dimming on the broad compromise immigration bill Esther had worked so hard to draft. Many US labor leaders weren't happy with the legislation's increase in the number of temporary workers, whom they worried could sabotage wage guarantees and other protections they'd fought hard for, and they made it clear to their champions in the Senate, including Vermont independent Bernie Sanders, a self-proclaimed democratic socialist, who had recently moved over from the House. Meanwhile, hard-liners such as Sessions, who had sought to kill the DREAM Act back in 2003, continued to fight anything that would even resemble amnesty. As summer 2007 rolled around, the decade's last big push for comprehensive reform fell by the wayside.

With broad congressional immigration reform essentially dead, groups whose support had directly and indirectly nurtured the young undocumented immigrants began to turn their attention toward a very different kind of campaign, that of freshman Illinois senator Barack Obama. The Harvard-trained lawyer and Hawaiian-born son of an anthropologist from Kansas and a Kenyan scholar, who'd been raised in Indonesia, was now running for president. Like Sanders, Obama was wary of the Secure Borders, Economic Opportunity and Immigration Reform Act of 2007, but in the end, he had voted in favor of bringing it to a full vote. He seemed the most sympathetic presidential candidate that immigrant rights proponents had seen in their lifetime.

It wasn't long before the lines between the immigration reform movement and that of the nascent Obama campaign would begin to blur. Obama had cut his teeth on community organizing in Chicago and had already won recognition from the Center for Community Change. He understood the power of his volunteers lay not just in sharing his story with potential supporters but in sharing their own stories and in developing the same leadership skills he had learned as an organizer on the streets of Chicago.

The Obama campaign received a hand from Harvard Kennedy School Professor Marshall Ganz, whom the senator had met while in law school. Ganz, the son of a rabbi, had marched with the farm-worker activist and hero Cesar Chavez in the 1960s. Ganz's class required students to develop personal stories or "narratives" through which they could better connect with people and ultimately achieve political and social change. He began to train Obama campaign workers. Eventually he invited in a few local young activists to audit his Harvard class, including Carlos Saavedra, who had attended the NCLR conference in Philadelphia two years before. Telling their life story was what the undocumented activists already did instinctively. Now they would learn to hone that skill not just to inspire others, but to inspire them to action.

As the young activists were shaping their stories and beginning to take them to the streets, something else began to change, something part of the natural course of life and of political movements: teenage rebellion. At first, the young leaders were happy to receive invitations to speak from veteran activists. But increasingly, they felt as if the older activists viewed them as props, trotting them out to pull at the heartstrings and then sending them back to their seats.

In the winter of 2007, the Center for Community Change's Fair Immigration Reform Movement organized a meeting of its member groups on the campus of Gallaudet University in Washington, DC. The goal was to plan a strategy in response to Bush's last, lame-duck push for immigration reform. The students asked for a meeting room of their own to exchange ideas. The organizers of the conference were taken aback. Meet alone, without the adults? The idea hadn't occurred to them. They scrambled to find a space and came up with an overflow room packed with coats and bags. Julieta Garibay, Juan Rodriguez,

Tam Tran, and the other students looked around and almost laughed. They had literally been relegated to the coatroom. The next day, they declared independence.

Jose Luis Marantes, a mentor to Juan and Felipe at SWER, was among those who addressed the older advocates.

How many of you believe in the youth movement? he asked. The veterans, including Josh Bernstein, applauded.

How many of you believe that this movement can't be won without the power of the youth? he asked, again to applause.

How many of you are willing to give up your jobs to make way for youth to lead this movement forward? This time the room was quiet.

The students wanted to split off from the veterans to create their own group, an organization that would focus on the passage of the DREAM Act. They would call the new coalition United We Dream, in a nod to the campaign Josh had with Marie Gonzalez and in honor of a smaller, similarly titled initiative in Massachusetts. As they made their case, Josh stood off to the side. In many ways, his work with these students was done. He would step back as they stepped forward to fight for the DREAM Act on behalf of other young immigrants like themselves.

HARETH WAS A SOPHOMORE in high school when the presidential election heated up in 2008. She had been so inspired by marches two years before that she eventually volunteered for the campaign of a fellow Bolivian running for the Arlington County school board, Emma Violand-Sánchez, or "Dr. Emma," as Hareth called her, but that was as far as her political activities went. Like Felipe, she fiercely guarded her own immigration status, looking after her sisters while her parents worked. She worried about her parents. Her father was exhausted all the time and talked about a slowdown in construction. He still helped Hareth with her math homework, complaining about the newfangled ways teachers taught geometry. But increasingly, she noticed that his beer with dinner became two or three. Hareth tensed when he came home with alcohol on his breath, but she shoved away that fear. Her father was fine. They were fine.

Along with her parents, she watched TV in May 2008, when, during an interview with Univision nightly anchor Jorge Ramos, Obama promised that if elected, he would make comprehensive immigration reform a top priority during his first year in office. In fact, the senator's promise followed that of his rival and fellow Democrat Senator Hillary Clinton, who'd promised to present Congress with a bill during her first hundred days in office. But to Hareth, Obama seemed fresher, more believable. Maybe this guy was worth watching.

In Miami, Felipe also cheered after hearing Obama's promise. He, too, was worried that Clinton's promises were political, given the tough 1996 law that had passed on her husband's watch. And he liked Obama's background in community organizing.

This was a campaign Felipe could get behind, an election they might actually have a chance to win. He and Juan spent months canvassing and getting out the vote, even if they couldn't cast a ballot.

But their main focus remained local. Jose Luis Marantes from SWER had been pushing Felipe to speak out about his status, but he had demurred. It wasn't safe. He just wanted to be a regular student. Still, the idea of stepping forward gnawed at him.

But as he watched Gaby's relatives fight a looming deportation case, Felipe decided he had to come forward. *Here I am, the student government president*, he thought. *If I say who I am, I can really change people's minds.* He helped Gaby organize a march in the spring of 2008 from Miami Dade College to DHS's downtown office. During the march, Felipe finally went public with his immigration status.

They dubbed it their "undocumented and unafraid" march, a phrase that felt more of an aspiration than a declaration. Yet the words inched further toward truth each time they uttered them.

On the day of the march, Felipe wore a pin with the question *Undocumented?* He and the others covered their mouths with black duct tape, silently protesting the constant fear that kept so many im-migrants silent. Maybe they would be arrested, maybe they would be deported, but at least it wouldn't happen in the shadows while the rest of the country slept or went about their breakfast routine.

Dozens of the participants left their identification cards and other documents in their cars in solidarity with friends who had no valid immigration papers. Looking at the group, it was impossible to tell who was or wasn't documented. Felipe was terrified and thrilled all at once.

They walked past discount luggage stores and fashion outlets, merengue music blaring from the open storefronts, just as it did in Central and South America, where many of the area's small-business owners hailed from. They walked past vendors selling hot dogs and empanadas and toward the cluster of state and federal court buildings.

At DHS, officers stood outside with guns at the ready. Felipe froze, terrified that they might actually shoot him. Only later did he realize that the men and women in uniform were simply stationed at the ready, according to standard procedure. No one at DHS planned to shoot at the ragtag demonstration by fewer than a hundred students. No one was arrested. The group barely made the local news that night, but Felipe had discovered two things: he had been scared, but he had not run; and the officers could have arrested him, but they had chosen not to.

The march was liberating, and Felipe began to speak out more. Yet as exciting as life seemed on the political side, in his personal life, Felipe felt as if he were sinking. He was finalizing his divorce, and once again the sense of failure washed over him. Juan took to check-ing in on his friend every day to make sure he got out of bed and ate, sometimes even dragging him out of the apartment. Juan had recently broken up with his girlfriend, and at times the sexual energy between the two men was so intense Felipe could barely breathe. Still, they both brushed off the tension. To Juan, it seemed Felipe was another straight friend, looking to experiment. Felipe was too terrified to sug-gest otherwise.

Then one unbearably hot afternoon, the two men took a break from work and strolled upon the grass at Bayfront Park across from the carousel, watching the prestorm whitecaps surge across Biscayne Bay. Felipe thought about the march, about his friends fighting deportation orders. He thought about his desire to be honest with the world about his immigration status. Why then, should he have to remain silent about something even more essential? His heart beat against his chest. He tried to distract himself, mentioning the latest news from the Obama campaign, from their new immigrant friends in Texas, New York, and Los Angeles. Then he stopped. *Screw it.*

"I've decided to be happy," he blurted out.

Juan nodded. "Great."

"I've decided," Felipe said slowly, taking a deep breath and hoping his voice didn't tremble, "to be happy, whether it's with a girl or with a guy."

Silence.

The breeze stopped. Felipe could see a couple laughing together across the grass. He waited for Juan to say something, anything.

Slowly a light seemed to flicker behind Juan's eyes. He took off his glasses and squinted at Felipe. "Wait! Do you mean me?"

Juan sat back for a second; then he leaned over and kissed Felipe, hard. Felipe felt as if he were floating. He had never been so happy and so terrified. He wasn't out. They were in a public park in Miami. He could be deported for any reason, at any moment. And he didn't care.

They stayed there along the bay for longer than they could remember, Felipe more at peace than he'd ever been. Juan stared at Felipe, his mind whirring, wondering if it were really possible that two young men could make a life together.

In November, Obama won roughly 57 percent of the Latino vote in Florida, slightly more than Bush had won just four years before. As he heard the news, Felipe thought of Obama, growing up with his mother and then leaving her as he became a teenager, and his thoughts turned to his own life and his own mother, living thousands of miles away. Outside, a party had already started. Felipe went into the street that night, mingling with his celebrating neighbors, optimistic about his future. Two months later, Felipe and Juan rang in the New Year's with newfound organizing savvy, a boatload of political confidence—and each other.

4

DARK CLOUDS LEAD
TO A TRAIL

Felipe Matos and Juan Rodriguez enjoy lunch on a brief break in St. Augustine, January 2010. (COURTESY OF ALEJO STARK)

Dario Guerrero watched Obama's 2008 election with his parents, impressed that a "black guy" would for the first time be living in the White House and hopeful that the new president might help reverse the slowdown in construction his father was seeing.

But in truth, Dario was far more excited about getting his driver's license, breaking his three-mile track record, maybe getting the attention of some of the cooler girls in his class, and finally getting to enroll in a college-level math course. He was at the top of his class at one of the nation's top public high schools, the California Academy of Mathematics and Science, nestled in the Dominguez Hills campus of California State University. He had qualified for Principles of Engineering, a class that provided dual community college credits. One evening, as his mother made dinner, Dario sat at the dining table overlooking the backyard and carefully filled out the college credit forms.

"Mami, I need my Social Security number," he called to his mother. Rocio wiped her hands clean and fetched the number from papers she kept in her bedroom.

A few days later, the phone rang. It was an administrator from the California Academy. Dario took the phone into the back corner of the family's narrow kitchen, where the rumble of the washing machine would drown out the noise of his family. He leaned against the quartz counters his father had recently installed using leftover stone from one of his projects.

The school administrator didn't mince words. The Social Security number Dario listed did not match his name. Dario apologized. His mother must have given him the wrong digits.

You do have a Social Security number, don't you? the woman pressed him. If he didn't—

Why was she asking him this? It was just a stupid mistake. But her words made him nervous. He looked across the kitchen window at the giant playhouse his father had put together for his little sister, Andrea, a miniature wood-shuttered home complete with white fence and a framed heart above the door. He stared at the swing set next to the little house and thought of all the times he'd pushed Andrea, her long black hair floating behind her.

The administrator asked again. *Do you have a Social Security number?*

Of course he did. Dario promised to get back to her the following day and hung up. What if he didn't? Dario had heard of the cases, on TV or whispered by his parents and friends. People who didn't have Social Security numbers. Those people were put on buses and sent back to Mexico or wherever. But those people lived in hiding . . .

Later that evening, Dario grumbled about the call to his mom.

We need to talk, she said.

Dario sat on the dark brown couch in the living room with his parents. Quietly, they explained that for years they had been using his younger, US-born brother's Social Security number for Dario. Now that the two were at the same school, the administration must have flagged it, or maybe the technology to identify errors was getting better. It didn't matter. There was nothing they could do.

Yes, they explained, they had come to the United States on tourist visas, just as they'd always told him, but they had overstayed the visas. He had been too young until now for them to say more. They hadn't been sure at first that they wouldn't return to Mexico if the economy improved and the crime receded. They hadn't wanted to burden him with their secret or risk him telling the wrong person.

But at least now you are in the process of getting citizenship, Dario prompted.

No, we aren't. They couldn't. There was no path, no line, that they could get in to make things right. They didn't qualify for the so-called millionaire's visa, the EB-5, which would have enabled them to stay if they invested $1 million in the United States and created at least ten new jobs. And they didn't qualify for any other visa. But Obama had promised to take action. And for the moment, they weren't in danger. Immigration officers weren't looking for them. That night, Dario sat at the computer on the cramped desk in his room, across from the bunk beds he shared with Fernando, Fer, as he'd taken to calling his younger brother, and he began googling "illegal immigrant" and "college."

JUST AS THE IMMIGRANT RIGHTS GROUPS had hoped, President Obama bolted out of the gate on immigration reform. He broke tradition, plucking key immigrant advocates out of the back offices of Congress and the cramped quarters of the Washington nonprofit world and bringing them into the White House. In a surprise move, he asked the National Council of La Raza's Cecilia Muñoz to join his domestic policy team on immigration. She agreed to meet with his then chief of staff Rahm Emanuel, who would later become mayor of Chicago. Cecilia figured she might at least get some intel on the new president's immigration strategy even as she declined the job.

But after the meeting, Emanuel called again, and this time he passed the phone to the president.

"The president told me he wouldn't take 'no' for an answer," Cecilia recalled. She eventually took a job managing the White House's relationship with state governments and later became the administration's top liaison with the nation's Latino groups.

In February 2009, Cecilia's friend Esther Olavarria was tapped for the Department of Homeland Security to help the agency refocus its enforcement measures on those whom the government considered the greatest threat.

A few months later, Ted Kennedy was diagnosed with brain cancer, and by August, the "Liberal Lion" of the Senate would lose his last battle. Esther became even more determined not to let his vision of reform die. The Democrats held both houses in Congress—not by much, but they held them. With Kennedy gone and McCain now taking a back seat on immigration as the backlash in Arizona continued to grow, the administration sought out a new set of partners to carry the mantle forward: New York Democratic senator Chuck Schumer and South Carolina Republican senator Lindsey Graham. Together, maybe they could present Congress with an immigration proposal that would not only strengthen the border and increase the number of temporary work visas issued but also create a path toward citizenship for the 11 million people living in the country without authorization. It had to be something the Democratic-led Senate couldn't refuse and something enough GOP lawmakers would be willing to join. Some days, Olavarria had to pinch herself: the change she'd wanted to effect for nearly a decade was finally at hand. In the House, a group including Florida representative Lincoln Díaz-Balart secretly met to come up with their own framework.

Then, like the national economy, the president's immigration motor sputtered and stalled. In July 2007, the investment bank Bear Stearns had liquidated two of its mortgage-backed security hedge funds, just as the stock market hit a near-record high. Only in hindsight would that combination of events be understood as the red flag for the financial meltdown that lay ahead. A month later, the entire US housing market went under, threatening to take with it the savings of millions of Americans and the world economy. By June 2009, unemployment topped 9 percent, more than double the figure from the same month of 2007.[1] During his first months in office, the president sought to rein in Wall Street and stave off financial collapse.

Then came health care reform. It was the top priority for the Obama administration after shoring up the nation's financial structure. The battle was fierce and bitter, and the result was an imperfect solution—better, the president and his supporters believed, than what had existed but still satisfying no one. And now the president had spent even more of his personal and political capital.

Meanwhile, so-called birther conspiracy theorists, who'd first raised their heads during the election season, had once again begun to circulate their theories about the origins of the new president. A fringe group, many of whose members also vehemently opposed immigration reform and whose claims were stoked by big media names such as CNN anchor Lou Dobbs,[2] insisted once again that Obama's short-form Hawaiian birth certificate was a fake. The president himself might even be an "illegal alien," alleged one birther, Californian

Orly Taitz,[3] who later accused Obama of creating a plan to traffic "hundreds of thousands of illegals . . . and dump them on the unsuspecting population."[4] It was an accusation Donald Trump would later latch onto.

Obama's promise to Univision anchor Jorge Ramos "that we will have in the first year an immigration bill that I strongly support and that I'm promoting"[5] now seemed wishful thinking. Nor was Congress rushing to act. For the new Democratic leadership, as well as most Republicans, the idea of legalizing the status of millions of people in the country so they could better compete for work in the midst of a recession was now close to a nonstarter.

In Miami, Felipe watched his hopes of change slowly burn out. He and Juan had moved in together, and he was no longer shy about referring to Juan as his boyfriend, at least to his small circle of friends. But despite graduating at the top of his class in June 2008 and being named among the top twenty community college graduates in the nation, he had to take a year off school because he couldn't figure out a way to pay for the rest of college. His server job at the nightclub kept milk and peanut butter in his fridge but not much else. He kept busy with fellow immigrant activists. Following the training he and Juan had received from Carlos and other disciples of Harvard's Marshall Ganz, he joined them to train more groups of young, undocumented immigrants in Florida, Ohio, Colorado, and Nevada—key congressional, as well as presidential, swing states, where strategists in Washington realized the Latino vote could be key.

Yet there were days when Felipe found it difficult to get out of bed. It wasn't just his disillusionment about the president's unkept promise for the overhaul of the country's immigration system, or his struggle to pay rent. That summer he attended a workshop organized by a local nonprofit whose mission was to stop queer kids from attempting suicide. The idea was that by teaching educators how to have frank talks with parents and teens about the issues, the teens would feel less alone.

Ostensibly Felipe went to the trainings to learn how to help others, but soon he began to think about his own family. Juan had come out to his father two years before. Initially, his father had kicked him out of the house. But after a few months Juan's dad had called. *Are you eating, m'hijo?* he'd asked. They rarely spoke about Juan's love life or much of anything else. But now Juan's father would occasionally introduce Juan to his own gay friends. Juan and Felipe laughed about the introductions, but Felipe knew how much even the awkward gesture meant to Juan.

Maybe, thought Felipe, it was time to tell his mother back in Brazil. After all, through the organizing trainings, he'd become pretty good at telling his story: his arrival in the United States and now even his relationship with Juan. He had come out to everyone who mattered—except to the one who mattered most.

Everything he'd done so far had been tied in some way to making his mother proud, to making her sacrifices worth it. Why couldn't he tell her about this? He and Juan were creating something, each pulling back sometimes, pushing each other away, but it was the best relationship he'd ever known. Felipe wanted to tell her about the person who made him want to get up in the morning, the person whose social awkwardness sometimes made him want to bang his head against the wall, yet whose caresses made him ache with longing. He wanted to tell her about the person whom he could lie next to at night and finally fall into a deep, panic-free sleep.

One October evening in 2009, while Juan was out, Felipe sat in their tiny living/dining room and dialed his mother's number in Rio de Janeiro. The electronic ring sounded hollow, so far away.

He'd practiced what he would say. But as the words tumbled out, they didn't sound quite as smooth.

Olá, Mamãe, how are you? I'm calling you because I have something to tell you. Remember Juan? You know that he's not my roommate, right?

His mother was confused.

Juan is also my partner.

Okay. Juan is your partner. So?

Partner as in boyfriend.

There was silence on the other end, marked only by the distant sound of voices overlapping from another line. Slowly Francisca seemed to be making sense of this information. Finally she spoke. She said she would leave it in God's hands, and then she changed the subject.

Okay, you do that, totally fine, Felipe told her, breathing a sigh of relief. All things being equal, the conversation had gone pretty well.

The next day his mother called back. Her voice was rough. She was agitated. *Felipe, you are going to hell. You must stop whatever blasphemous acts you are partaking in. You need to find a new wife, or go back to your old wife!*

Felipe tried to keep his voice steady, not sure how much to argue, how much simply to let her spew her fears. He knew it had been too easy. After all, his mother had in recent years become a born-again Christian. Still, he hoped her anger would blow over. He'd wait it out, like he waited out Miami's summer storms.

It did not blow over. His mother called back for days.

You are a disgrace to God. She implored him to change. Felipe had heard strangers call him "illegal" or "faggot." But his mother's voice through the telephone wires sliced through months of carefully sewn protections.

The world could hate him, whatever. But his own mother?

He stopped picking up the phone.

If it's my life's purpose to make this one person proud, and I can never do that, what is left? he asked himself.

A few nights later, while Juan was out, Felipe walked to the bathroom and stared into the mirror. There had to be something to ease the pounding in his head, to quiet that internal voice telling him he was dirty, unworthy, failing. He opened a bottle of Tylenol and began swallowing capsules.

Juan arrived home around 8 p.m. The apartment was dark and oddly quiet. Felipe was in bed. Juan sighed. Felipe was either sick or depressed again. He tried to wake his boyfriend, to see if he wanted to eat something, but Felipe barely stirred. Finally, after much prodding, he awoke but turned to the wall.

"Go away, leave me alone. I just need to sleep."

"What happened?" Juan wanted to know.

"I took some pills," Felipe finally confessed.

"What do you mean, you took some pills?" Juan asked very slowly.

There was no answer. Juan ran into the bathroom. He yanked open the medicine cabinet, and spotted a Tylenol bottle. He shook it—not quite empty but with far fewer capsules than he remembered.

How many pills had Felipe taken? *Four? More?*

Felipe said he couldn't remember. Juan turned on the lights. Felipe was pale. Juan knew then it was definitely more than four.

He carried Felipe to the restroom and told him he had to throw up. Felipe couldn't. He just wanted to sleep.

Juan took a deep breath. He could handle this. The idea of a Tylenol overdose seemed almost laughable, but he remembered reading somewhere that it wasn't.

"I can't let you sleep. You might not wake up," Juan said. He could feel his anger rising. *How could I have left Felipe alone? How could Felipe have done this?*

His mind flashed to his own suicidal thoughts after high school graduation, when, despite being valedictorian, his status had meant that the only job he could get was in a warehouse. He'd talked friends down from hurting themselves before, other young immigrants worried about coming out, facing deportation, or the deportation of their families. But he'd done so mostly over the phone, a neutral aide who could put them in touch with friends or family nearby. He tried to think clearly. He had a license but no car. If he called the police or 911, maybe they would help—or maybe they would start asking questions about Felipe's immigration documents. He wondered if calling medics would start the wheels of Felipe's deportation.

Juan asked himself, "If Felipe dies on me, will I hate myself more if I didn't call the police, or if I did?"

Finally, Juan decided to call his friend Subhash Kateel, a local labor organizer, who had been at the forefront of the effort to protect the rights of Muslim immigrants in New York following the September 11 attacks. Subhash was a decade older, and his calm gaze from behind his black wire-rimmed glasses often defused a situation. Subhash immediately agreed to come over. But Felipe wasn't having it. He refused to go to the hospital, pulled on his shoes, and walked unsteadily out the door.

By the time Subhash arrived, Felipe and Juan were sitting on the curb at the corner of the block. Felipe was too weak to flee. His friends carried him into the car, and Subhash drove to Mercy Hospital, the city's only Catholic acute care hospital, hoping the Church's history of aiding immigrants would ensure no one called ICE.

Even after the doctors pumped Felipe's stomach, and even after they told the young men that if they'd waited any longer for help, Felipe would have suffered severe, irreparable liver damage, Felipe refused to speak to Juan. He was furious at having once again failed at something big, ashamed to have ended up in the hospital and to have put himself at risk of deportation.

Before he left, Subhash called Maria Rodriguez of the Florida Immigrant Coalition. She met them at the hospital and sat by Felipe's bed, singing softly to him just as she would to her young son.

Felipe would later remember something else about that night, a nurse who came to check on him. Neither Juan nor Subhash nor Maria would recall her. Maybe she was a dream, but she seemed so real at the time. All he wanted to do was sleep, and Juan wanted to stay the night, but the nurse insisted visiting hours for anyone but immediate family were over.

Juan explained in Spanish that he was Felipe's brother. The nurse asked where he was from. *Colombia*, Juan responded. The nurse raised an eyebrow. Her patient was from Brazil.

She gazed steadily at Juan. *What's your name?*

Juan Rodriguez. The nurse glanced at Felipe's listed name.

She looked from one frightened young man to the other.

Okay, he's your brother, she said finally and let Juan curl up in a chair.

At first Felipe was grateful. But then, the more he thought about it, the more he wasn't grateful. He was angry.

I am tired of having to depend on others' kindness, he thought.

The hospital agreed to let Felipe go home only after his sister found him a therapist. Felipe and Juan didn't talk much about the hospital, or even about his depression. In some ways, it was a relief for both of them.

But the fear that Felipe would disappear again into depression, or worse, kept Juan up at night; it was a fear he didn't dare share with many friends or organizers. For the first time in a long time, he felt at a complete loss.

That fall, Felipe received a scholarship to attend St. Thomas University in Miami. As he recovered, Juan threw himself into organizing for the student group SWER. A few weeks later, a group of the students decided to do something big to generate the same energy they'd felt marching through downtown the summer before: they would stage a protest outside the Broward Transitional Center, some forty miles north of Miami. The innocuously named facility housed hundreds of South Florida immigrant men and women facing possible deportation. The fate of most would be decided by immigration judge Rex Ford,[6] whose courtroom lay behind the detention center walls and who was known as being among the toughest immigration judges in the nation, deporting people at a rate higher than many judges even along the US-Mexican border.

The young activists brainstormed ways they could draw attention to what they were only beginning to recognize as a nationwide stepped-up deportation policy. President Obama was supposed to be their champion. But now they were seeing more forced departures of friends and relatives, including students like themselves. They argued back and forth but finally decided to set up empty desks and chairs outside the center's walls and to hold up signs and use a bullhorn to call out their message: education, not deportation. It was their new catchphrase, a slogan that would later become the name of one of the first national immigrant youth campaigns.

As Felipe threw himself back into school, it was a relief to Juan to get away for a few days to attend a conference in New York. There he met Rico Blancaflor, a Filipino American and leader of the Posse Foundation, a nonprofit group that provided support to help at-risk youth succeed in higher education. The two hit it off and began talking about the informal social networks or "posses" necessary for first-generation students to make it through college. Those networks seemed to overlap with the informal ones immigrants in the United States relied on, regardless of whether they made it to college. For Juan, these networks felt like a modern-day "underground railroad" of people like Subhash, Maria, school counselors, and sympathetic classmates.

The two men joked about organizing an immigrant underground railroad relay walk to raise support for the nation's most vulnerable immigrants. But soon they grew serious. Rico suggested a corporate marathon-type event with teams and T-shirts. If they started organizing now, they could maybe pull it off in a few years, with events in every major city across the country.

Juan listened. *Three years? We don't have three years*, he thought. *I could lose Felipe before then.*

On his way home from New York, Juan got a call from the young protesters in Broward. They had followed their action plan to the letter. A handful of local TV cameras came out to record their protest at the detention center. But when they stood up on their makeshift desks to peek over the detention center walls, they discovered that not only was no one on the other side paying attention but workers were constructing a new wing, adding new beds. Soon Broward Transitional Center would be detaining even more immigrants. All the weeks of planning, the transported school desks, and the guerrilla theater seemed pathetic.

By the time Juan got home to Miami, he had made his decision. He was going to walk, all right, just as he and Blancaflor had discussed; he'd walk from Miami to Washington to make his case in person.

He explained his plan to Felipe.

But what are you asking for? Felipe wanted to know.

Juan wasn't sure. Congress didn't seem to be in any hurry to tackle broad immigration reform, and yet the veteran activists weren't likely to give it up and just put their support behind the DREAM Act.

Felipe stared at Juan. This all sounded crazy, but it was just crazy enough that it might work.

Juan started lacing up his blue Nikes and walked out into the rainy night. Felipe turned back to his studies. A little while later, he dialed Juan's cell phone. No answer. He dialed again. Nothing. Felipe's heart began to pound. Finally Juan answered.

Wait, did you mean you were leaving now? Felipe demanded.

Yes. Are you in or out?

Yes, yes, okay. They would do it. But they would do it right, Felipe insisted. *I want to be able to say good-bye to my sister!*

Juan stopped. Maybe there were others who would march with them. They needed a posse. *Okay.* Juan agreed to turn around and return home.

It was Felipe who came up with the idea of starting the walk on January 1, 2010: a new decade, a decade in which immigrants would tell their own stories. As the two began brainstorming, Juan could see the light come back into his lover's eyes.

They started calling friends.

Gaby picked up the phone on the second ring.

"Where are you?" Juan asked. Gaby was driving home from downtown. Come over now, they told her. They had an amazing piece of news, but they had to share it in person.

She didn't hesitate.

When Gaby arrived, the young men wasted no time.

"We are going to walk to DC, and we want you to come with us," they told her.

"Great," she told them. "I've been wanting to do this for years."

Gaby had been wanting to do something big ever since the day three years before, in the dawn hours of July 26, 2006, when federal agents knocked on the door of her home.[7,8] They came with police officers, surrounded the house SWAT team style. Terrified, Gaby's older sister let them in, even though she wasn't required to. Gaby was protected because of her student visa, but her parents, pastor Gustavo Enrique Pacheco and Maria de Fatima Pacheco Santos, and her two older sisters, were hauled off and questioned for hours.

Gaby had come with her family from Guayaquil, Ecuador, at age eight on a tourist visa. Her parents had even bought property before they came, hoping it might give them the option of staying and eventually earning permanent residency. But by the time of the raid, they had tried and failed to get legal status, and most of the family was in the country illegally. Immigration and Customs Enforcement officials claimed that they chose the house and the aggressive entry because they were looking for a similarly named "fugitive." The officers never found the fugitive they said they'd come looking for.

The Pachecos insisted the raid was retaliation against Gaby's activism. The Miami Dade College student had been the president of the Florida Association of Community Colleges, representing more than a million students statewide,[9] and she had frequently met with legislators in Tallahassee, urging them to approve in-state tuition for undocumented immigrants in Florida, and had even organized a student rally at the capitol earlier that year, which had been covered by local media. Meanwhile, her father had spoken out in his role as a pastor on behalf of undocumented immigrants at a rally only months before.

Gaby's older sister Erika later told her lawyers that one officer said he'd seen her on TV, confusing Erika with her activist sister, while Gaby testified that another officer told her it had been a bad idea to go around speaking on TV and that yet another officer had an entire file folder on her. She maintained that officials had agreed to release her family temporarily only if she would remain quiet.

The US government didn't exactly refute the family's claim. Immigration judge Carey Holliday wrote on March 18, 2008, that Gaby

Pacheco "freely chose to draw unwanted attention to herself and her family," adding "People who live in glass houses should not throw stones."[10]

Gaby thought over the risks. Walking to Washington would mean she would likely lose her student visa and thus her legal status. But it would also raise the profile of her case and might help her and others win more permanent protection.

Many other friends turned Felipe and Juan down. Some held immigration status through school and, unlike Gaby, were afraid to lose the only security in their world of uncertainty. Others had to support their families and couldn't quit their jobs or simply didn't think it wise to miss so much school. Many were wary about what would happen as they marched up the eastern seaboard, through the heart of what had once been Ku Klux Klan country.

A couple of nights after Gaby agreed to join them, they called their friend Carlos Roa, an architecture student whose family had fled the regime of Hugo Chávez in Venezuela.

Carlos's mother had just died, and he could barely focus on his studies. Walking away from his life didn't sound too bad. It made perfect sense. His own life was in turmoil. He didn't have a place to live. He was working, taking two classes, and paying out-of-state tuition, barely eating.

But with the family still distraught over his mother's death, Carlos wanted to explain the plan to them and win their support before he officially agreed. His father was on board, but Carlos sought the blessing of his aunt, the family matriarch, who had achieved legal immigration status and owned a comfortable home in the Miami-Dade suburb of Weston, known colloquially as Westonzuela for its fast-growing Venezuelan exile community.

Carlos wasn't keen on going alone but worried that Felipe and Juan might antagonize his conservative relatives. He turned once again to Maria Rodriguez, who agreed to tag along with Carlos and his father for the meeting.

The meeting did not go well. They sat on the formal mustard-colored sofa and quietly sipped coffee as Carlos's aunt called him crazy and predicted the "rednecks" would get him.

Carlos's older sister was angry, too. Like their aunt, she was already a resident, and she hoped one day to sponsor Carlos, never mind that it might take decades.

That is still better than putting yourself at risk, she told him. Carlos looked to his father for help, but he remained silent. Carlos was crushed.

Outside, as they left, Carlos let his anger spill out. But his father stopped him. *They don't understand. They've never been in our shoes,* he said, adding, *I'm proud of you, hijo.* That was all Carlos needed.

Now there were four.

VETERAN IMMIGRATION ATTORNEY Ira Kurzban shuffled briefs at his desk in his small law office on Coral Gables' elegant Miracle Mile, a cool escape from the South Florida sauna outside. Never mind that it was already October. It was one of those days when he missed the seasons of his native Brooklyn. His secretary buzzed him. The students were here.

Juan, Carlos, and Gaby entered Ira's office, taking in his numerous awards, the Haitian art decorating the walls, and the photo with Haiti's former populist president, Jean-Bertrand Aristide.

Ira waited until they sat down. "So, what kind of trouble are you going to cause this time?" he asked with an impish smile.

Three years before, Ira's phone had lit up with an inquiry from Eduardo Padrón, the balding, dapper president of Miami Dade College, asking for help in Gaby's case.

Ira hadn't let the college president finish. He was in. It was precisely this combination—undocumented young immigrants with connections to sympathetic high-powered lawyers, academics, and civic leaders—that was beginning to make Florida such a powerhouse on immigration reform.

Despite Florida's poor showing during the 2006 protests and its reputation as mostly a place to launch spaceships, to party, and to develop liver spots, the Sunshine State was fast becoming a breeding ground for these young activists. A complex and at times combustible combination of hemispheric turmoil, hope, opportunity, and political calculation set the stage. Cuban exiles; South and Central American and Caribbean immigrants and asylum seekers; Puerto Rican transplants;* the growing Spanish-language media empire; and those famous Electoral College votes—all helped make Florida the right place at the right time.

But it wasn't just about the large number of Latin American and Caribbean immigrants who'd made their home in Florida. It was also advocates and activists such as Cheryl Little, Maria Rodriguez, and Subhash Kateel. It was also Eduardo Padrón, a Cuban immigrant, one of the "Pedro Pan" children sent to the United States alone by their parents to escape the communist government, who had risen to power cultivating close ties to the city's conservative Cuban and Anglo elite.

It was also Ira Kurzban, the son of Romanian Jewish immigrants, who had managed to build a successful career as one of the nation's top immigration lawyers, even as he often championed the politically unpopular, and who had written *the* book on immigration law: a six-inch-thick tome used in universities across the country and emblazoned with his name.

Kurzban had mentored Cheryl Little and Esther Olavarria. And back in the 1980s, he and his colleagues had won landmark judicial rulings on behalf of Haitians fleeing on rickety rafts from the decades-

---

* Orlando talk show host and former GOP state legislator Tony Suarez explained Puerto Ricans' support for immigrant rights beyond simply shared language and culture: "There is not a Puerto Rican family in the U.S. who doesn't have someone who is married to a Dominican, an Argentinian or a Mexican who may have someone in their family affected [by the immigration laws]." (Laura Wides-Muñoz, "Fla. Puerto Ricans Could Play a Key Election Role," *San Diego Union-Tribune*, August 1, 2012.)

old repressive regime of Jean-Claude "Baby Doc" Duvalier, which had given him an unusual confidence among immigration attorneys.

In a harsh 1980 opinion siding with Ira's clients, South Florida District Court judge James Lawrence King wrote that the US government had a "systematic program designed to deport [Haitians] irrespective of their asylum claims."[11]

Ira later successfully argued on behalf of some 1,700 Haitian immigrants before the Supreme Court,[12] alleging that Haitians were being unfairly locked up as they awaited their political asylum hearings. Or, as he bluntly put it, if you were black and seeking political asylum in South Florida, you ended up behind bars.[13]

His success with those cases made him believe anything was possible. So when Felipe's group visited him, Ira once again envisioned the beginning of a David-versus-Goliath battle.

He looked at the students. They weren't people who had many years of experience. They weren't professional advocates. They weren't politicians. Yet he saw himself in their determination.

He wrote them a check for $1,500 on the spot.

The money helped pay for the first of half a dozen pairs of shoes they would wear on the walk and other supplies. And it afforded them the confidence to know someone of Ira's caliber believed in them.

Local lawmakers were also sympathetic. South Florida Republican representative Ileana Ros-Lehtinen, Lincoln Díaz-Balart, and later his younger brother Mario, long championed the rights of legal immigrants and also supported the DREAM Act activists early on.* For them, it was not only good politics in their immigrant-heavy districts, and what they viewed as the moral thing to do, it was also personal.

Both Ros-Lehtinen and the elder Díaz-Balart had fled Castro's Cuba with their families as young children. (Castro had actually been a close friend of Díaz-Balart's father prior to becoming a revolutionary and

---

* In 2007, Ros-Lehtinen hosted meetings for two Colombian high school students, Alex and Juan Gomez, who faced deportation, and she later helped the young men gain a temporary reprieve.

had even been married to his aunt.[14]) These lawmakers knew about starting over in a new country and about escaping political upheaval and repression.

The immigrant story also hit close to home for the recently termed-out former speaker of the Florida House of Representatives, Marco Rubio, who would soon run for the US Senate. His own parents had left Cuba initially for economic reasons but made the United States their home for good following the revolution. He, too, understood firsthand the breadth of immigrant stories. He had grown up the son of working-class immigrants not only in the protective Cuban-exile bubble of Miami, but also in the heavily Mexican American immigrant communities of Las Vegas. And later he married into a family of Colombian immigrants.

"My dad was 30-something years-old when he came to this country and had to start his life brand new. So my generation in many ways inherited a lot of dreams and hopes,"[15] he recalled. He seemed to understand that but for the grace of God, Fidel Castro, and the Cold War, his parents might not have made it into the United States legally, either. Rubio would, of course, later shape-shift on immigration as he struggled to win consensus for reform within his party in Washington, but in the Florida legislature, he was known as someone who not only had tried to provide in-state tuition for the young immigrants but had also kept harsher enforcement proposals from reaching the state Senate floor.

Felipe and the others calculated that they would have at least some cover from these local politicians. Secretly, they began to meet at Felipe and Juan's tiny apartment in Miami's Little Havana. Despite having lived there nearly a year, the couple had barely furnished it. Gaby made a table out of a wooden crate, hemmed a wine-colored tablecloth, and made matching cushions. Now they could get down to business. The four sat around the low table each night as they discussed the plan.

They would walk 1,500 miles up the eastern seaboard in a meandering path that would allow them to pay homage at key 1960s civil rights sites. They called their walk the "Trail of Dreams," referencing their moniker as DREAMers, but also as a nod to the Cherokee Nation's forced 2,200-mile "Trail of Tears" from the eastern South to Oklahoma more than a century before.

They had yet to settle on what they would actually ask for when they got to Washington. They argued back and forth: comprehensive immigration reform? The DREAM Act?

Gaby thought of what Marie Gonzalez told her when she'd first called her right after ICE raided the Pacheco home. Gaby needed community support to help her win deferred action, Marie explained. She needed to convince the government, just as Marie had, to use its discretion not to deport her or to "defer action" on her case.

Once the US government initiated deportation proceedings against a person, Immigration and Customs Enforcement authorities could at any time use their discretion to recommend an immigration judge close a deportation case. That wouldn't give the person legal status, but it would take him or her out of the government's crosshairs. Immigration and Customs Enforcement could also ask a judge to reopen a case, which would allow the immigrant to argue his or her case for asylum or another path to legalization. But such successful cases were rare, and if the person lost that case, his or her deportation was all but guaranteed.

Deferred action was different. Immigration authorities didn't have to go to a judge for that. They could use their own discretion, and though the action was temporary and could be revoked at any time, it meant the immigrant would have some legal protections and could then apply for a work visa.

Ever since Marie had told Gaby about deferred action, Gaby had begun to see it as the best available option for cases far beyond her own.

It became, she joked, "like *My Big Fat Greek Wedding* response, where the aunt wants to put Windex on everything." Every time she heard something about any undocumented immigrant, her response was "deferred action, that's your solution."

Their friend Subhash Kateel took it one step further. They should ask for a blanket deferral for anyone the government did not view as a high deportation priority, starting with the youths. Such an executive action wouldn't need to go through Congress since it was temporary and merely an expansion of what Immigration and Customs Enforcement was already doing on an individual basis. Subhash had worked in New York to help individuals who had been wrongly incarcerated or who had lacked due process during deportation proceedings, work that had intensified in the wake of the September 11 attacks. His experience had taught him the power of executive intervention, and he believed that much more could be done by the president, even if legislation was stalled. Tapping into the power of that branch of the government might be the immigrants' best chance.

Subhash's argument made sense to Felipe, Juan, Gaby, and Carlos, and it helped the group avoid having to choose sides between the limited DREAM Act legislation and the broader push for comprehensive reform.

For now, Felipe and the other students agreed that they would press Obama and his administration to protect them, rather than focusing on Congress, which seemed unlikely to act. They wanted the president of the United States to end deportation of families and to use his discretion to allow people like themselves to stay and work in the country at least until Congress took action. They also wanted to ask that the president provide similar protections for the parents of US citizens.

Once the foursome agreed, they took their plan to the larger movement. The reaction was not what they had expected.

"You can't just walk!" Maria Rodriguez insisted. "You don't even have coats. It's warm in Miami in January, but not up in the Carolinas."

Others worried about an undocumented gay couple walking through the heart of what had once been the Confederate South.

"Do not do this," cried Cheryl Little, whose organization provided legal support for the students during one meeting. "I can get you released from jail, but I can't resurrect you!"

As their attorney, Cheryl advised against the plan, yet she couldn't help but admire the group, just as Ira had. After all, she thought, if the 1960s civil rights activists had listened to their lawyers, they might never have marched on Selma.

In Washington, the fledgling United We Dream coalition was somewhat more enthusiastic, if a little dubious. The group wanted the four students to use their platform to raise awareness about the DREAM Act.

But the greatest pushback came when they announced their plan to the broader immigration reform community at a conference in Las Vegas. Their plan met a mix of disbelief, dismissal, and outright hostility. In what would become a harbinger of the tensions to come, some veteran Washington advocates believed the group would put too much of a spotlight on the DREAM Act, rather than on broader immigration reform

One activist suggested they go and organize in Iowa, where one of the biggest raids had occurred the previous year. Several advocates called the walk a suicide mission, echoing Cheryl's concerns about their safety and the fruitlessness of such an endeavor.

"Everyone thought they were crazy," Jorge Ramos later admitted.

Still, Felipe, Juan, Gaby, and Carlos were undeterred, determined to do the walk with or without the support from the Washington establishment.

In November, Cheryl and Maria helped organize a press event at a local church in Miami's Little Haiti neighborhood. The four announced their plans alongside a group of farmworkers who agreed to fast in support. A dozen local reporters and national correspondents, accustomed to the farmworkers' protests, filled the church pews. As Juan began to speak, the journalists sat up in their seats. Who were these kids who spoke English so well, who dressed like typical college students, and who carried themselves with confidence, even a sense of entitlement? They began to take more careful notes.

Maria also reached out to the group Presente.org, co-led by the journalist and activist Roberto Lovato, who agreed to do media outreach.

Presente.org had recently generated enough of a public outcry to help oust anchor Lou Dobbs from CNN following years of the anchor's hyperbolic rhetoric about undocumented immigrants, including linking them to falsely inflated leprosy numbers. The group was ready for a new campaign.

As Felipe and his friends prepared for their walk, they read Martin Luther King Jr.'s "Letter from Birmingham Jail," and watched the old black-and-white footage from *Eyes on the Prize*, the documentary series about the 1960s civil rights protests.

They didn't expect the snarling dogs or tear gas African American marchers had faced in the 1960s. Still, they planned to march through areas where the recent influx of undocumented farmhands and construction workers was often viewed with a mix of fear and frustration, a part of the country where only six years before anal sex had been a felony. They wanted to better understand the region's history.

They asked each other the hardest questions they could think of. "Are you okay with getting punched but not punching back?" That one seemed relatively straightforward. "Are you okay with one of us getting raped and not attacking back?" They pushed further: "Are you okay with dying?"

And each time Felipe or Juan would say, "If you're not okay, you need to leave."

They also asked themselves what they would do if they didn't achieve their goals. But for Felipe, that was a question he couldn't answer. He didn't know what the march would bring. He just needed to march. Whether one person reacted or a hundred thousand did, this was now his mission.

The Saturday after Thanksgiving, they trekked to the massive outdoor Sawgrass Mills factory outlet mall in Broward County, buying matching white Nikes, the first of three pairs of shoes each would go through on their 1,500-mile journey to Washington.

5

A TRAIL OF TEARS
AND DREAMS

Carlos Roa, Gaby Pacheco, Felipe Matos, and Juan Rodriguez link arms as they near the end of the Trail of Dreams in Arlington, Virginia, April 2010. (COURTESY OF ISABEL SOUSA-RODRIGUEZ)

On January 1, 2010, just as Felipe had envisioned, he, Juan, Gaby, and Carlos stood on the steps outside Miami's historic Freedom

Tower, across from the Miami Heat's basketball arena in the heart of downtown. About a hundred family and friends gathered, as well as reporters from the *New York Times*, the *Miami Herald*, its Spanish-language sister *El Nuevo Herald*, local TV reporters, and other journalists looking for an alternative to the traditional Miami Beach New Year's hangover story.[1]

Felipe tried not to let his nerves show as the noon sun rose high over Biscayne Bay, and he looked to the small crowd that had gathered, but his usual smile was absent. The elegant, sand-colored tower that Miami Dade College had agreed to let them use had been built during Prohibition and modeled after the bell tower on the cathedral of Seville. It had served throughout the 1960s and 1970s as a reception center for Cuban exiles.[2] Now it was a gallery and cultural center for the college. But older Cuban Americans still sometimes referred to the building as "El Refugio" (the refuge), a place where the US government had first welcomed them with open arms.*

The symbolism wasn't lost on Felipe.

"People want liberty, economic liberty, political liberty, but the opposite is happening," Felipe told a correspondent for the Mexican paper *La Jornada*. "With this walk we are announcing to the world that we are coming out of the shadows."[3]

The four walkers wore blue sweatpants and long-sleeved white T-shirts emblazoned with "Trail of Dreams" and "Fast for Families." The latter was the motto of the group of farmworker activists who had driven up nearly an hour from the nation's winter strawberry fields in and around the Southern Florida agricultural town of Homestead to show their solidarity. Many of the farmworkers were accompanied by wide-eyed young children, clasping their mothers' hands. One woman had lost her husband to deportation. Another wore a DHS tracking bracelet around her ankle as she waited for the US govern-

---

* The powerful Cuban exile and South Florida businessman Jorge Mas Canosa bought the building shortly before his death in 1997. The family oversaw its restoration.

ment to determine her fate. They weren't new to protests. They had fought for immigrant and farmworkers' rights for years.

But unlike the students, they couldn't afford to take off work and walk for months at a time. And unlike at least Felipe and Juan, who could pass as white and addressed the media in fluent English, the farmworkers' indigenous heritage was clear. They spoke mostly in plain Spanish sentences as they described their barely livable wages, abuses in the field, and the constant threat of immigration raids.

The farmworkers' presence was essential as the students kicked off the Trail. The farmworkers couldn't walk, but through their fast in solidarity with Felipe and his friends, they would activate their network of other farmworkers across Florida to provide the students support. A couple of the women fussed over the group, giving them hugs.

As they stood with the students, the farmworkers also anchored the call to action in the broader story of the 11 million immigrants who had yet to come out of the shadows. And they anchored the moment in history. Nearly half a century earlier, farmworker organizer Cesar Chavez's fledgling union* had joined Filipino grape pickers in a pro-test and a more than 300-mile march from Delano, California, to Sacramento to demand better wages.[4] That walk hadn't changed things overnight, but it had set the stage for a massive California grape boy-cott that ended after five years with a collective bargaining agreement for some ten thousand agricultural workers.

The Florida farmworkers might not join the Trail, but the four students weren't walking alone. Cheryl Little's group, the Florida Immigrant Advocacy Center, had donated $3,000 for a refurbished RV that would accompany the walkers for emergencies. The center would also provide pro bono legal support. Maria Rodriguez's group was running

---

* Chavez was a complex figure for the immigration advocates. He had championed the fair treatment of farmworkers, even as he had strongly opposed illegal immigration precisely because he believed it lowered wages for those already here. Yet he eventually had supported a path to citizenship for the same reason: because he believed it would level the playing field.

logistics, helping map out the trek and setting up places to stay along the route. Half a dozen women and men would keep track of the walkers, coordinating stops at churches and other solidarity groups along the coast.

Maria found a volunteer driver for the RV, a former associate instructor from Indiana University named Felipe Vargas, who could also provide first aid—and an extra set of eyes on secluded stretches of road where rattlesnakes and alligators still roamed. Other volunteers would join up for stretches of the walk. The RV would provide a safe place to sleep when church basements and volunteers' couches were scarce.

Despite the precautions, Felipe's sister, Carolina, worried about her little brother's safety. She drove forty-five minutes on New Year's Day to attend the rally and see him off.

Promise me you'll come back, she whispered to him in Portuguese.

Felipe wondered if he could really promise that much, but he nodded and hugged her.

In fact, the group would soon learn that Immigration and Customs Enforcement did not plan to arrest them—as long as they didn't engage in illegal activity. A contact in the Department of Justice would keep track of them. But the day he left, Felipe had no idea what lay ahead.

As Maria had predicted, the four students weren't well prepared. That winter was one of the coldest in the Sunshine State's history. It was a balmy 65 degrees in Miami the day they left, but the temperature kept dropping. And while the students were busy contemplating life and death, none had thought to buy a winter jacket. By the time they reached Boynton Beach, some seventy miles north of Miami, the temperature had dropped to an extended record low high of 50 degrees during the day. The group made a quick shopping detour for jackets, balaclavas, and gloves.

For city kids whose experiences with nature generally involved a trip to the turquoise waters of Miami Beach, the pure physicality of the walk—often at least sixteen miles a day—and the intensity of the exposure to stretches of untamed Florida habitat were shocks to their systems. Their days frequently started at dawn and ended at midnight. Early on, they'd decided to give up coffee so as not to lose time in the morning. Everyone was cranky. Their feet were soon covered in blisters, and they quickly ran out of bandages, which slipped off halfway through the day anyway. Felipe took to protecting his feet with small pieces of duct tape. By day six, Felipe had to visit a Vero Beach–area podiatrist, who taught him how to pop his blisters with a sterile needle, and told him to change socks frequently and use moleskin bandages and antibiotics.

Halfway through January, Gaby threw her hip out and found herself flat on her back writhing in pain. A visit to a chiropractor arranged by the nonprofit group Voices of Justice, plus a couple days of rest, and she returned, but the pain in her hip and back meant she would ride in the RV on more than one occasion throughout the rest of the trip. So, too, would Felipe, who also suffered debilitating back pain. Only Carlos and Juan would walk the entire way.

To track their travel and boost their visibility, the group kept a blog. One of Felipe's first posts was entitled "I Think I'm Pregnant . . . ," with a tongue-in-cheek list of reasons, including "I am always hungry; I am always craving ice cream. . . . I don't fit into my pants anymore. . . . I have swollen feet; I have lower back pain . . ."[5]

Their ranks swelled to well over a dozen at times. People would walk with them for a few hours or a few days. Some even walked for a few weeks. Others opened their homes for a night so the students had a place to stay. But as they headed north away from their friends, families, and longtime allies, the days got longer and sometimes quieter, the landscapes wilder.

"I kept telling myself to put one foot in front of the other and that's it. I cannot deny that I feel homesick. . . ." Felipe wrote.

But Felipe was also captivated by the lush beauty of his adopted home.

"All one could see was an amazing and intricate system of gentle waters that flowed down south towards my beloved South Florida,"

Felipe wrote after a day walking through a newly restored section of the Everglades.

"The sky was blue but one could see a storm approaching in the horizon and smell the wetness in the clouds. For a couple of hours, all I heard was the sound of small birds, the cars coming in my direction, and the wind."[6]

Daily they passed roadkill species they'd rarely, if ever, seen alive: possums, armadillos. Few drivers stopped when they hit an unlucky animal. Felipe guessed most never even noticed. But walking, one could see the sad details of each animal. One afternoon they passed a deer that had been hit and lay at the side of the road. That night, as they arrived at a potluck party thrown in their honor by a local nonprofit, Felipe asked what was for dinner. "Venison," one of their hosts responded, killed that afternoon.

He did not eat it.

A month into the walk, they reached Paynes Prairie, a state preserve about ten miles south of the University of Florida in Gainesville, where bison and wild horses roamed and whooping cranes alighted at the side of marshes, just out of the reach of alligators. They covered more than twenty-two miles that day, and the quiet was both uplifting and isolating. As beautiful as the meadows and marshes were in the early-morning light, it was easy to wonder what the group was achieving, all this walking in the middle of nowhere. They checked the blog and followed the comments, but even with social media, it was hard to know if anyone in Washington was paying attention.

But there were also moments like the time on the outskirts of Orlando, when they stopped at a coffee shop to use the restrooms and noticed the staff behind the counter whispering and smiling. Carlos approached the employees to chat. It turned out they had seen Felipe and his friends on TV. Moments later, the coffee shop servers poured the group free coffee and presented them with $40 in donations they had spontaneously collected.

Another time, someone called the police because their RV was parked illegally, but the owner of the parking lot had seen their story in the paper and declined to file a complaint.

Near midnight on January 27, the night before Gaby's twenty-fifth birthday, she was getting ready for bed when she heard a serenade outside the window of the Gainesville home where they were staying. It was her father, who'd made the six-hour drive (or, for Gaby, twenty-seven-day hike) up from Miami to celebrate with her. He was singing the traditional Spanish birthday song "Las Mañanitas." The next day, the gang took a break and reunited with Gaby's family, savoring a rare restaurant meal.

As the skin peeled off the soles of their feet, their muscles burned and stretched, and their spirits flagged, Felipe and his friends received texts of encouragement from the farmworkers fasting in Homestead that put the red welts and swollen toes into perspective. After all, the farmworkers' blisters had long since turned to calluses. If those men and women were willing to fast, Felipe and the others could keep walking.

Throughout January, the students received media coverage by newspapers across Florida and local TV and radio outlets, as well as a few national mentions by the *New York Times*, the *Washington Times*, and the *Huffington Post*. Unlike Felipe and his friends, the fasting farmworkers earned little media attention following the kickoff. Three fasters were eventually hospitalized, and they decided to call off the effort. They would find other ways to support the walkers. Now it was up the Trail of Dreams.

In North Florida, the group discovered farm towns such as Mayo, where nearly a third of the 1,000 residents lived below the poverty line, and heard about how life had gotten tougher after the 2006 marches and the stepped-up raids.

When their driver, Felipe Vargas, asked why the local farm labor movement seemed to be stuck in a "dormant stage," the residents were quick to answer: "Fear."

Felipe and the others were no strangers to discrimination, but as relatively light-skinned, college-educated Latinos who lived in Miami, their experience with racial prejudice was more abstract.

A stop in the coastal town of St. Augustine, the first city in the nation founded by European settlers, brought things closer to home. They took a detour along the town's historic "Freedom Trail." At St. Augustine's small civil rights museum, Felipe learned how Martin Luther King Jr. and other leaders chose the city as the place to help reinvigorate the flagging civil rights movement. Fearing Congress would endlessly filibuster the 1964 Civil Rights Act, civil rights leaders had urged young black activists to stage nonviolent protests, including a "swim-in" at the Monson Motor Lodge. In response, the hotel owner had dumped pool-cleaning acid (a variant of hydrochloric acid) into the water as the teens swam, photos of which quickly circulated in newspapers and newscasts worldwide.[7]

Felipe was surprised to find that few locals even seemed to know about the hotel incident or the other sites on the city's Freedom Trail.

"What's the Freedom Trail?" an attendant at the visitor's booth said when they asked for directions.[8] How could people learn from history if they didn't even know what had happened? he wondered.

Soon after the group reached Georgia, they met local members of the NAACP for lunch in Albany. As they talked, the NAACP leaders mentioned in passing a Ku Klux Klan rally to be held halfway across the state the next day in the eastern town of Nahunta, home to some 375 mostly white households, about a third of which were barely scraping by. The Nahunta mayor had publicly grumbled about the event but essentially claimed his hands were tied. The city wouldn't give the KKK permission to march, but as long as the group didn't obstruct traffic, it couldn't stop it either. The Klan rally provided a reality check outside the bubble of religious allies and other immigrant advocates whom the four usually met with. The noon rally promised three distinct themes: prayer in schools, the rise of sexual predators, and the "Latino invasion."

Felipe and the students decided to check it out. After weeks on the trail of long but relatively quiet days, they were itching to come face-to-face with those who objected to them.

On the ride over Felipe was nervous, but when he stepped out of the RV and saw the ring of FBI agents, including their contact at the DOJ, separating the NAACP protesters from the KKK, he didn't know whether to laugh or cry. The robed men, old and young, with their pointy white hoods, seemed straight out of the history books.

Did I just get into a time machine? he asked himself.

"Mexicans don't have a patriotic sense," one speaker called out. "They should deport all the Mexicans. It's a plague is what it is, and they should be eradicated."

In fact, many more people had gathered in opposition to the Klan than in its support. Others had their phones out, filming the scene as if capturing a circus act.

Still the speaker's words made Felipe's stomach tighten.

Juan tried to laugh it off, especially one speaker's efforts to link immigrants and global warming. "How did we do that, with jalapeño peppers?" he asked with a smirk.

With so many law enforcement officers present, the KKK rally turned out to be one of the safest events the students attended along the trail. In many ways, the Klan itself seemed almost like a harmless throwback, a last gasp of a dying order. Felipe was more scared of the white supremacist movements that operated without sheets, that raised funds and recruited online, the trolls whose comments he knew were being deleted from their blog by the support team. Between 2008, when Obama was elected, and 2010, the United States saw the number of domestic extremist groups, mostly anti-immigrant and pro-white supremacy, increase by about two hundred, according to the Southern Poverty Law Center.[9]

Yet after they blogged about the event, one online response made the day feel worth it.

"As the granddaughter of a KKK member and grandniece of a grand wizard, I apologize for the ignorance of my ancestors and current members of that hate group," a woman who identified herself only as "Nancy" posted on March 1, 2010. ". . . While we loved our elders, we eventually saw what their twisted agenda did to people and families. . . . Continue your march."[10]

For Felipe and the group, scarier than the Klan were the times they tried to meet with local sheriffs and other law enforcement officials. Along the way, they set up meetings with the officials to ask them about their detention policies. Some listened in stony silence. Some never showed. But sometimes their response was surprising.

Only months before, *The Nation* magazine had published a story about Immigration and Customs Enforcement sub-field centers, including one in Cary, North Carolina,[11] where immigrants could be held, sometimes for days, before families could track them down. The four walkers joined a church group outside the detention center, located in a remote, woodsy office complex with the most minimal of signage. An Immigration and Customs official who identified himself as Brian met them at the entrance. One by one the protesters questioned him about the government's stepped-up deportation efforts and the treatment of the detainees at Cary. To their surprise, Brian listened and politely argued back in a series of exchanges the activists recorded.[12] The demonstrators were protesting against the wrong people, he insisted.

"I do not make the laws," he said, his shaved head and gray stubble towering half a foot above the rest of the crowd. "It's grassroots. Talk to your congressmen, talk to your senators. Get the law changed."

Eventually Felipe introduced himself and explained about the march. "I wonder if you get the chance to talk to the people you are locking up. When you lock up people, you are locking up students like me."

There was something almost comical about Felipe's earnestness. Brian looked at him as if he were wondering, *Is this kid for real?* Yet it was precisely Felipe's vulnerability that seemed to disarm him.

"I know you are just enforcing the law, but there's a cost—"

"There's a human cost," Brian echoed in agreement.

A few minutes later Felipe gave Brian one of the demonstrators' posters. "No human being is illegal," it read.

Felipe also asked for a hug. Brian leaned in awkwardly, giving a what-the-hell shrug.

Felipe handed him a card with the group's information, "so you can spread the word about the four students walking to Washington," he said.

"You guys are actually walking all the way to Washington?" Brian asked, eyebrows raised, for the first time seeming somewhat impressed. "Not in cars?"

Felipe explained that was why he had so many blisters on his feet.

Brian nodded his head and puffed out his lower lip.

As they left, the demonstrators noted that another agent had ripped up the poster they'd given him. Brian said he planned to keep the one they'd given *him* in the office to remind himself of the group.

"Really?" the group asked, incredulous.

"Yes. This is the first time something like this has happened to me," he said.

Often, though, the confrontations along the road weren't with law enforcement officials; they were internal. The four knew very well that despite the uncertainty in their lives, they were doing relatively well for undocumented immigrants. They'd worked hard, studying at odd hours, signing up for every club, some days barely eating, sometimes spending three hours a day on the bus to get to classes, grabbing every opportunity they could. But their efforts had been met with academic and social support. Although every member of the group but Juan could face deportation, they already had a leg up on many of their peers. All but Felipe came from middle-class backgrounds, at least in their home countries. At times, tensions flared between Felipe Vargas and the rest of the group, and van rides turned into political arguments. Sometimes he questioned his role as a Mexican American chauffeuring around "privileged South Americans." He wondered if the group had received its protection from law enforcement because of their light skin color.

"I ask myself everyday why is it that these dreamkids have not been picked up," he wrote in his blog.

". . . Being the only Mexicano on the trail it has been challenging for me on many levels to make sense of why I am walking and supporting 4 South Americans that came here legally and overstayed their visa," he continued. " . . . South Americans have always thought they were better than me. They have always made me . . . feel as [though] they knew what was best for us and had to speak on our behalf. In Indiana or in any newly emerging Latino community you find the same phenomenon . . . South American immigrants, often more privileged in our global class system, often more privileged in the public education system, and often privileged by our broken immigration system will be asked to speak for Mexicanos or Central Americanos."[13]

Felipe Vargas did not accompany them all the way, but in the end he decided the four young walkers did more good than harm. If they were willing to listen and help give voice to those who were not such stellar students, who did not have access to college, then, yes, they could very well represent him.

If the walkers' youth and earnestness impacted the officials they met, the children Felipe and his friends came upon along the trail seemed to have a similar effect on them.

One local civil rights activist who was helping set up meetings and speaking gigs for the group, Adelina Nicholls, of the Georgia Latino Alliance for Human Rights, would turn to the audience after each speech and ask if anyone had anything to add. One afternoon, an eleven-year-old boy named Oscar was the only one to raise his hand. Nicholls motioned for him to come forward. The short boy, with a bowl cut and big brown eyes, looked as if he were straight out of a Mexican pueblo, thought Felipe. Then the boy opened his mouth. Out came a Southern drawl as thick as molasses.

Yup, this kid is from Georgia, Felipe laughed to himself, embarrassed by his own assumptions.

Oscar hadn't planned to talk, and his bravado melted away as he stood in front of his audience. "Please don't send my dad away, President Obama," was about all the fifth grader could get out before his eyes filled with tears. His thirteen-year-old sister spoke, and she, too, began to cry. She had been called a wetback all her life, even though she and her brother were Georgia natives. Their dad, who picked pecans for a living and later told Felipe he was proud of helping feed people through his work, had been detained after officers stopped him, found he was driving without a license, and then discovered he was in the country illegally. Now he faced deportation, while their mother worked from home decorating cakes, too afraid to look for outside work.

Gaby walked into the audience and hugged the girl, her own tears spilling into the teen's hair.

The group stayed overnight with Oscar's family. That weekend, Oscar and his sister walked two days along with the students through the intermittent rain, cracking each other up with jokes as they twirled their bright-colored umbrellas and jumped puddles.

Sometimes, Oscar waxed philosophical. He compared his family's situation to that of African Americans in the United States in the 1960s, when they couldn't vote and were given only the lowest-paying jobs. Felipe would do a double take, reminding himself that the boy was just eleven. Only when the students once again broached the subject of their parents' immigration status did the siblings' preternatural confidence crumble.

"It was as if we opened Pandora's box," Felipe wrote a few nights later. " . . . Their pain was so evident that I couldn't do anything else other than cry as loud as they were."[14]

AT EACH STOP, local Spanish-language TV, fledgling news sites, and occasionally local English-language reporters showed up thanks to the constant pestering by Presente.org and Maria Rodriguez's team back in Miami. Media interest in the Trail of Dreams continued to grow. By March, they were earning press coverage in Georgia in Spanish and English, including a spot on the Atlanta-based CNN. Each of the walkers received attention in his or her native country, as well as in Canada, Spain, and even Taiwan.

Meanwhile, United We Dream, which had declared its independence at the conference back in 2007, upped the action as it helped encourage solidarity marches around the country. In late February, the National Korean American Service & Education Consortium, NAKASEC, helped organize an eighteen-mile Trail of Dreams in Los Angeles, while Latino activists farther south in Santa Ana led their own walk. Some two hundred immigrant students in Milwaukee also marched in solidarity that month. Later on, workers from Long Island's service industries marched to New York City and then to Washington, DC. Students in Manhattan organized a walk to DC. as well, with the group Make the Road New York. Some of the groups called for passage of the DREAM Act, others for comprehensive reform. Their actions, informally coordinated through United We Dream, made the veteran Washington advocates take notice.

In Chicago, Tania Unzueta, the aspiring journalist and activist who had spoken at the Windy City's 2006 marches, had begun to test strategies to help stave off deportations for friends through trial and error, compiling information on what kinds of letters worked, which calls were most effective, and which legal arguments were most successful. Yet even as she gained local prominence as an organizer, she was still relatively quiet about her own unauthorized status ever since Dick Durbin had helped her return from Mexico. It was one thing to advocate for a friend, another to give her story to reporters and risk deportation herself.

Now, spurred on by the Trail of Dreams, Tania and dozens of other young adults in Detroit, New York, and Cambridge, Massachusetts, finally came forward on March 10 and declared themselves "undocumented and unafraid."

The events were billed in press releases as part of a "National Coming Out of the Shadows Day," inspired by the similarly named event LGBTQ activists had organized decades before. Like Felipe, Tania and others were beginning to realize there was a certain safety in coming forward with their story, a network ready to react should something happen to them.

Still, many remained afraid. Even at the March event in Chicago, Tania was the only one of eight young immigrants who allowed the media to use her full name.

For undocumented immigrants in places such as Texas and Arizona, the risks of coming out were even greater. The United We Dream affiliates there were more hesitant to join in large, public ceremonies. Arizona was now on the verge of passing some of the toughest state immigration laws in the nation, including a proposal allowing police to stop and check the papers of those they suspected of being in the country illegally. Opponents called the measures—which also made failing to carry immigration papers a crime—a welcome mat for racial profiling. Some, including a charismatic young activist named Erika Andiola, joined the public protests despite the growing threats, but for many teens in Arizona, the declaration of "undocumented and unafraid" was still very much wishful thinking.

IT WASN'T EASY to come out in places such as Virginia, either. One afternoon during the spring of her junior year in high school, Hareth lay on the floor at her friend Antonella's, pretending to do homework. The two had long been close. Antonella was the head of their school's Latin American Student Association. An outspoken Argentinean with long honey brown hair, she lit up any classroom. Boys and girls alike were drawn to her.

But in recent months, she'd withdrawn, picking fights with Hareth for no reason. That afternoon, neither girl could focus. It felt as if a fog hovered between them. Hareth couldn't think of a way to cut through. Lately, all the talk at school was of college, and increasingly when conversation turned to the inevitable, Antonella became distracted and irritable.

Hareth was worried about her own future, yet she couldn't risk sharing her fears with Antonella, so she kept quiet. Hareth didn't want anyone asking too much about her own family, so she asked little of others.

They couldn't help it, though, and the discussion about graduation and college inevitably popped into their conversation. Suddenly Antonella burst into tears. *You just don't understand. You'll never understand,* Antonella said.

Try me, Hareth urged.

I'm undocumented, Antonella finally said.

Hareth was flabbergasted. Antonella, so smart, fearless, and popular. Hareth couldn't believe it. They had spent countless hours together. How could she not have noticed?

Easily, she realized.

Hareth looked at her friend. *So am I,* she said quietly. The two girls stared at each other, then began to laugh. Soon they were giggling hysterically. It was too crazy even to cry. They had both felt so alone, and now they were not.

Slowly they began to help each other. They learned that neither would be able to fill out a college application for any Virginia school because she would need a Social Security number or Alien Registration Number. Even if a school waived that requirement, neither could afford college without some form of in-state tuition or financial aid, which, like Arizona, Virginia would not offer them. Hareth was a good student but not a star like Dario, not the kind of student who could hope for a full ride anywhere, even under normal circumstances.

At a loss, the girls decided to broach the topic with the one adult who might be able to help: Robert Garcia, a retired engineer who years before had helped design the Washington, DC, Metro, and was the staff adviser for the Latin American Student Association.

They called him "Mr. Garcia," but behind his back, the beloved straight-talking Texan was known as "Mr. Monopoly" because of his resemblance to the game's bald, top-hat-sporting icon. Mr. Garcia was well connected in the community and an active member of the League of United Latin American Citizens, LULAC. They gambled that they could trust him.

The girls expected him to react with shock, or some surprise, but he showed neither. *There are many others like you at Washington-Lee High School,* he told them. It wasn't his place to share names, but he could offer a few groups they might want to reach out to.

BACK ON THE TRAIL, Felipe and his friends now found themselves in high demand from national immigration groups and under greater pressure to back one specific congressional bill. Still, the four tried to keep things light on the trail, belting out the theme songs to their favorite childhood cartoons, especially *Dora the Explorer.* They watched clips of themselves on the local news and teased each other when they sounded overly angry or strident, subbing in dramatic suspense music or interspersing YouTube squirrel videos to make fun of themselves.

But when they reached Raleigh for the United We Dream meeting, they couldn't ignore the growing tension over what they should be asking for upon their arrival in Washington. The youth-led coalition had failed to convince the veterans to back the DREAM Act. Now members were at odds over whether to defy the more experienced advocates seeking comprehensive reform and make a push solely for the act. United We Dream organizers wanted Felipe and the rest of the walkers to take a public stand in favor of the more limited bill.

The veteran immigrant activists no longer scoffed at the four. Frank Sharry, who had helped organize the worker caravan back in 2003, had by then founded the nonprofit group America's Voice, the unofficial communications arm of the immigration reform movement. He hadn't initially taken the group seriously. But he was beginning to see that the kids might have a thing or two to teach the veterans about communication.

The Washington groups wanted the marchers to use their growing publicity to do network interviews calling for comprehensive immigration reform. Some used the Trail of Dreams for fund-raising requests for broader reform, even though that wasn't what the group was asking for.

While Felipe and his friends argued over what to do, the veterans lobbied Tania in Chicago, and the emerging United We Dream leaders in New York and Washington, like Cristina Jiménez and Walter Barrientos, not to throw their support behind the stand-alone DREAM Act. If a sizable group of young undocumented immigrants made public that they didn't think comprehensive reform had a chance, it would doom the broader effort, the veterans pleaded.

Privately, the veterans knew comprehensive reform was a long shot, and they, too, urged Obama to use his executive authority to stop the deportations. But publicly, they focused on getting the president to keep his promise and harness the same energy he'd used to win health care and banking reforms in Congress to push a comprehensive overhaul of the nation's immigration laws.[15]

In March, the veterans organized a protest in Washington to pressure lawmakers to introduce a bill.[16] More than 100,000 undocumented immigrants and their allies attended, according to news reports at the time, though organizers put the number at twice that. The rally garnered some media attention, but it did little to sway either the president or lawmakers and likely meant far fewer people would come to Washington on May 1 for International Workers' Day and the completion of the Trail of Dreams.

Felipe, Juan, Gaby, and Carlos were exhausted. They had been walking for nearly ninety days. Each night, as Felipe's head sank into a new pillow and he closed his eyes, images of mothers crying and anxious children filled his dreams. When they started, it had been about the journey, about making it from one end to the other. Now he thought of Oscar and his sister. He couldn't let them down.

The group argued more about what they would do when they arrived in Washington. They wanted to take a stand, to end the march with a bang. Felipe and Isabel wanted to participate in a peaceful protest even if it meant getting arrested. But Carlos and Gaby feared deportation. Federal authorities had said they wouldn't intervene only as long as the youths abided by the law.

"People had all these expectations of what to do. They really wanted us to do something big when we got to Washington, but we couldn't come to a consensus," Felipe later recalled.

The young undocumented immigrants had never intentionally participated in civil disobedience to get arrested. Their fear of deportation was too great. Now they wondered, should they do something they knew might force the government to arrest them? Should they try to make it look unintentional? They debated whether they would be more useful to the movement as symbolic detainees or as free activists able to speak out.

While they were in Raleigh, Juan made a phone call that upended everything.

Juan called his sister, who was twenty-five but, due to a congenital birth defect, had a mental capacity closer to that of a twelve-year-old. It quickly became apparent that she was upset.

Where are you? Juan asked.

I'm at the sale, she responded.

What sale? Juan asked. *Are you at the mall?*

No, his sister replied. She and her father were having the sale.

What are you selling? Juan asked, confused.

His sister furiously explained that people were out front buying everything, even the TV.

Put Dad on the phone! Juan demanded.

Juan's father explained: he hadn't wanted to worry his son, but he'd decided to leave the United States and move to Canada.

Juan Rodriguez Sr. had once owned a construction contracting business, employing a group of men he could call at a moment's notice to do a job. But that had all ended in 2007. After years of an occasional ticket for driving without a license, his record had caught up with him. Another ticket for driving without a license in Hillsborough County had become a felony, and the family couldn't afford to bail him out.[17] He had spent six months in jail, missing the holidays, the birth of his youngest daughter, and Juan's high school graduation.

After that, he was terrified to drive again. He lost work, relying on friends for rides to take him to the odd construction job.

Around that time, Juan's sister was also aging out of the public services she'd long received to help her live as independently as possible. In Canada, the public health system would be more likely to help her. Maybe there his sister could get support, even residency, his father reckoned, and then he could find legal status as her guardian.

Juan was floored. He'd been responsible for his sister since he had been nine, cooked the family meals since he was eleven. He had never been allowed a voice in the house until he'd moved out. Finally, just as he and his father had gotten into something of a groove, the family was leaving.

Juan's father promised to come through and say good-bye. They would meet the group a week later in Henderson, North Carolina. Juan Sr. had little to fear about driving now; he was on his way out.

As Juan awaited his family, the group received more bad news.

On March 12, eighteen-year-old Miami Dade College student Leslie Cocche was waiting for her train at a Tri-Rail station in Broward County, backpack in tow, just as she did every day to make the hour-long commute to classes. Several immigration agents approached her, asking about her immigration status and requesting her identification papers. When the Peruvian native, who had come with her family to the United States at age ten, couldn't provide the right documents, the agents handcuffed her and took her to the Broward Transitional Center, placing her into deportation proceedings.[18]

Leslie had been waiting for the same train Felipe had taken for years to attend Miami Dade College. *That easily could have been me,* he thought. His frustrations bubbled over. It felt as though the president had just been lying to them, assuring immigration advocates that DHS was now focused only on detaining "criminals." Leslie was not a criminal.

As their arrival in Washington grew closer, Felipe and the others began to worry more and more that despite all the publicity, they would arrive, attend a rally or two, and go home with nothing gained. The students turned inward, against one another, picking up on months' worth of slights and ignored insults: who had walked more, who was doing more of the grunt work.

After Juan's father came to say good-bye in Henderson, Juan snapped. The entire group began arguing once again, and suddenly Juan announced he was done. He would go to Canada with his dad. Here he was, walking thousands of miles to keep people from being deported, and he couldn't even protect his friends or his father.

I created this, and I can destroy it, he thought as he laced up his shoes, just as he'd done the night he'd decided to create the walk.

Carlos insisted he'd keep walking by himself if he had to. He wasn't about to turn back. But Juan was adamant. He was done.

He turned to Felipe. "You're coming with me to Canada, right?"

"No." Felipe said it quietly. He couldn't leave. He had given his word, and that was more important than money in the bank, his mother had always said. And actually, it was pretty much his only money in the bank.

They had said they would walk to Washington, and they would walk to Washington.

Juan stared at Felipe in surprise. No, he would not compromise. He was done. Then he stopped and sat down. He could not leave Felipe. He could not leave his friends, the movement. Okay, he would go to Washington. The four looked at one another. They hadn't felt this alone and impotent since they'd begun the walk.

It wasn't the last time their commitment to one another would be tested. For the most part, Felipe and Juan had kept their relationship discreet along the trail. They were being hosted by an array of organizations, some Catholic, some Southern Baptist, not known for being particularly welcoming to gay men. It was a deal they had made in order to be able to do the walk, and they knew their actions (or lack of action) made it easier for their ground team to find them housing along the way.

At one point, they had all agreed to donate blood to make a statement about immigrants' willingness to give back to their community.

Juan had pointed out that if he were honest about his personal history as a man who'd had sex with other men, he would be rejected as a donor. He wasn't about to go back into the closet for a blood donation, he told the group, and they agreed he should do what he felt was right. But Felipe was afraid. He didn't want to be outed publicly. "Do what you need to do," Juan told him. When the nurse did his intake, Felipe declined to mention his relationship with Juan and offered up his arm.

But Felipe couldn't refuse the LGBTQ blogger who asked to interview the two in North Carolina, and it was then that Felipe and Juan publicly came out as a couple. In an early-April blog, Felipe wrote for the first time along the Trail about his feelings for Juan.

"The Trail of DREAMs is a loud cry for justice, but on a more personal level, it's been an affirmation of my identity," he wrote. ". . . I am a man who dreams of one day being considered equal in the eyes of society next to my partner, Juan Rodriguez—the wonderful man I fear being separated from at any moment when all I wish is to spend the rest of my life with him."[19]

Some of the solidarity groups began to take notice and brought it to the attention of the logistics team, whose members were themselves exhausted and working around the clock to ensure safe landing spots for the walkers each day. Everyone was on edge, even more so because in Arizona, Governor Jan Brewer was poised to sign her state's harsh new immigration bill known as SB 1070, which had already inspired copycat versions in legislatures across the country.

As the group reached Arlington, Virginia, in late April, Juan and Felipe got word that their hosts would prefer them to keep their relationship quiet. Juan spoke to one of the women on the logistics team. She was sorry to have to ask them to keep it quiet, but she had barely slept in days. She'd called some hundreds of places to get them shelter each night over the course of their four-month journey. She was running out of options and needed to find them safe places for just one more week. She was volunteering her time, neglecting her own children. And now, rather than being grateful, Felipe and Juan were complaining because they couldn't hold hands in public.

"I have been notified that one of the group's associate organizers has 'kindly' requested that Felipe and I not 'act gay' at the arranged social gatherings on Sunday. In fact, it is 'preferable' if any sign of my relationship to Felipe is not mentioned or made visible in any manner to those who will be present," Juan wrote in a hastily typed response to the Trail's support team. "I don't know if this hurt me the most, or if I was more wounded by the fact that someone from my own team relayed this information to me."[20]

It made Juan physically sick to always be hiding his true self. Felipe had tried to kill himself in response to rejection over his sexuality. Maybe if he hadn't also been so vulnerable because of his immigration status, things would have been different. But this was their reality. Felipe remembered the time early on the trip when he and Juan had been playfully shoving each other as they arrived on the outskirts of Athens, Georgia. It was about 10 a.m., the air was cool, but the sun was already high.

A beige sedan swerved toward them.

"FAGGOTS! FAGGOTS!" a man yelled.

Juan pushed Felipe out of the way just in time. "If we hadn't moved, he would have hit us," Juan said.

He remembered the time they'd been asked to give blood and he had been afraid to be honest.

This time he would not be silent.

After months of talking about human dignity for all, talking about civil rights, and urging immigrants to take pride in their own stories, no matter what they were, he felt a visceral pain at being told he could share all stories but this one. Felipe, Juan, Gaby, and Carlos sat down together. They had long ago decided that Gaby would speak for them in most public places. They wanted her voice represented as the only woman, and they also recognized that she was often perceived as less of a threat and was better able to communicate their message.

Gaby said no; this time it would be up to Juan and Felipe to speak. They agreed that Felipe would talk at the church in Arlington about immigration and civil rights—and also about homophobia. The four walked into the meeting, with a renewed sense of united purpose. Before them, several hundred people, black, white, and Latino, sat at U-shaped tables to allow attendees to eat lunch and listen at the same time. A young woman who lived in Arlington got up and told her story. She was facing deportation, and she was terrified. She needed the community's help. Then Felipe stood up. Now it was his turn to seal the deal—for the young Virginian immigrant, for Juan, for himself, for the rest of the group, for the millions who couldn't be heard.

Felipe looked out at the pastors in the audience, the other allies. He thought of what he needed to say to convince them to help this young woman. These were the people who could save her if they flooded congressional offices and immigration officials' telephones and email accounts with enough messages. These were the people they needed to come to the rally they'd planned for when they crossed the Potomac River into Washington.

Felipe began to talk about David and Goliath. He knew the Bible backwards and forwards from his church days, and he'd always been drawn to the story of David, the youngest son, who as a teen had slayed the giant. Some versions of the story put David at age fourteen when he killed Goliath, the same age Felipe had been when he arrived in Miami. It was the story he most identified with. His passion worked its magic.

The speech earned foot-stomping applause.

But Felipe felt sick. He had not mentioned Juan. He had not mentioned homophobia.

Afterward, they all posed for pictures, smiling, with arms around each other.

As they walked out of the center, Juan leaned over. "You betrayed me," he whispered. Felipe's heart cracked. Then they both forced smiles once more and were whisked off to the next event.

6

ARRIVAL AND THE AFTERGLOW

Immigrant leader Tania Unzueta speaks to a reporter as part of a "coming out of the shadows" event in Chicago, Illinois, March 2011. (SARAH-JI/LOVE AND STRUGGLE PHOTOS)

Felipe and the other walkers arrived in the Washington area almost a week early, having covered ground faster than they planned. Now they had to wait. They were relieved to have a few days to rest but anxious, after so many months, to finish what they'd started. It was hard to believe they'd come this far. Felipe thought back to how close the whole thing had come to falling apart in North Carolina. They had gained national and international attention, winning the respect of many of the naysayers. Yet back in the nation's capital, they were once again at the mercy of the Washington players.

And within that circle of powerful change makers, chaos reigned. A few days before, Senator Lindsey Graham,[1] the South Carolina Republican who had stepped in to lead the GOP immigration reform effort in the Senate, dropped his support.[2] He had failed to convince even a handful in his party to join him on the remake of the 2007 comprehensive bill. Some Democrats in the House pushed ahead even as they knew that without Republican support, it was likely doomed.

Democrats held a sizable majority in Congress, but not all of them were on board with comprehensive reform, and with dozens of contested Democratic House seats up for grabs in elections that year, they knew they would see defections within their party on the bill. They needed at least some GOP votes to get past a filibuster.

On April 28, four days before they'd officially walk into the nation's capital, Felipe, Gaby, Juan, and Carlos drove into the city, parked their RV, and held a news conference at the National Press Club,* accompanied by Cheryl Little, who'd come up to provide support. As they walked toward the Press Club for their unofficial arrival in Washington, reporters flanked the four.

"You are walking so fast," someone called out.

"Sorry, we're used to it," Gaby said with an apologetic grin.[3]

---

* The walkers also met with South Florida Republican representatives Lincoln and Mario Díaz-Balart and Ileana Ros-Lehtinen, who had cosponsored the latest version of the DREAM Act in the House, as well as with Senator Durbin, who advocated for a similar measure in the Senate—although it seemed clear that any DREAM Act provision would now be wrapped into the comprehensive legislation.

They were peppered with the same questions they had been asked all along the trail and answered reporters distractedly, without breaking stride.

"Are you really undocumented?" one journalist asked.

"Yes," a weary Gaby replied to the interviewer. "I actually lost my status to do this." By taking leave from Miami Dade College, she had lost her student visa.

As Felipe neared Constitution Avenue, someone asked him and the others if they'd achieved their goal. "No," they answered—not until the administration took action to stop deporting those without serious criminal records.

"If they don't do anything, Latinos will not come out and vote in November," Carlos called out.

Someone asked Carlos if he feared being detained. "I lost the fear of being deported by walking 1,500 miles," he responded.

That same day, aboard Air Force One, Obama appeared to officially signal the death knell for a comprehensive bill in rare casual comments to the traveling press corps. "We've gone through a very tough year, and I've been working Congress very hard, so I know there may not be an appetite immediately to dive into another controversial issue," he told them.[4]

The president may have spoken the truth about Congress's unwillingness to act, but his comments infuriated immigrants' Washington advocates and their Democratic allies. Only months before, the president had made an impassioned speech for comprehensive reform. Esther Olavarria, who had worked to salvage and update Ted Kennedy's bipartisan bill under the leadership of Lindsey Graham and Chuck Schumer, was crushed.

"Even presidents have bad days," his top adviser on immigration, Cecilia Muñoz, told the advocates in an attempt to explain the public torpedoing of any hope for comprehensive reform that year.

While the Democrats continued with the Washington Kabuki theater-like ritual of presenting their immigration bill, even though it had little chance of passing, Felipe and the walkers remained true to their original mission, sporting T-shirts urging people to text the president to stop deporting young students and their families.

The walkers had asked to meet President Obama and to deliver more than 30,000 signatures they and their allies had collected in support of their request for deferred action for those who would be eligible for the DREAM Act. Through the veteran activists, they got word the president had declined but would send his trusted aide Valerie Jarrett. The four students refused. They had walked 1,500 miles to meet the president. They tried to drop the petitions off with the Secret Service outside the White House, but the agents wouldn't accept them, either. Things were not going as planned. The day before, upon returning to their RV, they had found the door wide open, their laptops gone.[5] Gaby dialed the police, but when they asked for her name, she briefly hesitated, still frightened of what would happen if she gave it.

Still, they had reason for hope. Although outwardly, comprehensive reform remained the focus, behind the scenes there was growing support for deferred action. The week before the Florida students had arrived in Washington, Durbin and Republican senator Richard Lugar of Indiana, had sent a letter to DHS secretary Janet Napolitano urging her department to issue a broad deferred action order for DREAM Act–eligible immigrants.

The senators expressed appreciation for Immigration and Customs Enforcement's help in addressing individual DREAMer cases. "However, deferred action for DREAM Act students would be more efficient than the current ad hoc system," the senators wrote. They noted that too often the decision to defer action came as a last-minute reprieve. "The decision to grant deferred removal in a DREAM Act case is frequently made shortly before the removal date. This is an inefficient use of limited resources."

What they didn't describe was the havoc such uncertainty wreaked on the lives of students, who each year received a letter confirming another year of deferred action, often only after much prodding, as in the case of Marie Gonzalez. Each summer, as the July Fourth weekend approached, she mentally and physically prepared for her ten-year exile, only to have the whole thing called off at the eleventh hour.[6]

The letter boosted the students' spirits. Someone had been listening. Inside the White House, experts quietly stepped up their research into what the executive branch could do, including ending the workplace raids and attempting to work with Immigration and Customs Enforcement to refine the priorities of who should be detained. But the president believed in working through the democratic process, Cecilia Muñoz maintained. And that meant exhausting all possibilities within Congress.

On May 1, Felipe, Juan, Gaby, and Carlos walked across Arlington Memorial Bridge into Washington beneath clear blue skies. Hundreds of supporters followed them. Some had walked 250 miles in solidarity. Others had taken buses to join them. Many had risked being stopped along the way by immigration officials. Felipe and his friends had shadows under their eyes. Their hair was bleached, their faces were sunburned. They were exhausted.

But they had made it. Tears filled Felipe's eyes. *We did it. We actually did it!*

By the time they reached the White House, some 5,000 people had gathered. Many held signs against the deportations and in support of the DREAM Act, but there was also a strong showing in reaction to a new cause for alarm: Arizona SB 1070. Anger among immigrants over the Arizona laws had coalesced into May Day marches around the country, which had overshadowed the students' arrival in national media coverage but also gave urgency to their cause.

The protests focused on SB 1070, scheduled to go into effect in late July, which required local law enforcement officers to determine the immigration status of a person if the officers had "reasonable suspicion" to believe the person was in the country illegally. Immigrant rights groups argued the law was an open invitation for racial profiling of Latinos, Asian Americans, and Middle Eastern Americans. Much like the Sensenbrenner bill, the law included penalties for harboring and transporting undocumented immigrants.

Also like the Sensenbrenner bill, it had once again scared people onto the streets in some seventy cities across the country.[7] The marches were smaller than the massive demonstrations of 2006, but they were focused in their call to oppose the law and stop similar proposals from passing in other states. According to the *New York Times*, at least 50,000 people took to the streets in Los Angeles on May 1, 2010, with 25,000 in Dallas, and more than 10,000 each in Chicago and Milwaukee.

In Washington, Felipe, Juan, Gaby, and Carlos each left their worn trail shoes and a rose at the gates of the White House around midday. The sun beamed down from the clear sky. Oscar, the little boy they'd met in South Carolina, had come to DC with his parents. Thanks to Gaby's quick efforts and work by the team's lawyers, his father was in the process of getting deferred action. Oscar greeted the group with a hug.

The four students stood shoulder to shoulder in their matching T-shirts yet seemed oddly disconnected from the scene. They sat apart as nearly three dozen protesters, including Democratic representative Luis Gutiérrez of Chicago, were detained for sitting on the White House fence. The crowd cheered in support of the congressman and the others led away by police, hands fastened behind their backs with white plastic police ties.

Among those arrested were Joshua Hoyt, the head of the Illinois Coalition for Immigrant and Refugee Rights; Ali Noorani of the centrist National Immigration Forum; Deepak Bhargava of the Center for Community Change; and Gustavo Torres, who welcomed the walkers at his nonprofit CASA de Maryland organization. They hadn't all supported the four walkers from the beginning. Some had been downright skeptical. But now they were willing to get arrested on the students' behalf. Part of Felipe yearned to throw himself in with the allies and get arrested as well. It would be the most fitting end to the walk, he thought, the final act of commitment. Yet the bigger act of commitment was to his friends, who had all agreed to stick together. In April 2010, it was not yet commonplace to see young immigrant activists voluntarily get arrested. In fact, it was unheard of. The advocates would be detained and bailed out. Their lawyers would likely get any charges reduced or thrown out. But Felipe, Gaby, and Carlos could face deportation. And even if they didn't get kicked out of the country this time, if they ever did have the opportunity to apply for permanent residency, an arrest and conviction could torpedo their application. It would make them more vulnerable. They would have to be even more careful in everything they said and did. They had worked so hard to create a voice for themselves and their friends. They didn't want to lose it now.

Felipe grinned. They had completed what they'd set out to do. More than that, they now had a bigger, stronger network that would carry their dream forward. He was tired. And he was glad to hand over the baton. It was time for the next team to step up.

Reporters and videographers crowded around the advocates and Congressman Gutiérrez, who sported a T-shirt with the words "Arrest me not my friends," as he was taken in a van to be fingerprinted.[8] The bus with the detainees pulled away, and after dozens more interviews, the show was over. The four finally drifted back into the crowd.

Gaby took a cab to meet friends, declaring to her friends' laughter, "I don't want to walk anywhere anymore!"

Felipe and Juan headed to Dupont Circle with Felipe's sister, Carolina, and his niece and nephew. They sat on the grass, blowing dandelions. Nobody recognized them. He would need time to sort through everything they had seen and heard along the Trail. He would need space to decide what he wanted to do next. But for now, he was content to lie down next to his sisters' children and watch the bike messengers gather at the edge of the marble fountain. No more spotlight. *I get to be a normal person again*, he thought.

After 1,500 miles, it was as perfect an ending as he would get.

EXCEPT IT WASN'T AN ENDING. One of the groups organizing actions against the Arizona law asked the four young activists to lead a May 29 march in Phoenix. After that, there were calls for them to speak in

Los Angeles and San Francisco. Roughly a month after they arrived in Washington, the four were back on the trail, this time in a plane, headed to Arizona to meet with Sheriff Joe Arpaio. They needed a break, but they couldn't say no, especially not to a face-to-face with Arpaio, whom they'd heard so much about.

As they sat in the plane, looking down over the Gulf of Mexico, Juan leaned over to Felipe. "Will you protect me?" he asked, only half joking about the next leg of their trip.

"Yes!" replied Felipe. "But how?"

"Love me forever!" Juan declared.

Felipe could do that. He could definitely do that.

The plan was to hug Arpaio, a tactic of kindness they'd used on opposition throughout the walk. And they did. Some critics wondered how they could extend their arms to a man who seemed to actually enjoy raiding homes and rounding up immigrants.

For the group, it wasn't just about turning the other cheek. They wanted to show they were unafraid of him. They also wanted to transmit in some basic way the pain they had absorbed along their trail from the stories of people like Oscar and Leslie.

And they called his bluff. A sheriff who derided the notion of prioritizing certain undocumented immigrants had invited them into his office, then declined to arrest them. The toughest sheriff in the country had just demonstrated his support for exercising prosecutorial discretion.

It was clear the walk to Washington had left an indelible imprint on the political landscape. United We Dream leaders now pointed to the Trail as an inspiration. Even people such as United We Dream leader Mohammad Abdollahi, who would soon split off to form a more radical immigrant activist group, acknowledged years later, "A lot of people say the first notion they have of undocumented folks is the kids walking from Florida."

In Chicago, young undocumented activist leaders were beginning to seriously consider civil disobedience of their own. They now knew how to mobilize a network of friends and family, how to reach out to the media, how to flood immigration officials' telephone lines and email accounts with petitions to defer a deportation. If they were detained, they believed, they could organize a similar campaign on their own behalf. Felipe and the other students on the Trail hadn't been ready to get arrested. But they had opened door for others who were.

Taking a cue in part from the Trail of Dreams, Tania Unzueta joined Mohammad Abdollahi, whose family had fled Iran more than a decade before and had settled in Ann Arbor, Michigan, and together they set their sights on a nonviolent action in Arizona, at the offices of Republican senator John McCain. They made no effort to hide their plans. Tania and her group planned a sit-in at his Tucson office, knowing even a peaceful one could lead to their arrest and deportation. They worked with local activists and publicly counted down until the action. Tania called Dick Durbin's office and talked with his staff, and she kept the Washington contingent of United We Dream up to date as well.

Arizona was symbolic. Since it had passed the new immigration laws, similar measures had sprouted up in states across the country, many of them drafted in a coordinated manner through the national American Legislative Exchange Council, a business-backed group supported by the conservative billionaires Charles and David Koch.

Meanwhile, McCain, who had led the immigration reform effort with Kennedy in the mid-2000s, had backed away from both a comprehensive bill and the DREAM Act ahead of his run for the GOP nomination in 2008, echoing the more conservative cry "Secure the borders before reform."[9] Yet he was still among the adversaries they thought they could most likely sway. After all, he'd cosponsored immigrant-friendly bills in 2003 and 2005. In his heart, they believed, he was still supportive of their cause.

On Monday, May 17, 2010, five young activists walked into McCain's office. Along with twenty-six-year-old Tania and twenty-four-year-old Mohammad, the group included Lizbeth Mateo, twenty-five, a recent graduate of California State University, Northridge, and Yahaira Carrillo, twenty-five, of Kansas City, Missouri, both undocumented.

Tucson high school counselor Raúl Alcaraz, twenty-seven, a legal US resident, rounded out the group.[10]

McCain was facing one of his toughest primaries in years against a conservative Republican candidate who backed Arpaio's tough position on immigration, and he was still wounded by the attacks on his stance on immigration during the presidential campaign. It also seemed ridiculous to risk his campaign on a bill that was likely to fail. His staff welcomed the activists into the cramped office politely, and the senator even agreed to meet with them. But he wasn't going to budge.

Nor were the activists. They sat against the wall, all five dressed in caps and gowns, jeans and sneakers emerging from beneath. Tania's curly black hair spilled out from under her cap. On each of their gowns was pinned a button with a photo of two smiling young women.

Only days before, a pickup truck on a narrow road in Maine had slammed into a car carrying Tam Tran, who had shown her videos and testified before lawmakers in 2007, and Cinthya Felix, an undocumented activist originally from Mexico. The two had been killed in the collision. The desire to do something in Tam and Cynthia's honor had emboldened the small group. They stayed in the office all day, and when the offices closed, they refused to move.

In the end, authorities arrested everyone but Tania. At the last minute, she and the others had agreed she should leave. She was good with the press and could serve as their spokeswoman. She also was the most vulnerable when it came to detention because she had already been paroled back into the United States in 2001, which meant that under the law, an immigration judge wouldn't have the same discretion to allow her to post bond if immigration agents detained her; thus, unlike the others, she would have to fight her case from behind bars. Tania wasn't sure she wanted to risk that.

Instead she did countless interviews that evening, talking not only about undocumented youths but also about other struggles, including equal rights for those in the LGBTQ community. She wasn't making a random connection; besides their immigration status, there was something else four out of the Tucson Five had in common: like Felipe and Juan, they all identified with the LGBTQ community.

A surprising number of young immigrant activists identified as queer. It wasn't a coincidence. For some, it meant that from an early age, maybe before they had known they were undocumented, they had felt the emotional and mental burden of having to hide part of their identity. Coming out in one part of their lives—often as queer in their teens—had made it easier, more familiar, to come out again as undocumented and made doing so feel all the more urgent. Some of these young men and women also felt as though they had less to lose than other immigrants because they were already viewed by their own community as outsiders or even as troublemakers. And some queer activists were drawn to the movement's emphasis on telling and respecting each person's individual story. They had been rejected so many times that once they found that rare safe space in which to tell their stories, they clung to it.

That's not to say it was easy for them to come out. For Felipe and Juan on the Trail, it had felt safer to be public about their immigration status than about their sexual orientation. For Tania, who'd come out as a lesbian in college but kept her immigration status quiet for fear of losing her humanitarian parole, the opposite had been true.[11]

Many had witnessed the growing number of states rule in favor of same-sex marriage. The queer community's battle to be treated as fully human and with dignity under the law felt familiar, and the pressure tactics the LGBTQ activists used to get lawmakers to their side—telling their personal stories, engaging in filmed confrontations—were easily transferable. The LGBTQ rights movement was in many ways the foremost civil rights movement of these young activists' generation. They had seen the 1960s civil rights movement only in black and white, and farmworker boycotts had also faded away more than a generation before.

The cross-pollination between the groups would only continue to spread. By the end of 2010, with the health care reform fight mostly over (at least for the rest of Obama's presidency) and the nation slowly finding its way back from the great recession, the push for the DREAM Act heated up, just as did the fight to end the ban on same-sex marriage and the military's "Don't ask, don't tell" policy, which allowed the discharge of individuals if their sexual preferences became public. America's Voice, which had begun helping United We Dream disseminate its message, brought on board one of the chief LGBTQ political strategists in Washington.*

In a 2008 campaign letter, Obama supported repealing the federal 1996 Defense of Marriage Act, which defined marriage as the union between a man and a woman. Now once again, after the bruising economic and health care fights, it seemed there wasn't the appetite to do so. The LGBTQ community was furious. But like the young immigrants who had refocused on the DREAM Act, they quickly pivoted. If they couldn't get marriage equality yet, at the very least, they wanted an end to "Don't ask, don't tell."†

Many soldiers had been outed despite their precautions and forced to leave the military. Others, like the young immigrants, were simply tired of hiding their identity. LGBTQ advocates worked to publicize sympathetic stories of heroic soldiers discharged over their sexuality and of officers unable to get medical coverage for an ailing partner. In April, days before the Trail of Dreams ended at the White House, several LGBTQ activists shouted down the president at a California fund-raiser.[12] A month earlier, a group of military veterans organized by the activist group GetEQUAL chained themselves to the White House fence to protest.[13] The young immigrant activists took notes. The LGBTQ rights movement had more money and access than the

---

* Joe Sudbay, who'd spent three decades as a policy analyst and advocate, and who helped with the White House protest by LGBTQ veterans, began advising America's Voice during this time.

† "Don't ask, don't tell" was the compromise President Bill Clinton had acquiesced to early in his administration, a delicate balance meant to reward the lesbian, gay, and bisexual communities that had backed his candidacy by revoking the outright ban against homosexuality in the military while accommodating lawmakers' fear of openly gay military personnel. It boiled down to essentially: Keep quiet about your sexuality (and pray you don't get outed), and you can serve.

undocumented groups had. But even wealthy white gay men who could vote needed allies, and many now saw value in Latino political and cultural support to effect policy and social change. The two movements increasingly shared not only strategies but protagonists, as youths such as Felipe, Juan, and Tania were no longer willing to choose one fight over another.

IN JUNE, Obama finally agreed to meet with a member of the Trail of Dreams. He invited Juan, the only one with legal status, to the White House. Juan looked around. Part of him still couldn't believe he was there, not just at the White House but standing among some of the most powerful players in the immigration rights movement: the labor leader and civil rights activist Dolores Huerta, Frank Sharry of America's Voice, Eliseo Medina of the Service Employees International Union (SEIU), Angelica Salas of the powerful Southern California Coalition for Human Immigrant Rights (CHIRLA), and Janet Murguía of the National Council of La Raza.

Juan wore a yellow dress shirt, one of many his father had left behind on his way to Canada. He tried to tuck it in, but it was so baggy. He wanted to look right. He wanted to look like he owned a formal shirt of his own. He kept thinking about what Gaby had told him: he was there representing not himself but people who weren't allowed to be part of the conversation, people who weren't allowed to sit at the table.

As he looked in the mirror, he thought of his father. "I always thought of my dad like the Great Gatsby. Whenever he could, he tried to create these grand extravagances. Whenever he could, he would try to make us feel like one day we would be important people in the world. I don't think my dad ever imagined me to be a politician or anything, but it felt like my dad would always have wanted me to be an important enough person that the president would want to meet with me."

Juan knew he would have a limited time to make his case to the president. He'd talked it over with Gaby, Carlos, and Felipe. Gaby, who'd had the most experience in Washington, said that almost everything in the meeting was likely to be scripted. As the youngest and least experienced in the group, Juan was unlikely to get much if any time to talk. Anything he did would have to be physical, a visual demonstration of how he and so many other young activists felt.

Juan also felt guilty. They should have invited the undocumented: Felipe, Gaby, and Carlos. What he didn't know was that not only was it risky optics for the president to invite in a group of undocumented immigrants but on at least one previous visit, Secret Service agents had nearly detained undocumented White House visitors after running the standard background checks on them. That was the last thing the president's staff wanted.

Juan was ushered into the White House and eventually into the small dining room and waited along with the advocates, Cecilia Muñoz, and other White House staffers. The president entered and walked around the table, shaking hands with the visitors. Juan was among the last. He willed his hands not to tremble. The president put out his hand. Juan clasped his hands behind his back.

It's not the president of the United States that's greeting me, he told himself. *It's just a person, and he's the person in charge of enforcing policies that are dividing families.*

Juan looked up at the president. "I can't shake your hand," he said.

He barely had time to explain more, that this was personal. The president got the message.

Then what was supposed to be a friendly meeting turned tense. The president complained that the immigrant groups were constantly attacking him.

Juan remembered the president saying he understood the immigrant story, the vulnerability and fear, but that he could find millions of stories from people around the world who wanted to come to the United States. His job, essentially, as the nation's chief immigration officer, was to decide who would be allowed to come—who would end up earning $300 a week, not $300 a year.

The immigrant advocates wanted to keep a united front, show that the president was committed to moving immigration forward, that it was something he cared about personally and could get done, so as to keep up the energy in the field and the pressure on Congress. Juan initially agreed not to talk about the handshake moment.

And he didn't for a while. But he left the White House feeling torn. He understood the president didn't like being constantly attacked by his allies, but wasn't taking the heat kind of his job? Yet he appreciated that Obama hadn't tried to snow them. He was grateful to have had the opportunity to meet with a president who was so honest and raw.

Then once more he reminded himself that they weren't just a group of friends coming by for tea. This was the man responsible for breaking up so many families he knew, for separating parents from their children because they hadn't been able to get a driver's license and had driven anyway, or because they had been waiting for a train without proper ID on their way to school.

"If it were any other setting, I would have cried."

It felt once more as though no one had really listened to what he and the other members of the Trail had been asking for.

But the Obama administration had begun laying the groundwork. In June 2010, Department of Homeland Security assistant secretary John Morton issued the first of a number of memos—the so-called Morton memos—outlining the agency's priorities when it came to immigrant detentions. Terrorists and violent criminals were at the top of the list. Young undocumented immigrants who had grown up in the United States did not even make the list.

The memos were part of a broader effort within DHS's Immigration and Customs Enforcement agency to establish priorities for enforcement, "and actually have those priorities carried out by those agents, which doesn't sound like a big deal, but it was revolutionary in the ICE world," Napolitano would later recall after leaving the agency. "They really did not differentiate between the types of backgrounds of the people who were in the country illegally."

AT THE SAME TIME, a split was widening within the United We Dream coalition. Everyone was now focused on the DREAM Act, but some, including Mohammad Abdollahi, felt that the group wasn't doing enough to pressure lawmakers and the White House. They worried its leaders were being swayed by what they only half jokingly termed the immigration industrial complex—the mix of well-established Washington-based nonprofits, whose funders supported broad immigration reform but not necessarily broad structural and socioeconomic change. And then there was the Democratic Party, which Mohammad and others felt wanted to make sure whatever happened with immigration would benefit the party first and foremost. Among the Democrats' considerations: the fact that legalizing undocumented immigrants without giving them citizenship wouldn't do much to bring new voters into the party.

Simmering tensions had begun to show. On the one hand were the young activists like Gaby, who had become increasingly accustomed to the pace and style of Washington, even as they pushed for change. On the other were organizations and activists from the middle of the country, like Tania, and those in the Southwest and in California, who did not feel their voices were sufficiently heard in Washington.

In July 2010, young activists upped the ante by holding a silent protest in the offices of Democrats, including Senate majority leader Harry Reid. Others sat outside the office of Democratic senators Dianne Feinstein of California, Chuck Schumer of New York, and Bob Menendez, the tough Cuban American from New Jersey. Another group of activists held a protest in the atrium of the Hart Senate Office Building, while still another camped out in McCain's Washington office.

The sit-ins infuriated some Democrats, who saw themselves as the young immigrants' champions. Both Menendez and Gutiérrez took particular umbrage at the young activists' recriminations. Both men had cosponsored versions of the latest comprehensive immigration reform bill. And they hadn't been afraid to challenge the Democratic Party when they felt it wasn't looking out for their constituents or was disrespecting fellow Latinos. Now they were being told by a bunch of kids that despite their years in Congress, they were out of step and too cautious?

As the students sat in Reid's office, again in caps and gowns, they spoke with Gutiérrez by phone. The Chicago lawmaker, born to Puerto Rican parents, encouraged them to leave. It did not go well. Mohammad Abdollahi recorded the call and later posted it online,[14] a hardball tactic that proved effective in embarrassing his target in the short term.[15]

"For you guys to walk away from there, what has to happen?" Gutiérrez asked them. The students' political inexperience showed as they struggled to articulate exactly what they wanted the majority leader to do. They gave mini-speeches. Finally they clarified what they wanted; they wanted Reid to put the DREAM Act onto the Senate calendar for a vote.

"What if it fails?" Gutiérrez asked.

"*La vida es un riesgo.* Life is a risk," one young woman answered, unfazed.

"You know something. You guys are all adults. You know exactly what you're doing," Gutiérrez responded in the exasperated tone of a parent. He resented being attacked when he was one of the few lawmakers willing to engage directly with the students in the first place.

It was not a tone the students wanted to hear. They huddled around the phone. Now they were angry. They accused Gutiérrez and other lawmakers of endlessly debating, pointing fingers, but failing to act. They understood that Gutiérrez had put himself on the line with his party on comprehensive reform, but that effort seemed to be going nowhere. The students promised the DREAM Act would only be a first step, that they would come back to fight for comprehensive reform. Their proposal was a foot in the door.

"We are tired of waiting," one student said, "we have people [who've been undocumented] here for ten years, for nineteen years, since they were one year old."

Gutiérrez said he was sympathetic but disagreed. "I'm not quite sure your getting arrested and possibly deported actually advances [things]," he warned. The congressman reminded them of who had gone to jail during the White House rally at the end of the Trail of Dreams. It was the older allies, including himself, who'd been arrested, not the students or any other undocumented youths.

The rejoinder felt like a low blow.

His arrest had been symbolic, they shot back. As a sitting congressman, Gutiérrez had little to lose.

"Every time somebody says the whole thing can't pass, only part of it, it weakens us. It divides us. It confuses us," Gutiérrez tried again. "We once had a united movement for comprehensive immigration reform. Now we don't."

Gutiérrez went on to remind the students that there were families that had been waiting decades for reform and had seen loved ones deported. Mohammad interrupted, reminding the congressman that as a result of the sit-in at McCain's Tucson offices, he and others from that group were now in deportation proceedings.

"So for you to sit here and talk to these five, six youth that are sitting in this office and to put them down . . . instead of supporting them is a shame!" he said, his voice shaking.

It wasn't just Gutiérrez. The young activists would have a tough time convincing lawmakers to go for the DREAM Act as long as the veteran advocates, with whom the Democrats had close ties, pushed for comprehensive reform. In a July interview with Los Angeles' biggest Spanish-language newspaper, Reid said as much, telling *La Opinión* that he was waiting for the "immigration advocates" to give him the green light to pivot from a comprehensive reform effort to the DREAM Act.[16]

Those advocates were, for the most part, still urging Reid and Gutiérrez to go for another stab at comprehensive reform. Some, such as SEIU's Eliseo Medina and Angelica Salas of CHIRLA, saw supporting only the DREAM Act as equivalent to selling out: forget about the gardeners, the nannies, just take care of some privileged kids who couldn't go to college.

"You're saying we should pivot from fighting for eleven million to one million and we're not even going to win because the votes aren't there?" they questioned.

By then Frank Sharry had become a convert to the potential power of the undocumented students, if not the DREAM Act itself. "Yes," he answered. He was thinking about the movement. It wasn't so much 11 million versus 1 million. "These young people are emerging as authentic leaders of their own struggle. We need to support them," he insisted.

Frank also had a bigger strategy in mind beyond the DREAM Act. These youths were clearly going to go ahead on their own anyway. And even if the DREAM Act failed, which still was more than likely, the campaign to pass it might at least turn the screws on Republicans to put something in its place. It was a way to advance the legislation, he believed. For him, backing the young undocumented activists wasn't so much a policy play as it was part of a cultural and political battle.

By continuing to attack the Senate majority leader, the young immigrants could have pissed Reid off enough that he would have given them the cold shoulder. Everyone wanted the Senate majority leader's attention, and Reid could have spent his political capital on any number of bills that year.

Except that he was fighting for his political life in Nevada in a race against the Tea Party–backed GOP candidate Sharron Angle. Since 2000, the number of Latinos in the state had grown from under 20 percent to more than a quarter of all residents.[17] Angle was already running ads describing Reid as "the best friend an illegal alien ever had" and even had one ad targeting the DREAMers. If the longtime senator were to have a chance, he'd need Latino voters, and the energy and determination of the undocumented youths would help. Reid, too, was coming around to the idea of the DREAM Act. A young woman named Astrid Silva had begun showing up at many of his events, handing him slips of paper with bits of her story on it. She'd come to the United States from Mexico as a four-year-old, crossing the Rio Grande with her mother on a rubber raft. "I have never, ever as much as stolen even a piece of gum, but I feel like a criminal," she wrote in one letter. Reid also met with Roman Catholic cardinals, including Los Angeles' Mahony. His wife, the daughter of a Russian Jewish immigrant, also urged him to act.

At a progressive conference held in July in Las Vegas, Reid promised to bring the bill up if he could get sixty votes in the Senate. In the middle of his Q-and-A session, students who had been sitting quietly in caps and gowns stood up and silently protested what they saw as one more effort to stall. By late summer, Reid agreed to tack the proposal onto a military appropriations bill, although that version would fail.

As Felipe and Juan watched the political process play out, they couldn't help but grow excited to see other undocumented youths step up the pressure on lawmakers, but they also felt increasingly out of their element. They were not comfortable in the Washington environment, where the right political alliances were so important. They wanted to go back home and to the grassroots work they thrived on.

The students' tactics were working, though. More and more young immigrants were stepping in to take on the fight. And more veterans were coming out publicly for the DREAM Act. Even if the concept left a bad taste in their mouths because it excluded so many, they, too, could see the impact the young immigrants were having on both lawmakers and on the American public. Opposing a campaign led by telegenic young immigrants was not what political leaders wanted to do. As Frank Sharry had already realized, this was not a moment to miss. In cities across the country, older immigrant advocates, emboldened in part by the youths, now began to hold more sit-ins and protests for comprehensive reform, as well as increasingly for the DREAM Act.

IN CALIFORNIA, Dario Guerrero, like most DREAMers, followed the congressional debates from afar, occasionally watching them on TV with his parents. But for the most part, he tried to ignore politics. It all seemed so far away from his daily life. He wasn't the only one of his childhood friends who was undocumented, and though he didn't advertise his status, it didn't seem like a deep, dark secret either; it just was. More immediate were the college applications. The Internet told him his choices were simple: shoot for the moon, the handful of elite schools that could afford to offer full private scholarships, or go to community college, the cheapest option, paying for one class at a time. The Massachusetts Institute of Technology recruited him and even flew him out to visit the campus. But it quickly became apparent that it could not accept him without the right documentation. On that trip, he wandered over to the Harvard University campus. He remembered his teachers joking about how one day he might even go to Harvard. He hadn't even known what it was back then, just somewhere important, yet the idea had embedded itself, floating in the back of his mind for years. Why not apply? He had nothing to lose. Dario searched for advice on applying as an undocumented student. Soon he connected with an online thread of other students in the same situation. For fun, Dario and a few buddies began documenting their research, playing around with his dad's old camera, making a short video about their experience applying to college as undocumented immigrants. On a whim, he attached the film to his application. The university would know his status anyway; he might as well own it.

Dario tried to tell himself it didn't matter, tried not to care too much as he and his friends discussed immigration at lunch or while his parents watched the news. He asked his girlfriend, a US citizen, if she'd consider marrying him. She stalled. *Something's got to pass*, he thought, watching the protests back east.

NOT ALL YOUNG IMMIGRANTS were excited about the DREAM Act. Some 65,000 undocumented students were graduating from high school each year,[18] but at best about 10 percent graduated from college— and two years of college was one of the requirements for citizenship under the DREAM Act; that or military service.[19] Others had arrived in the country at too old an age to qualify for the proposal. Edgar Alejandro Aldana Viramontes was among them. He had arrived in California with his family from Guadalajara, Mexico, during the winter of 2003, just two months after his sixteenth birthday. When his family had settled near Pomona, California, about thirty miles east of Los Angeles, going to college had been the least of his worries. His family was among thousands drawn to the plentiful agriculture and construction work and the small-town feel of southeastern California, but life was far from easy.

Alex, as he quickly became known at school, hoped that the move would improve things for his parents, whose industrial chemical business back home had floundered. He hoped it would end the fighting between them and the beatings his father inflicted mostly on his older brother and mother. Instead, things had gotten worse. Two years after they had overstayed their tourist visas, they were still living with an uncle and his wife, sharing two rooms. Alex's father had found work in construction, but money was still tight. Alex's older brother often stayed out all night. His little sister cried at school. His father easily flew into rages.

Alex begged his mother to leave. She refused. Alex was small for his age, with shaggy black hair hanging over his eyes, shy yet determined, often lost in a book, dreaming of one day moving to Los Angeles. He threatened if his mother didn't leave, he would. A school counselor at his sister's school tried to intervene as well, encouraging Alex's mother, Laura, to seek help as a victim of domestic violence.

But Laura couldn't believe anyone would help someone like her, an "illegal." And as bad as things were, the situation was familiar. Leaving opened up the possibilities of even worse scenarios. She worried what would happen if her husband called the police to hunt her down. Most battered women in Southern California went first to an emergency shelter, then transitioned to low-cost long-term housing with help from the state and federal governments. As an undocumented immigrant, Laura didn't qualify for that aid, nor did her Mexican-born children. Then one day, as his parents fought, Alex stepped in, and his father grabbed him by the neck. The next morning, Alex finally told his own school counselor what was going on, triggering action Laura couldn't stop; she would have to leave her husband or risk having social workers come to the apartment and possibly take her children away.

Mother and children made their exit the very next day, staying a night with a school official until a space opened up at a shelter an hour's drive away in neighboring Riverside County.

Alex spent his senior year of high school working full-time at night as a dishwasher in a Japanese restaurant to earn money for food and rent, often falling asleep at school the next day. Once a strong student, he no longer considered college his next step. He just needed to survive. Eventually he reconciled with his father and got a job in construction with him. And he did move to Los Angeles, finding work in HIV educational outreach to at-risk immigrants. It was through this work that it often fell to him to break the news to other young immigrants he met that the DREAM Act they had been hearing about on the radio might very well leave them out because they had arrived too late or had not graduated from high school. Alex increasingly resented the attention lavished on the valedictorian types. He wished he could see more young people like himself testifying in Congress, those who weren't stars but who were working to support their families and contributing to the economy. Did his work to halt the spread of AIDS really have less value to the country than a two-year college degree in communications? What about the guys who had spent years building the San Bernardino and Pomona homes so many Californians were flocking to?

BACK AT WASHINGTON-LEE HIGH SCHOOL, Hareth Andrade-Ayala was now a senior. Her adviser, Mr. Garcia, put Hareth and her friend Antonella in touch with activists he knew. In the fall of 2010, the girls organized a small group (made up mostly of boys who had crushes on Antonella) to volunteer for the growing DREAM Act campaign. They joined other more experienced organizers working the halls of Congress. The first day they walked up Constitution Avenue toward the Dirksen Senate Office Building, Hareth swallowed as she stared up at the bronze doors. "I didn't know you could just go in," she whispered.

She asked one of the leaders of her contingent what they were going to do. "A sit-in," he told her. More and more students were adopting the practice of dropping into offices and threatening to stay until they could meet with staff, and to Hareth, the whole scene seemed almost quaint. It was something she'd read about in her high school history books. They were going to the office of the junior senator from North Carolina, Kay Hagan, joining up with a few students from her state, and weren't going to leave until she agreed to meet with them. Elected just two years before, Hagan was among some five Democratic senators still on the fence over the DREAM Act, and activists believed they could bring her to their side. Hagan was a former bank vice president, a centrist Democrat, and the niece of Florida's last elected Democratic governor. But less than a year into her job, she was already under attack from groups backed by the Koch brothers, who, in addition to funding the American Legislative Exchange Council, were supporting the nascent Tea Party movement. Opponents of the president's Patient Protection and Affordable Care Act had also begun amassing money to unseat her.

Hagan wanted to be careful about alienating the state's white conservative voters, many of them low- and middle-income earners, who increasingly saw the wave of new immigrants to North Carolina as a threat to their own livelihoods. Still, the freshman senator seemed open to discussion.

The teens spent that first afternoon camped out in her lobby. Hagan's staff was friendly and eventually agreed to hear out the students.

"What am I supposed to say?" Hareth asked the organizer leading the sit-in.

Tell your story.

"What do you mean, tell my story?" she asked. That would take hours.

The organizer's response: make it shorter.

Hareth was indignant. She'd never told her story publicly, and she wasn't about to cry. She watched as several students recounted some of the most intimate details of their family histories to complete strangers. Some did cry. She was embarrassed for them. She was also in awe. The staffers were visibly moved and agreed to pass the message on to their boss. Hareth marveled at their success.

So this is lobbying, she said to herself. *I can do this. No problem.*

Only later would Hareth learn the staffers' response was standard practice—often a polite way to nowhere. And only later would she begin to feel the toll it took on her to relive the worst moments of her family's story again and again.

A MARRIAGE, A DEATH, AND A VOTE

Marie Gonzalez walks to church on her wedding day, accompanied by her mother, Marina Morales Moreno, in Puntarenas, Costa Rica, November 2010. (COURTESY OF MARIE DEEL)

Marie Gonzalez took a bus to Washington in September to lobby in support of Senator Reid's DREAM Act push. As she stared out the bus window at the blur of flat midwestern farmland, she thought of how many trips she'd made to the nation's capital. Maybe a dozen. There had been fewer in recent years. She had tried to focus on her studies at Westminster College. Money had gotten so tight her last year that she ended up sleeping on her friends' dorm couches. Then came graduation. She had fallen hard for Chapin Deel, too. They had kept dating well after he graduated. Now, it felt strange to head once more to Washington. Coming from Jefferson, Missouri, she'd never had many nearby friends in the movement and had always felt some distance from the other young advocates who had learned the ropes locally and often traveled to national meetings in tight groups. That distance was more acute this time. She watched the new crop of undocumented leaders flooding Washington with both joy and sadness. Seeing people like Gaby Pacheco take charge was thrilling. She wanted to stand up and cheer. But there was guilt, too. Soon she would no longer be among them.

Nearly a year before, in November 2009, Marie's cell phone had rung as she sat in her cubicle at the Farmers Insurance call center. She still daydreamed about someday putting her political science degree to use working in Washington or as a social worker or finally applying to law school. But for now she was just glad to be able to earn a paycheck.

It was a cool November afternoon. Chapin was on his way to pick her up from work, but they would have to take a detour, he warned her. A friend was having car trouble thirty minutes away in Kansas City, and he needed a lift. Marie sighed. Chapin's buddy had roommates. Why couldn't they pick him up?

Once again DHS had delayed her work permit renewal, which she also needed to renew her driver's license. The work permit had finally come, but she was still waiting to get her license. The government rarely gave her an explanation for the delays. Sometimes the work authorization renewal took a couple of months, sometimes more than six.

The upshot was that she had to depend on Chapin and other friends for a ride. There was no easy public transportation in Jefferson City, and unlike many undocumented immigrants across the country, Marie refused to drive without a license. Grudgingly, she agreed to tag along.

She tapped her pen on her desk and looked around at the other cubicles, where a dozen or so employees served as the front line for incoming claims. Chapin had helped get her the job, and the work allowed her to send money back to her parents in Costa Rica. Her bosses didn't seem to mind her precarious status.

She imagined the simplicity of her colleagues' lives. If they needed to drive to work, they could drive to work. They wanted to go to an R-rated movie or go out with friends and order a beer? Easy, they pulled out their ID. Sometimes it felt easier to mourn not having a driver's license than not being able to see her parents for more than four years. Now when she talked to them, they barely ever asked about serious things. Marie wanted so much to tell them about her job searches, the gnawing question about her and Chapin's future, but lately it was the latest local gossip they talked about, as if anything real were too painful a reminder of everything in her life they were missing.

Chapin arrived late and was preoccupied. They barely spoke on the ride to the city. Marie hunched in her seat, still thinking about the permit, work, her parents. Finally Chapin pulled into the parking lot of a red, wood-paneled Kansas City steak house called the Golden Ox. It was a place where ranchers had once gathered after selling their cattle at the Livestock Exchange Building next door. Now the historic restaurant drew a mix of old-timers and hipsters. Marie fumed. This was supposed to have been the restaurant they'd one day go to for a special occasion, not to meet Chapin's careless friend.

She got out, slammed the car door, and strode toward the restaurant. Instinctively she stopped, waiting for Chapin to catch up with her. But he hadn't moved. Marie turned back. Chapin stood there with a nervous grin, eyebrows raised in silent entreaty. As she approached his side of the car, he bent down on one knee and held a small box open toward her. Marie shook her head.

Oh, my God! Yes!

It was time. No more waiting. Marie threw her arms around him.

Chapin had visited Marie's parents, Marvin and Marina, in Costa Rica over the summer. He had wanted to meet his future parents-in-law and get their blessing. It was strange to go without Marie, be presented to her entire family alone with his rough Spanish. But they didn't have another option. Marina and Marvin had met him at the airport and taken to him immediately. Marina had even given Chapin the diamond that had come loose from her own engagement ring. He'd combined that one in a band with a small diamond from his grandmother's wedding ring, leaving space for yet a third stone, a new one, something of their own.

The Golden Ox wasn't the kind of place that offered champagne, but the owner comped the couple a small bottle of wine. Over dinner, Marie laughed as Chapin explained that he'd waited so long, he really didn't think he could wait another minute to get to the restaurant. For years she had resisted marrying Chapin for status. They'd broken up several times. Once she'd even given up and bought a one-way ticket to Costa Rica before Chapin had talked her into canceling it. She had hated the idea Chapin or anyone else would think they were together for convenience. But also, she had been only nineteen when she'd met him. She'd wanted to be sure. She kept hoping maybe she'd be able to get permanent residency and *then* marry him.

Yet each year it seemed less and less likely that her deferment would be renewed. The last time she'd reapplied, her work permit had been delayed by nearly six months, making her unable to get any real job and leaving her daily life in flux. In the spring of 2009, she'd even started to look for work in Costa Rica. But once again, at the last minute, and thanks to yet another letter from Durbin, DHS had come through just days before the Fourth of July and given her a reprieve.[1]

As she approached her twenty-third birthday, her opposition to marriage began to seem silly. Who else was she going to spend her life with?

They decided to get married in Missouri as soon as possible. Given that the spousal green card process could take between six and nine months, they used the time to organize a proper Costa Rican church wedding, which her parents could attend. They chose Thanksgiving 2010, so friends and family might be able to fly in and join them.

Now, nearly a year later, the invitations had been sent, and their US friends and families had bought their tickets. Still Marie's application had not been approved, and her temporary visa had yet to arrive. She couldn't leave the country without risking that the application would be denied. The case was complicated because even though she'd been granted a temporary reprieve each year, she still had a pending deportation order. She called the DHS hotline, but no one seemed to be able to give her a clear answer.

To make matters worse, Marie's father had been diagnosed with testicular cancer. Two surgeries later, he was undergoing chemotherapy. She ached to be by his side. The days ticked down. The September trip to Washington, some two months before the wedding, was a welcome distraction, although the bus ride took more than twenty-four hours. Once again Marie went to lobby lawmakers for the DREAM Act. This time, it seemed, maybe they had a chance.

There has been so much hard work. I have to be there for my own sake, and for those who can't be, she thought.

Before going, she took stock of the Missouri delegation. Democratic senator Claire McCaskill had opposed the DREAM Act in the past but now seemed open to at least considering it. Republican senator Kit Bond was firmly in the no camp. And Representative Roy Blunt, a fellow Republican running to succeed Bond, faced attacks from Democrats over whether he and his former wife had years before hired an undocumented immigrant to do housekeeping and tried to expedite her asylum case. Any hope that Blunt might be willing to consider a more moderate stance on Marie's case or any other withered.

In the end, Marie spent most of her time lobbying lawmakers outside her state. After months of working at the insurance company, it was exciting to once again be part of something bigger, something that could affect the lives of so many. Despite all the heartache, she still loved Washington, still wanted someday to work there.

She was a bit envious of the younger activists. Like many other DREAM elders, she'd pitched herself to the nation as the perfect immigrant, the immigrant whose story everyone could stand behind. After all, hadn't the slogan and the T-shirts for her case read "We Are Marie"? And especially in the early years, in a conservative town where so few had gone public about their status, she had been terrified that one false move—even driving without a license—would not only get her deported but also erase that "We" for her and for thousands of other young immigrants whom she represented.

The teens roaming the halls of Congress these days seemed so much freer. Just by showing up, they were taking risks she hadn't. Marie had been forced out. She had already been in deportation proceedings when she spoke on Capitol Hill back in 2004, with little left to lose. But these youths were putting themselves at greater risk by voluntarily revealing their status. And there were so many of them.

By 2010, Marie had been telling her story for more than half a decade. She'd become more jaded after the failure to pass immigration legislation in 2007. Each trip had become harder. Every time she recounted the moment DHS took her parents to be questioned, she revisited the terror of suddenly realizing the government viewed her and her family as criminals. Every time she recalled the day her parents had to leave Missouri, her chest constricted with the utter panic of saying good-bye.

Now she was so close to having the chance to move on and become a citizen. There were so many she was leaving behind, not just those staking their lives on the DREAM Act but also those who wouldn't be eligible. She felt guilty simply for enjoying the thought of the relief she would soon have.

In October, she wrote a blog post, a plea of sorts to her friends and fellow advocates. Ostensibly, it was about her departure from Washington, but it also spoke to the much greater departure she would soon make: "I know that many of you wish that I could just wait a bit longer and see what happens, but I can no longer wait. My life has long been in limbo, and with my father's illness I will not sit from afar and watch."[2]

In late October, Marie received word that her file had been sent to the wrong processing center and now no one could find the application. As the holidays approached, Marie and Chapin were forced to push back their flight until Thanksgiving Day to squeeze out extra time to sort out the visa delays. The wedding was set for the Saturday after Thanksgiving. Marie had called the DHS inquiry line telephone number so many times that she knew it by heart. Advocates and pro bono lawyers once again intervened on her behalf. Finally she received notice that her casework had been found. Her interview would be scheduled in Kansas City for Tuesday, November 16, when Marie and Chapin would answer a battery of questions to prove that theirs was not a sham marriage. Sometimes Marie felt like her entire life consisted of proving to the world that she was not a fraud.

Three days after the interview, on Friday, November 19, Marie headed back to Kansas City for the FBI fingerprinting to ensure that she had no criminal background and to keep her identity on file for the future. Her lawyers assured her the prints would be screened by early the following week.[3] On November 23, forty-eight hours before their Thanksgiving Day flight, Marie and Chapin chugged down their coffee. More bad news: the fingerprints had yet to come back. No one knew why. Their wedding was scheduled for Saturday, and still Marie did not have permission to leave the country. They drove back to the Kansas City DHS office again. The security officers at the front desk recognized her. *Still no luck?* they texted, as surprised as she was.

Determined to make the plane, Marie and Chapin decided to wait at DHS for news. Although the agency would be open the day before Thanksgiving, immigration officials had told Marie they would be processing only deportations. Marie began emailing all of her old immigration contacts, including Josh Bernstein.

When the clock ticked 5:30 p.m. and they had to leave, the guards at the front entrance tried to console Marie as she sobbed.

She called her father in Costa Rica. Friends and family had already begun arriving. She was going to get on the plane, she told him. She was done. She didn't care if she couldn't come back.

No, m'hija, he told her. *Don't be rash.* They could always reschedule the party. But for Marie to lose her US home now, after everything they'd been through? That was crazy talk.

On their drive home, Chapin, usually so calm and collected, pulled over to the side of the road, got out, and banged his broad fists against the car, his tears streaming into the wind.

That night, there seemed only one thing left to do. They met up at a bar with the only close friends who were still in town, friends of Chapin's who hadn't been able to afford the flight to Costa Rica. They downed tequila shots as it slowly sank in that they were going to miss their own wedding and stumbled to bed past midnight.

The phone rang at 7:30 the next morning, jolting Marie wide awake. Her head throbbed as she answered, still half asleep. It was Marie's lawyer. Someone had found her fingerprints. Marie was scheduled for an appointment in two hours back at the Kansas City DHS office. *Get to DHS!* the lawyer roared.

Marie and Chapin grabbed their keys and jumped into the car. Marie was still in sweatpants, evidence of the previous night's makeup and the salty remains of her tears still on her cheeks. When they arrived, the guards at security high-fived her. *Don't ask questions,* they said.

A few hours later, it was done. Finally they were free. The next day, as they sat on the plane, Marie considered the miracle that had occurred. They had come so close to missing it all. And if there hadn't been "*We* Are Marie," if she had been just one of a million other Maries, she probably would have missed it.

Marie barely recognized her father at the airport. It had been five years. She had seen pictures, but looking at him in person was different. The chemo had robbed him of his thick black hair and mustache. He was thin and slightly stooped. Still, he grabbed Marie in a bear hug. Finally.

Some forty people were already at her parents' home in Puntarenas when they arrived, the home she had helped her parents build by sending part of her salary to them each month. A local photographer was there, snapping pictures. A Costa Rican radio reporter wanted an interview, too. Marie desperately wanted to be left alone with her parents, to curl up in her mother's arms, but she reminded herself that this was bigger than her story. And she was here in part thanks to the media. Patiently she answered question after question.

Finally they began to focus on the day at hand. Marie's mother had already baked the prewedding Thanksgiving turkey at Marie's grandparents' house. Mother and daughter drove to retrieve it. Marie salivated as she carried the crisp heavy bird to the car. They returned some fifteen minutes later. Everyone was outside. Marina told some of Marie's American friends to help her bring the turkey and mashed potatoes inside. No one moved. Come inside, Chapin said.

Marie's dad had collapsed. Marvin was lying in the small living room. Someone had already called an ambulance.

Mi amor, I don't feel well, he said to his wife, clutching his chest. An American friend of Chapin's who was a doctor kneeled by his side.

When the ambulance came, Marie jumped into the back, accompanying her father, making sure the EMTs knew he was allergic to aspirin. *No, this is not happening,* she told herself.

Medics whisked Marvin inside as soon as they arrived at the hospital. Someone guided Marie and her mother into another room. The doctor peppered them with questions. He barely looked up.

The questions went on and on. Finally Marie asked where her dad was.

The doctor pushed back his chair. First he gave them an extensive list of Marvin's ailments. It had been the side effects of the chemo, not the cancer, that had triggered a heart attack. There was nothing more they could do, he said. Marvin was gone.

Marina collapsed. She demanded to be taken to him. It wasn't until she was allowed to see his body, Marvin's face looking for the first time in months as if he were truly in no more pain, that she was able to gather herself.

The wedding would go forward. Everyone was too overwhelmed to figure anything else out. Marie spent Thanksgiving night making both funeral and last-minute wedding arrangements. They picked out a casket at a neighbor's home mortician business, driving to an ATM in the middle of the night because the neighbor wouldn't accept a credit card. They paid someone else extra to build the traditional above-ground tomb overnight so the concrete would be dry by morning.

Marie had barely slept for two days, but her grandfather insisted they have coffee and snacks for the mourners who had begun to flock to the Gonzalez home as word spread of Marvin's death. They buried him on Friday. On Saturday, she was back in the same chapel where her father's casket had lain, making the final adjustments to the flower arrangements, and hanging white Chinese lanterns. Marie's grandmother ironed her empire-waist white lace dress. And Marie walked to the aisle behind her six bridesmaids without her father, her black curls cascading down her shoulders. Her mother wore black.

Marie put a picture of her dad in a flowered shirt on her phone and placed it at the empty chair at the head of the table during the reception. Afterward, they took her thin bouquet of stargazers and white lilies and placed it on top of her father's grave. Marie wondered that she had not run out of tears.

She had planned to return to Kansas City and maybe even make one more trip to Washington if the DREAM Act came to a vote. But she was still in Puntarenas helping her mother on December 8 when the House of Representatives passed a version of the DREAM Act, once again sponsored by Democratic representative Howard Berman of Los Angeles and Republican Lincoln Díaz-Balart of Miami. And she was still there six days later, when Reid finally announced that he would bring the DREAM Act to the floor of the Senate.

Throughout the late fall, long after Marie left, the young immigrants had been a relentless presence in Washington. Week after week they canvassed Capitol Hill, using the skills they had honed in the in-state tuition and other local fights. It wasn't just the sit-ins Hareth had participated in. They met with lawmakers to lobby them old-school style. They "bird-dogged" senators as they headed to the underground subway that ferried them from one side of Congress to the other. United We Dream organized daily "pray-ins" in congressional offices. The activists sat in the Senate cafeteria in their caps and gowns and held "study-ins." They made up Christmas carols supporting immigration reform and gave impromptu concerts for lawmakers.[4] They hadn't felt so hopeful since Obama won the 2008 election.

The day before the vote, Carlos Saavedra, the Bostonian cofounder and leader of United We Dream, posted on Marie's Facebook page, "Marie N. Deel, thank you for who you are, you were the key to building a strong immigrant student movement—you have inspired me to be a better person. You were one of the keys to bring us to this moment!"[5]

On December 18, 2010, Marie sat down at her mother's kitchen table and turned on her computer. She stared at the screen, waiting for the Internet to kick in. She had spent the last three weeks almost in shock, operating on autopilot. The image of the Senate floor flickered to life. Senators began filing into the chamber. Marie kept one eye on the hearing and the other on her social media feed. She couldn't think ahead. She couldn't think back. She was exhausted. Yet part of her was still, to her own surprise, excited about the vote. No way would she miss the debate.

THAT SAME MORNING, Hareth packed into the gallery above the Senate floor along with hundreds of other millennials from around the country. One girl wore a cap and gown cut from a pattern of an American flag. Some held hands. Others prayed silently. Hareth scanned the wall behind her, taking in the white marble busts of vice presidents past ensconced in the nooks behind her. All around the balcony, a sea of young people sat stiffly in their skirts, suits, and ties, their mostly dark hair framing anxious mahogany eyes. Hareth had opted for a burgundy sweater, jeans, and a pink jacket: warmth, comfort, and respect, in that order.

Beneath the gallery, on the Senate floor, dozens of mostly pale men, many old enough to be her grandfather, chatted and joked with one another as they strode across the blue patterned carpet. Hareth willed herself to remember every face, every marble bust and ornate molding, every bang of the gavel. This was the moment when the US government could finally move her, and all those around her, from invisible to visible. She closed her eyes. Many in the gallery had crossed the Mexican-US border with their parents, often before they could remember, or at least remember much. Many had flown to the United States with their family on tourist visas and never returned. Some had come with only one parent. Others, like Hareth, had initially come with no parents at all.

The memory of her arrival still played at the edges of her consciousness, often when she was least prepared: her mother's last glance as she said good-bye, the strangeness of the language, the aching feeling of loneliness in her gut, the rolling tug of uncertainty. She sensed that familiar roll now. She tried to convince herself it was the breakfast sandwich.

Only a few hours before, she had met other volunteers at the Lutheran Church of the Reformation a block away and scarfed down donated breakfasts. Some young activists had begun chanting, "We're fired up!" in an echo of the 2008 Obama campaign chant.

"We're fired up? Really, what does that even mean?" she'd muttered, watching them, almost embarrassed.

At seventeen, Hareth's heart-shaped face, shaggy bangs, and shiny pin-straight black hair still gave her an air of soft innocence younger than her years. It was her eyes that caught people off guard: playful one minute, unyielding the next.

More chants had followed as they marched down East Capitol Street.

"Ain't no power like the power of the people, because the power of the people don't stop!" Antonella and another friend, Karen, had begun chanting along with the crowd.

Hareth had looked around at all the strangers moving together in the cold morning air. Their chants had echoed in her head, then bounced along her tongue.

"Ain't no power . . ." she had mouthed, first in her head, next in a quiet whisper. Then she'd thrown her head back and opened her lungs wide. "AIN'T NO POWER!"

At the Capitol grounds, the chants caught in her throat. She'd been inside the Senate buildings already, but the Capitol, with its sloping lawn and wide steps, was a vastly more intimidating marble castle. All roads led here.

From her wooden seat in the gallery, Hareth looked down at the flag and the black marble desk in the center of the great hall. Above the vice president's empty chair were carved the words "E Pluribus Unum." Out of many, one.

Yes, she thought. *That is us.*

Below, Senate Majority Leader Harry Reid outlined the business of the special Saturday-morning session. They would start with a vote on House Bill 5281: the Development, Relief, and Education for Alien Minors Act of 2010. By taking up that version, they wouldn't have to send the bill back to the House for another round of votes. They were not actually voting on the House bill but rather taking a cloture vote: deciding whether to end debate and hold an up-or-down vote on the proposal. For that, they needed sixty votes. If they couldn't get cloture, the bill was essentially dead. If they did, the bill would likely pass.

If it passed, it would be the most significant immigration reform in more than two decades. Although far smaller in scale than the 1986 law, it would allow more than 1 million children and young adults with "good moral character" to step onto a path toward citizenship. Those who earned a high school diploma and completed at least two years of higher education or entered the military could eventually apply for US residency. In the meantime, they would be permitted to work, as well as study.

It was a long path, to be sure—nearly ten years if no delays were involved. But it was a path nonetheless, meaning that someday, even further down the road, they would be able to bring in their own parents, putting millions more unauthorized immigrants on the path to citizenship.

The vote was much more of a Hail Mary pass than Hareth knew. A month before, the Democrats had lost the House in the Tea Party's sweep of Congress. Within weeks, a new set of more conservative lawmakers would convene, and the DREAM Act would have no chance. So there they were, nearly a hundred senators[6] on a cold Saturday morning less than two weeks before Christmas, taking a vote that could reshape the nation.

If they failed to win the vote, the Senate would move on to the next item of business, including the cloture vote on an effort to repeal the military's controversial policy of "Don't ask, don't tell" for the LGBTQ communities. Like the young immigrants gathered in the gallery, queer activists viewed their bill as a last chance to move the ball forward before the new Congress was sworn in.

The speeches were beginning. Hareth sat back and squeezed her friend Karen's hand.

"I rise in support of the two very important votes we are having today. The DREAM Act is a moral imperative," New York Democratic senator Kirsten Gillibrand said when it was her turn to take the floor, addressing both the DREAM Act and the repeal of "Don't ask, don't tell" in one speech.[7] Of the DREAM Act, she said, "Young people who have come to this country through no fault of their own, who want nothing but to achieve the American dream, either through education or through military service—but they want to be part of this community and be able to give back to this community and in a country that was founded on immigrants, where the richness of our heritage and culture, and the breath of our economy, is due to our immigrants, we want to make sure every one of these young people can become an American citizen."

South Carolina Republican senator Lindsey Graham spoke against both bills, even though he had once been Esther Olavarria's hope for Republican support in the Senate. He began with "Don't ask, don't tell": "Repeal as it is being envisioned today could compromise focus on the battlefield," he insisted, adding that military leaders opposed ending the policy.

Graham then turned to immigration, and it was almost as if he were speaking directly to Hareth. "To those who have come to my office, you are always welcome to come, but you are wasting your time. We are not going to pass the DREAM Act or any other legalization program until we secure our borders," he said, adding he opposed the concept of the stand-alone bill that failed to address the larger immigration issue. "The best thing for the United States Senate to do, the House to do, the administration to do, is work together to secure our borders before we do anything else."[8]

Hareth thought back to the previous spring, to the night she had sprawled across the floor of Antonella's bedroom and they had discovered each other's status, how her life had changed since then. She shifted in her seat and turned her eyes from the Senate floor back to the balcony. Gaby Pacheco from the Trail of Dreams was there. She also saw Carlos Saavedra and Julieta Garibay in the crowd. She was too shy to wave. Besides, they looked preoccupied.

They were. Both knew it was unlikely the bill would make it. Despite all their work, Kay Hagan and others had refused to commit, fearing repercussions at the ballot box. On the way to the Capitol, Carlos had confessed to Julieta how worried he was. He'd promised his younger brother he'd get the bill passed in time for his graduation. That time was now.

Although she was just thirty, Julieta, the nursing graduate from Texas, was among that core group considered DREAM elders. Only days before, Carlos had called her with bad news: in a deal to push the bill through, Reid and Durbin had agreed to cut off eligibility at age twenty-nine.

This DREAM Act they're going to pass, it's not going to include you, he told her.

Julieta had been fighting for the bill for more than half a decade. And now all that she had worked for—if it passed—would leave her in the dust. It was a bitter pill to swallow, but she thought of all the young immigrants she had mentored, who were depending on her. How could she leave them now? She had promised to fight for them, and she would. Before she could even fully process the information, reporters had begun to ring, asking for a response. Someone asked if she'd consider going back to Mexico. She'd laughed. She'd actually tried that. Like Tania, she had returned in 1998 after high school, thinking it was the only way she could go to college. Except she had actually enrolled at the university there, but her academic Spanish had been too poor, and she'd felt lost in the culture.

If one listened closely to the senators' speeches that morning, it wasn't hard to tell where at least part of the day was headed. Speech after speech argued for and then against repealing "Don't ask, don't tell." Some senators, including Graham, said letting gay and lesbians serve openly would put the military at risk. But most of those who opposed the change argued in favor of waiting a little longer or letting the military set the timetable. It wasn't so much a question of "Should we, or shouldn't we?"; it was a question of when.

The discussion about the DREAM Act was different. It wasn't about stalling for time. A wide gulf still existed between those who supported the bill and those who opposed it.

"I'm asking for what is in effect an act of political courage," pleaded Dick Durbin, who had pushed to get Reid to bring the bill to the floor. "If you can summon the courage to vote for the DREAM Act today, you will join ranks with senators before you who have come to the floor of this United States [Senate] and made history with their courage, who stood up and said the cause of justice is worth the political risk."[9]

Playing on the military theme of the day, he rattled off the names of accomplished youths who were unable to serve their country because of an immigration status they had no choice over, including David, with a 4.2 average as a senior at the University of California, Los Angeles, the leader of the school band, who wanted to join the air force.

But Arizona Republican John Kyl wasn't having it. The senator called the bill a placebo. "The DREAM Act is an attempt to cure a symptom," he said. "Treating symptoms of the problem might make us feel better because we're doing something for a particular group of folks, but it can allow the underlying problem to metastasize."[10]

South Carolina Republican Jeff Sessions weighed in most expansively, touching on the fears of many Americans, even those who sympathized with the youths in the gallery: "If we pass this amnesty, we will signal to the world that we are not serious about enforcement of our laws or our borders. It will say you can make plans to bring in your brother, your sister, your cousin, your nephew, your friend into the country illegally as a teenager, and there will be no principled reason in the future for the next Congress sitting not to pass another DREAM Act, and it will only be a matter of time before that next group that is here illegally will make the same heartfelt pleas we hear today."[11]

IN A SMALL fifth-floor apartment in Atlanta, Felipe kept one eye on the C-SPAN speeches as he readied his laptop screen to video chat with his peers in cities nationwide. He'd spent the last few weeks in rural North Carolina communities, trying to put pressure on Senator Hagan.

"She kept saying all the support for the bill was coming from the big cities," he said of the campaign. "Since the state is mostly rural, she needed to hear from them." So he and others had persuaded mayors from small towns to send her letters. Hagan had seemed impressed, and Felipe was optimistic.

Ever since the Trail, undocumented teens around the country had looked to Felipe for encouragement. The responsibility both energized and exhausted him. That day, his role, as usual, would be to bolster the troops. "Hello, Memphis! Hello, Austin! Hey, Kansas City!" He called out to the groups on his computer screen.

Felipe and his friends mostly ignored the speeches. He had heard so many speeches on the issue that at this point he could argue both sides if he wanted to. One hour passed. Then another. Glancing up again at the TV in the corner of the small apartment a volunteer had opened up to the group for the day, Felipe suddenly noticed the clerk calling for a vote. Everyone grew quiet.

The senators strode to the front of the floor one by one and cast their voice votes. It was all so casual yet orderly. The act picked up votes from three Republicans: Bob Bennett of Utah, as well as Richard Lugar of Indiana, who had cosigned the letter with Durbin urging Obama to halt the deportation of DREAM Act–eligible students until the vote. "Yea," came the voice of Alaska senator Lisa Murkowski, too.

Veteran Republican senator Orrin Hatch, also of Utah, who had sponsored the first Dream Act bill back in 2001, had skipped the vote for a family event, calling it a "cynical exercise" to rush it through during the lame-duck session of Congress. Democratic senator Joe Manchin of West Virginia was also a no-show, attending a family Christmas party. So, too, were Republicans Jim Bunning of Kentucky and Judd Gregg of New Hampshire.

Maine's two moderate Republicans, whom the young activists had hoped to sway, voted no.

But to their surprise, McCaskill cast a "yea." Privately, her daughter had been lobbying her in favor of the vote, even as she had remained on the fence up to the last minute. In the end, her daughter's arguments won out. "Merry Christmas, honey!" McCaskill told her daughter after the vote.[12]

Hagan went. She could cast the deciding vote if necessary, but it was already clear, with forty votes against the bill, that her vote would not be enough to swing the outcome. They would still be four short of reaching the sixty needed, yet Felipe held his breath. He could take heart at least that they had helped change her mind.

"Nay," she said.

"The motion is rejected," the Senate clerk announced. "Under the previous order, there will now be two minutes of debate."

The shouts from the gallery were inaudible on TV but loud enough in the hall that the presiding senator that morning, Delaware Democrat Chris Coons, twice banged his gavel. "The Senate will be in order!" he shouted.

It was all so swift. Hareth had closed her eyes as Karen held her hand in a vise grip. She wasn't sure she could listen. Her heart pounded, making it hard to concentrate on the voices below. Now someone was pulling on her sleeve. Time to go.

Wait. What?

It was over. She'd missed it: 55 to 41. Five votes. They'd lost by five votes. The senators were already moving on to the next item of business. Every dream she'd conjured up over the last year as she had lobbied on the Hill, every dream she could remember, dissolved. Hareth willed herself not to cry. Later friends would accuse her of being cold, but her mother had taught her early on not to waste time with tears.

Quickly the Senate repealed "Don't ask, don't tell" by a margin of sixteen votes. Now the senators were debating a strategic arms treaty and preparing to confirm federal judges.

As the young immigrants filed out of the gallery, still in shock, they passed a group of jubilant LGBTQ activists. Hareth stared at them. They'd won, and the DREAMers hadn't? How could that be?

"It took us seventeen years," one man called. The young activists winced. They couldn't wait seventeen years.

Outside, the chanting started up again: "Undocumented and unafraid!"

The media began filming. All those clips Hareth had seen of immigrant activists over the years had been from moments like this, she suddenly thought. *And now I am part of this.* Whatever "this" was. There was no turning back.

Gaby Pacheco stood in front of a cluster of microphones, trembling inside. She was furious. The Democratic lawmakers were congratulating themselves and those who had voted in favor of the DREAM Act, already blaming those on the other side of the aisle for the loss.

She didn't want to hear the finger-pointing. This was not a courageous vote, she told the phalanx of reporters. It was not courageous to vote on the side of justice. It was simply the right thing to do.

Gaby found herself being ushered through the Capitol, down a series of hallways, and to the Senate majority leader's office, where a number of the veteran immigration advocates were preparing for an interview with Univision.

Gaby wanted to speak, but looking around the room she felt suddenly stuck. They would use her name and her image to represent DREAMers, to show support for Reid and for the Democrats. She had campaigned for Reid, she had supported him, but a failed vote during a lame-duck session of Congress was not what she had hoped for.

After the interview, Gaby approached Reid and leaned into his ear. "You know this is not enough," she whispered. "You can do more, and you know the president can give us deferred action."

In the White House that afternoon, aides who had fought for a repeal of "Don't ask, don't tell" celebrated, while their colleagues who'd pushed for the DREAM Act fought back tears.[13]

In Costa Rica, Marie mechanically made the necessary phone calls to reporters who had come to rely on her for quick responses. But sitting at the table in her mother's Puntarena home, she felt far away from it all.

Her father's death, the bill's failure. She had already half wanted a break from the activism. Now she knew she desperately needed one.

THE DREAM ACT'S FAILURE was not the end, not by a long shot. But it felt that way to many of the young immigrants Felipe comforted that day in Atlanta and across the country.

"This is a setback. We will win the war," he said, throwing out any military cliché he could think of. He spoke with Jorge Ramos from Univision and helped coordinate a national response for United We Dream. On camera, his smile rarely wavered.

In Los Angeles, a few miles away downtown, Juan sat in a conference room at the nonprofit Coalition for Humane Immigrant Rights of Los Angeles. The room was packed, seats and standing room filled way beyond the official sixty-person capacity, laptops lining the tables. For three days, Juan had arrived at 5 a.m. to work the phone bank, calling lawmakers to encourage them to vote in favor of the bill.

Each student would call and tell a senator's staff the same thing: "I am a Dreamer. My future is at stake, and you have the power to change my life forever."

As soon as he heard the final nay vote, Juan began calling undocumented friends back in Florida. "I just needed to hear their voices. I was begging them not to give up."

He called Felipe, but there was no time to talk between interviews and check-ins.

Juan saw an interview on TV with another undocumented activist, Renata Teodoro of Boston, and he stopped to watch it. The twenty-two-year-old Brazilian native and her sister had grown up in Massachusetts and had been living on their own for two years, ever since their mother and brother had been deported. Asked what she would like to tell other young people like herself, Renata responded, " I want to ask them all to cry, because we have a right to cry. There are so many people who are going to push us to go out the next day and be hopeful . . . but right now I just want to cry."

The words hit home. Juan had so many microphones shoved in his face, and he knew the press wanted something pithy, something about them being strong. But he had nothing to say. Renata was right. There would be time for the next battle. Now was the time to cry.

Not until hours later, as Felipe finally slumped into a seat at the Atlanta airport en route home to Miami, was he able to dial Juan again. Alone at last among strangers, his practiced confidence faded as Juan picked up the phone.

"Why do they hate us so much?" he asked.

8

NEW PATHS

Dario Guerrero waits to talk with a professor while his sister Andrea plays in Cambridge, Massachusetts, May 2013.

D ario Guerrero was finishing his homework in the Cal State Dominguez Hills campus library, where his magnet high school was housed, when his phone buzzed in late December 2010. He'd followed the vote in the Senate but only barely. He'd been focused on school and sports and college applications.

Now he looked down at the caller ID, puzzled. It was a Boston area code. His heart began to race. He answered the call and ran out to the front steps of the library.

An admissions officer from Harvard University broke the good news. Dario had won an undergraduate spot, with enough financial aid to cover academics, room, and board. A letter confirming the admission was on its way. Dario's mouth hung open.

"Thank you. Thank you. Thank you!" he repeated. He couldn't think of anything else to say. He hung up the phone and jumped into the air, pumping his fist as he let out a whoop of joy.

He called his mom that afternoon. She couldn't believe it, but she was happy at first mostly to hear that someone was going to pay for him to go to college. She'd heard of the school, knew that Dario had dreamed of going there, and had even talked with him about applying. She also knew he wanted to drive a fancy car and live in New York someday. She had humored all of his ambitions equally. Only later, after she began telling the other moms she volunteered with at Andrea's school about the news, and saw their expressions, did it slowly sink in what acceptance into Harvard University might mean for her son.

"You did it, *m'hijo*, you did it!" Dario Sr. cried that night. DREAM Act or no, his son was safe for now.

A few weeks later, Dario's father asked him to go for a ride and give him some help with work. Dario groaned, thinking his father wanted assistance unloading materials from his truck or some other task, but he agreed. They arrived in Beverly Hills, where his father sometimes worked, and on a side street they stopped in front of a parked red Ford Mustang convertible. It wasn't new, but it was sleek and shiny and pretty much everything Dario had dreamed of.

"*Félicitaciones!*" his father said, grinning. "You earned it."

Dario wanted to tell his father he was crazy, that he didn't need that car, that he shouldn't have spent money on something like this, even if a friend had done him the favor of refurbishing it. He didn't even have a license because of his immigration status. But all he could do was grin stupidly.

It wasn't a completely foolhardy purchase. Dario Sr. had made the calculations. Yes, it was risky to have his son drive, but they lived in suburban California. Every undocumented immigrant he knew took that risk on a daily basis. His son would likely be driving or in a car with friends driving no matter what, and he trusted his son over his son's friends behind the wheel.

More than that, the fifteen years Dario Sr. had lived in the United States had taught him a few things about how to avoid the police and immigration authorities. Driving a nice car, provided one drove responsibly and without loud music, was one way. Officers were more likely to stop an old car and to assume the driver might not have a license or legal status than a well-cared-for, expensive model.

Buying a car from a dealership, with all its requirements for insurance, not to mention getting a loan, was tough without legal status. One day he'd passed the Mustang with a FOR SALE sign on it. He'd had to get it. They could get basic insurance from Adriana's Insurance Services, whose TV ads assured potential customers coverage *con o sin licencia* (with or without a license).

Dario Sr. smiled to himself. Who would ever imagine that a kid driving a red Mustang was without papers, without a license?

In September 2011, Dario drove with his parents across the country to Boston, in the minivan, not the Mustang. Even before they'd found his dorm on Harvard Yard, part of him yearned for them to leave. He was finally starting life, freed from family but also from that box "illegal immigrant." From here on his identity would be Harvard student. His mother wanted to stay and help him unpack. No, no, he protested, shooing them out, just as students across the freshman quadrangle were doing. He was fine. There was a welcome party to go to, new kids to meet.

As they pulled away, Dario's father noted to Rocio how few Mexican families they'd seen. Maybe there were some *güeros*, wealthy Mexican students, but he wondered if there were any other working-class students, immigrant or not, like his son. And yet this was everything he'd wanted for his eldest child, he reminded himself. He brushed away tears and pulled onto Interstate 95.

IN EARLY 2011, a group of United We Dream leaders met in Arizona with Michele Rudy, a mentor and an organizer with the Center for Community Change. If they couldn't pass the DREAM Act, they would focus on the executive branch, as the Trail of Dreams group had sought. A smaller, more informal group met again in Miami for a more therapeutic retreat.

"I wish someone had sat down with us and said, 'Hey, you're going to be exhausted, you have to find some balance.' I didn't even know what burnout was," Boston activist Renata Teodoro said of those first months following the 2010 vote.

The Miami meeting was in part an attempt to find the balance. So many of the nascent movement's leaders had come into activism through personal desperation. Now they began to ask themselves if this would be their life's work and if they were willing to stick with it over the long haul.

Juan Rodriguez saw Renata at the Miami retreat and approached her. "Your interview after the Senate vote allowed me to shed tears and keep on going," he confessed shyly. "You were the reason I could get through."

The retreat was a safe place, away from the media and the politicians, in which to shed tears and take stock. The weekend renewed activists' convictions, but it couldn't erase their exhaustion and heartbreak. Many activists, including Felipe, went home to rethink their role in the movement. Some of the activists officially announced their split from United We Dream, establishing the more publicly aggressive National Immigrant Youth Alliance.

For Hareth, the 2010 Senate vote had been something of a tease.

Unlike the leaders who had been involved for much of the previous decade, she had just gotten her feet wet. Now what? She was graduating, and, unlike Dario, there was no call from Harvard. Her dream school, the University of Virginia, was out of the question. She wasn't eligible for in-state residence tuition, and she didn't have an international student visa. Tuition and books alone would cost around $45,000 annually. The number might as well have been $5 million. As she tried to figure out her next step, Hareth reached out to her mentor, Emma Violand-Sánchez, then a school board member and longtime supervisor of the Arlington Public Schools' English Language Learners program, whom Hareth had campaigned for after the 2006 marches. Like so many K–12 educators before her, Dr. Emma was frustrated by the idea that the country would invest in more than a decade of education for immigrant kids, then leave them hanging when it came to the final years necessary to earn more than a minimum wage.[1]

Dr. Emma invited Hareth, her parents, and several other families to help start a nonprofit that would seek private scholarships for undocumented students. She connected the students with local mentors, teachers, and lawyers she knew, many of them Bolivian, to get teens like Hareth into and through college.

The parents began meeting, too, sometimes in homes or in community spaces. Soon, the Virginia-based Dream Project became a support network not only for students like Hareth but for their parents as well. Unlike their daughter, Mario and Betty were too terrified to "come out" at work or in public. In these spaces, though, they began to open up and share their stories, just as their children had. Betty and the other mothers organized fund-raisers, bake sales, gala dinners. They didn't raise a lot of money, but it made Betty feel she was doing *something*.

Still Hareth wanted to do more. She waited for signals from the national leaders. Would an email pop up in her in-box telling her where to go? Eventually a friend and local organizer in Maryland, who was working to get in-state tuition for undocumented students there, told her to stop waiting for guidance. This was DIY activism. She didn't need money or a budget. She and her friends needed to keep making their voices heard any way they could, even if on a small and local basis. So they did.

They took photos of themselves carrying a cardboard sign that read "I am a DREAMer," and posted them on Facebook, asking friends to share. On weekends, they stood at a busy Arlington intersection near Hareth's apartment with signs, waving them at drivers waiting for the light.

"What is a DREAMer?" some drivers asked.

"It's me," Hareth replied, answering their questions about what it meant to live without immigration papers until the light turned green.

In the spring of 2011, Hareth was among the Dream Project's first scholarship recipients, receiving $2,000 toward college. She had settled on Northern Virginia Community College. It was near, it was affordable—albeit just barely—and Hareth was cautiously excited. Still, she would need more money to make it through the first year. She thought about taking a job under the table like her parents.

Then she got an invitation that would change her life. Following the Senate DREAM Act vote, the University of California, Los Angeles' Center for Labor Research and Education had been looking for ways to reenergize discouraged undocumented activists and keep them politically engaged. It wanted to keep pressing for the DREAM Act, but it needed a new direction. After talking with students, the center's director, Kent Wong, settled on the idea of a scholarship and fellowship program. The students would receive money to attend the college of their choice and a desperately needed vote of confidence in their future. The Center would offer them a weekend of organizing training, followed by a fellowship at a community or labor group. It seemed like a win-win both for the students and for the labor movement, which would build a new generation of sympathetic young activists. The result: Dream Summer, the first nationwide scholarship program for undocumented youths.

Wong reached out to United We Dream and its affiliates to find candidates. Hareth's name was added to the list. But she was still

seventeen, the youngest candidate, and Wong wavered about including her. "Can we take the risk? She could be deported on her flight
out here. She's a minor," he worried.

The other young activists laughed. *We could* all *be deported*. Hareth
was old enough. She knew the risks.

While her friends went off to beach week during the days before
graduation, Hareth headed for Los Angeles. The June training was her
first trip on an airplane since she'd arrived in the United States more
than a decade before. She was excited but nervous. The labor Center
asked immigration lawyers to remain on standby in the event any of
their students were stopped by immigration authorities midtrip. The
Center set up a hotline to field questions in case of emergencies. Betty
called the emergency number nearly every hour until she received
confirmation her daughter had arrived.

Hareth spent only the weekend in Los Angeles, but the brief training left its mark. There she met Marco Quiroga, who had immigrated
from Peru as a toddler and who shared with Hareth and the others
his fears about coming out to his family as gay. It was his sexual identity, he added, that made him so determined never to return to Peru,
where police used water cannons to break up peaceful LGBTQ demonstrations,[2] and where gay men regularly faced hate crimes that went
unpunished.[3]

Hareth returned to Arlington and split her fellowship between the
Virginia Dream Project and the small nonprofit, Edu-Futuro (Education for the Future), which had sponsored her. Many of the other
Dream Summer participants took their newfound organizing skills to
lobby state lawmakers in Sacramento in favor of two California bills
that could help undocumented students. One would make them eligible for private scholarships at state colleges and universities. The
other would open state-financed scholarships to them. They argued
for both, but with no taxpayer dollars required, the private scholarship
bill was the easier sell. In July, the legislature passed that measure,
thanks in part to the students' strong presence; they had repeated
many of the tactics that had been used in Washington for the DREAM

Act but this time with more success. It was a small victory, more a symbolic one, but one that began to blow wind back into the students' sails. By October, the governor had signed the second bill into law, too.

FELIPE SPENT MUCH OF 2011 working with Presente.org, the group that had publicized the Trail of Dreams. But after more than a year of absorbing the stories of children who had lost parents or were terrified of losing them, he struggled to keep going. Some nights, he found himself just sitting in his car crying as he listened to bad pop songs on the radio.

Yet he knew what they had done mattered. He continued to see the Trail's influence spread. In June 2011, the Pulitzer Prize–winning journalist and former *Washington Post* staffer Jose Antonio Vargas came out about his undocumented status in a piece for the *New York Times Magazine*, detailing the years he'd spent hiding his identity from friends, bosses, and sources.

"On the surface, I've created a good life. I've lived the American dream. But I am still an undocumented immigrant. And that means living a different kind of reality. It means going about my day in fear of being found out. It means rarely trusting people, even those closest to me, with who I really am," he wrote.

The Trail of Dreams had helped change that.

"Last year I read about four students who walked from Miami to Washington to lobby for the Dream Act, a nearly decade-old immigration bill that would provide a path to legal permanent residency for young people who have been educated in this country," wrote Vargas, who was born in the Philippines. "At the risk of deportation— the Obama administration has deported almost 800,000 people in the last two years—they are speaking out. Their courage has inspired me."

Like Felipe, he was no longer willing to live a lie. "I'm done running. I'm exhausted. . . . So I've decided to come forward, own up to what I've done, and tell my story to the best of my recollection."[4]

Moments like that kept Felipe going as he began to chart his next steps. Yet at home he was increasingly restless. Despite their having lived together for more than two years, Juan refused to talk about their future. Felipe couldn't control politics, but his personal life was different. He wanted reassurance that his partner would be there at least tomorrow and preferably many days after that. He hinted at marriage, but Juan shut him down.

"So where is this going to go?" Felipe asked.

"I don't know. Tomorrow I might not even be here," Juan answered. He had to be honest. He wouldn't promise Felipe he'd always be his partner.

Juan's father had been married four times. He'd had kids each time, and each time he'd left them. Yes, Juan was crazy about Felipe, but to promise forever? He didn't believe it was possible.

Felipe tried to make do with the present. He wasn't ready to leave, but he began to wonder what would happen if you had to love someone a little less every day—purely out of self-preservation.

In the fall of 2011, Juan's relatives on his father's side gathered for Thanksgiving. Significant others were included, but not Felipe.

To their surprise, Juan's grandmother on his mother's side invited Juan to visit her in Charleston, South Carolina, over the New Year and explicitly asked for Felipe to come. Juan's mother had remained in Colombia, and he had been raised by his father. He wasn't particularly close to his grandmother. But he and Felipe had never been to Charleston, and they needed the vacation. And, most of all, they were desperate to be in a place where they were both welcome.

Felipe was so nervous, he wrote talking points to ensure he'd make good conversation with Juan's *abuela*. As they approached the city after nine hours in the car, Felipe was exhausted and looking forward to collapsing. But Juan had other ideas. He suggested they get dinner and walk along the historic district's Waterfront Park before heading to his grandmother's home. The late-December night was near freezing. Once again, Felipe had forgotten to pack a winter coat. His stomach was growling. He had to pee.

Why couldn't they just go to the house already? he demanded.

Trust me, Juan begged.

So they sat by the harbor beneath the clear sky and crescent moon. Felipe looked out at the port, the lights of boats dotting the water. Ravenel Bridge glowed in the distance.

"This is where most of the slaves came into this country," Juan said, pointing to a shopping center. "This is where the ships unloaded the slaves . . . and this is where they were sold." He pointed to the old slave mart, now a museum of African American handcrafts.

Felipe shook his head. Anyone else would be admiring the stars, but no, Juan had to make a political statement. They held hands as they walked down the streets, and Juan continued his impromptu tour, stopping before the Daughters of the Confederacy and the other historic remnants of the antebellum South. Normally Juan's seemingly endless passion for justice was a turn-on, but that night, as his teeth chattered, Felipe found his single-mindedness more irritating than inspiring. Maybe they could pop into a nearby restaurant and grab a bite or at least use the bathroom, he suggested. But Juan pressed on.

As they walked, Felipe felt as if the streets cleared before them, families giving them wide berth. He wondered if it was in his mind or whether two young men holding hands on a winter night was really enough to frighten the locals.

Finally, Juan led Felipe to the steps of the Department of Homeland Security's Customs and Border Protection building, a massive neoclassical edifice that looked as if it belonged on Capitol Hill. It had been commissioned as a custom house before the Civil War as part of the union's futile effort to stave off Southern secession. Felipe and Juan sat silently beneath the white, Corinthian columns.

Juan looked over at Felipe and finally seemed to notice how cold he was. He began to talk, the words tripping over themselves. "I really wanted to bring you here," he began, "because this is the hub of a place that wanted to destroy us before we were born: the racism, the homophobia." He kneeled before Felipe on the cold steps of the Department of Homeland Security building. "You've made this universe more bearable. I wanted to reclaim this place for love." He pulled out a small box, a wedding favor from the recent marriage of two friends that had held Moroccan chocolates. Now, nestled inside, were two silver rings.

Felipe's breath billowed out, a wisp in the cold air. He grinned and kissed Juan, holding him tightly, not caring who saw.

Yes, I will marry you. Yes, I will protect you and stay with you.

As they headed back, the night seemed to tiptoe around them. No more fear. At least not tonight. He wondered if it was possible to burst open with happiness. Later Juan confessed to Felipe that it was the approach of their fourth anniversary as a couple that had spurred him to action. It seemed as though all of his father's relationships had fallen apart around the fourth year. Maybe it was a curse. He still wasn't sure he believed in marriage, but he knew he didn't want to lose Felipe. They celebrated the rest of the weekend. Felipe lost his conversation notes, and it didn't matter.

They returned home and began to make wedding plans. One afternoon, Felipe sat down with his five-year-old nephew and showed him a book about two men getting married. His nephew dutifully listened to the story, then turned to his uncle. *Okay, can we play soccer now?*

Sure, we can play soccer now.

They couldn't actually get married in Florida, where same-sex marriage was still illegal. Instead they threw a massive party in Miami and planned a quick courthouse wedding and honeymoon in Boston, where gay marriage was already legal.

Activists from across the country and family from across the hemisphere came to the Miami celebration. Friends donated the cake. Felipe wore a gray suit; Juan dressed in white. They both sported lavender cummerbunds and bow ties and matching nail polish. They held an unofficial ceremony in a local park. Felipe's sister walked him down the pavement toward the white canopy. His mother did not attend.

That evening they danced and ate until Felipe thought he would collapse.

In mid-May, Felipe graduated from St. Thomas University, the first in his immediate family to earn a university degree. His husband cheered from the crowd.

With things more stable at home, Felipe began to look for change on the professional front. His immigration status remained the same, but he felt more grounded now, had more energy to focus outward. It seemed as though no matter what they did, the immigrant advocates would never have enough sway, not alone anyway. They needed a broader base. Felipe turned to his friends in the LGBTQ community. Maybe now it was time to learn from the inside how the nation's other powerful—and far better heeled—civil rights movement worked. Soon he was back on the ground, helping to teach LGBTQ activists, often wealthy and white, about the basic principles of organizing and about the struggles of undocumented immigrants like him.

It's like when someone has a huge infection, and you say, "Let's just treat his arm," Felipe thought. Finally he was treating the entire body.

THAT SAME MONTH, Hareth was finishing her first year at Northern Virginia Community College. She had balanced school with her work for the United We Dream affiliate, the DREAMers of Virginia, helping fight deportation cases. UWD had begun working out of the Washington offices of the National Immigration Law Center, Josh Bernstein's group. But it had soon grown too big for the small space and moved into the offices of the National Immigration Forum.

The administration continued to insist that deportations were not targeting DREAMers. "We would show they were," said Gaby Pacheco, now working as United We Dream's political director. Whether they were targeting young undocumented immigrants or not, students were getting swept up in the raids. They called their first campaign "End Our Pain" in response to the stepped-up detentions in cities and towns nationwide. United We Dream focused on hundreds of cases, mostly DREAM Act–eligible students facing deportation. It wasn't always easy to identify them. Immigration officials certainly weren't publicizing the cases, and many families were too scared to reach out or didn't know how.

For Hareth, it was scary to think these young people's lives were partly in her hands, but it was also a relief to feel she could do something now that the legislation seemed to be going nowhere.

On Saturday, May 12, 2012, the same day Felipe graduated, Hareth lay in bed, enjoying her first taste of summer vacation. The house was quiet, and it felt so good to be lazy for once. She grinned and fell back asleep.

Her cell phone jerked her awake. She stumbled across the room to see a missed call. She listened to the message. It was the Arlington County jail. Her heart began to thump. She googled the number. It was a number used by inmates to call out. The phone buzzed again.

She hit "Answer" and slowly raised the phone to her ear.

"I'm sorry. *Lo siento*," she could hear her father's voice.

What?

"I'm so sorry," he repeated, his voice breaking. He sounded far away. It was so noisy in the background.

Hareth was awake now.

Quietly, Mario explained. He had been arrested for going through a stop sign at 4 a.m. Yes, he had been drinking.

Hareth looked over at Claudia, who was sleeping. Then she remembered that her mother had taken Haziel to cross-country practice. She steadied herself, asked if he had spoken to her mother.

No, not yet. He had called Hareth first.

She took a deep breath and forced herself to focus. She'd been through this drill with others at United We Dream. Now it was her turn.

She needed to get every scrap of information from her father that she could. The line could go dead at any minute, and it was only a matter of time before immigration agents might come to the jail where they were holding him. She asked him to tell her where he was, whether he'd been offered a lawyer. Coolly and calmly, she walked through the protocols she'd learned as if his were some case handed to her at the office, not the man who had tucked her into bed as a child, bandaged her scrapes, picked her up from basketball games, taught her how to draw.

She could feel his shame pour through the phone, and it broke her heart even as she wanted to shake him. But this was not the time for recriminations.

Three years before, Virginia had become the second state in the nation to fully implement an agreement with the federal government to participate in Immigration and Custom Enforcement's Secure Communities program. It was the latest evolution of an ongoing effort to coordinate between local law enforcement and DHS on immigration-related cases. Early on, Arlington County, where Hareth lived, had tried to opt out of the program, as had Massachusetts, New York, and Illinois. But by 2012, DHS had made the program mandatory.

When individuals were arrested, their fingerprints would automatically be run through both the FBI's database and that of DHS. If Mario's fingerprints did not clear, immigration officers would likely issue a detainer—a request that he be held for forty-eight hours (longer in this case, since weekends didn't count) until they could take him to the nearest available detention center, which might be several hours, or days, away. The family might not find out until he had arrived.

Secure Communities was based on a simple idea: that the government should know if someone who might have committed a crime had a legal right to be in the country. In practice, it was more complicated. Immigrant advocates, civic leaders, and many law enforcement agencies had long opposed the notion of local police and sheriff departments serving as an extension of immigration officials. They argued the fear of deportation made people in some of the most vulnerable communities less likely to serve as witnesses, offer tips, or otherwise work with police on crime prevention. Victims of abuse would be warier of turning in their abusers. Drivers stopped for even minor infractions would have an incentive to flee the scene.

The program also meant that many more people charged with minor infractions were now being placed in deportation proceedings, even if they weren't convicted. Of the more than 227,000 people removed[5] as a result of Secure Communities by the year Mario was arrested, roughly a third had felony convictions on their records serious enough to earn them punishment of more than a year in prison. In general, the largest group had only misdemeanor convictions.

As it turned out, it didn't matter if his fingerprints checked out. Under questioning from the officers, he had already confessed everything without having ever spoken to a lawyer, and he'd agreed to be turned over to immigration authorities. Like thousands of other immigrants, Mario had essentially initiated a process of deportation without even realizing it. He told Hareth he had believed the men in uniform who told him signing the confession would help him reunite with his family more quickly.

Her father's call time ran out. Hareth put the phone down.

She took a deep breath and then sank down. The tears began to fall, quietly at first, then harder, all the tears she had not shed when the DREAM Act failed, when her parents argued, when she thought there was no way she'd ever go to college. She clamped her mouth closed. She could not wake her sister.

Then she stood up. Hareth was only twenty years old, and she had just become the unofficial head of her family.

She called her mother, her aunt, and Dr. Emma, who agreed they would have to act fast and gave her the number of a young Bolivian attorney. The lawyer explained the logistics: the first action item would be to put money in an account for Mario to make calls.

They spoke to Mario again and began to get more pieces of the story. He'd taken friends out after a long day at work. He'd drunk too much. The bill had been too big, so he'd left his phone at the restaurant until he could return with the cash, and the only numbers he could remember belonged to Hareth and her mother. He had chosen Hareth.

Hareth imagined her mother waiting up for his return, worried sick when he did not come but having to pretend otherwise.

Mario had been only a block or so from their home when he was pulled over. He'd refused a Breathalyzer test, but even if he had tested below .08 percent blood alcohol, in Virginia officers could still have arrested him on suspicion of driving under the influence.

He'd been giving his friend Leonel, also undocumented and from Guatemala, a ride home. The officers had offered to let Leonel go, but Leonel had refused to leave Mario, even as he knew his loyalty would mean that his name would also be run through the federal system, likely guaranteeing his deportation.

Over the weekend, Hareth, Eliana, and Betty scrambled to pull together enough money to post Mario's bond of roughly $5,000, hoping that he wouldn't immediately be flagged by DHS and that they could get him out of jail before he was moved to a distant detention center.

Meanwhile, Mario quickly learned how things worked at the Arlington County jail. Some inmates had been there several years. Some worked in the kitchen for 50 cents an hour, using the roughly $30 they earned each week to buy chips and other specialties. The job was considered a privilege.

All those years driving through downtown, and he'd always passed right by the jail. *And I never paid attention to this place filled with so much suffering,* he thought.

On Monday morning, Mario looked out his cell's tiny window. Only blocks away was Francis Scott Key Elementary School, where Claudia was in fourth grade. He wondered what she knew and what she must think of him.

Claudia did not know, not yet. Betty had told her that their father had a lot of work. No one told Haziel, now a freshman in high school, but the adults all seemed to assume she had figured it out. It wasn't until days later, when Tía Eli came for dinner that Claudia finally learned her father's whereabouts. Furious at her brother and angry that the family was still trying to cover for him, Eli blurted it out: "He's in jail! He's not coming home!"

Behind her anger, Eliana Andrade was heartbroken. A deeply religious evangelical, she had spent years volunteering with new immigrants, warning them against the perils of drink, and encouraging families to take a stance of tough love and to follow the law. Now it was her brother, and she was torn. He had taken such a terrible risk, and he ought to face the consequences. Yet she couldn't bear to see the girls separated from him.

"I had seen so many cases like my brother's, and then it happened [to us], and I didn't have another choice but to help him," she said. "I didn't want him separated from the family."

The family finally spoke to the lawyer again on Monday. To figure out where her father would likely be sent, Hareth needed to get the number assigned to his case and his alien registration number from Immigration and Customs Enforcement. She would have to go there herself. Hareth's boyfriend at the time drove her to the nearest office. She had no license and was terrified to enter, but maybe, just maybe, she thought, she might catch a glimpse of her father before they moved him from the jail to whatever detention facility they planned to take him to. She never saw him. By Tuesday morning, the family had cobbled together the money and the necessary paperwork to pay the bond. But by then, Mario was gone.

ICE agents had banged on his cell door at 4 a.m. Tuesday morning. They'd shackled his arms and feet and loaded him and more than a dozen other prisoners onto a bus. Mario had no idea where they were taking him. He imagined himself being dumped over the border into Mexico.

Four hours later, they arrived at Immigration Centers of America Farmville Detention Center, a low-slung complex encircled by barbed wire about seventy miles west of Richmond. Throughout the 2000s, immigrant detention centers, which resembled low-security jails despite their name, could not be built fast enough, nor their beds filled quickly enough. Lawmakers wanted an end to the government's catch-and-release policies, whereby detained immigrants were often set free because there was no place to hold them. By 2009, Congress had approved money for a minimum of 33,400 detention beds, nearly double that of the previous decade—a number that generally became a stand-in for the minimum number of people Congress expected Immigration and Customs Enforcement to keep locked up each night.[6]

The Farmville facility was set in the woods, with only a water treatment plant for a neighbor, and was the largest in the Mid-Atlantic region, part of the Obama administration's effort to create a "civil detention" system, with more freedom of movement for immigrants whom the government wanted to hold but who were not necessarily charged with a crime.

The new facility "is mostly here to address the impact of Secure Communities," Robert Helwig, assistant director of Immigration and Customs Enforcement, told the *Washington Post* in 2010. "We do anticipate a surge in detainees."[7]

Back in the late 1950s, Farmville had briefly gained attention for voting to close its public schools rather than integrate. Now the recently opened detention center operated by the private Immigration Centers of America company was among the main sources of employment for the shrinking community. Opened in 2010, the center had created some 250 jobs and provided the town's budget with an extra dollar a day per detainee held. By 2015, between the per inmate fees and other taxes, the flow of private detention center funds to Farmville would reach nearly $300,000 annually.[8]

The Richmond-based Immigration Centers of America took in revenue not only from the detention center but also from the private transportation company that ferried detainees such as Mario from immigrant-heavy neighborhoods of eastern Virginia to the southwestern region of the state.

At Farmville, guards woke Mario around 5 a.m. for breakfast, and by 9 a.m., his stomach was once more growling. Some detainees complained about boll weevils in the food.[9] Detainees could buy extra food, but Mario recalled a small soup costing nearly $5. Telephone calls could be up to $16 a minute, and sometimes the password on the calling cards didn't work.

Food wasn't the only problem at Farmville. A year after it opened, a Salvadoran inmate had died of liver failure five days after arriving at the facility. The facility's nurse later told inspectors she had urged guards to provide him with more serious care and had been blocked from taking his vital signs.[10]

A 2011 planned inspection found the center not to be in compliance with more than a dozen federal guidelines,[11] including staff responsiveness to emergencies. In a follow-up review conducted just months before Mario arrived, federal officials described the facility as generally being well managed. Yet that review also noted the detention center still failed to meet certain standards, including things like requiring reasonable suspicion before strip-searching detainees and ensuring the person in charge of training staff had actually taken the required forty-hour training course.[12]

Mario was surprised to learn that many of the people in Farmville had green cards. They had been convicted of a crime, had served their time, and were now being deported. Some had lived in the country more than thirteen years but told him they had been pressured to agree to deportation rather than fight their case. If they did decide to fight, they had to do so mostly through video calls with the deportation officers managing their cases. Judges spoke to the detainees remotely from hundreds, if not thousands, of miles away.

ICE eventually deemed that process "ineffective," in part because the video calls were made only once a week, on Mondays. That meant that for someone like Mario, who arrived on Tuesday, a week would go by before he was able to talk to his case management officer.

As Mario waited for word from his family, he tried to remain upbeat. But it was the doors, the sound of the heavy metal slamming shut and screeching open early in the morning, signaling the departure of yet another group, that terrified him. The noise kept him from sleeping. The doors reminded him of how little power he had and of how much he had utterly and completely screwed up.

Hareth was afraid to visit her father. Not only was Farmville far away, but she worried she, too, might be detained. Only her Tía Eli, already a citizen, could go, and she was the most furious at her brother. But at least she was family, and while she was there, she visited Leonel as well.

On June 3, Hareth turned nineteen. It was the first time since her parents had arrived in the United States nearly a decade before that she hadn't celebrated her birthday with her father.

When the family finally did see him in court, it was via a video monitor. He had been taken to a room at Farmville to participate remotely. Many detainees missed their hearings, unaware they could participate via video, but the family had made sure Mario would be notified. He was wearing shackles on his wrists, a chain connecting them to his feet as if, it seemed to Hareth, he were a murderer or slave to be sold at auction. She tried not to think about how pale and thin he looked.

Hareth knew what people would think of her father, her family. Those who wanted the chance to stay should live an exemplary life, should be above and beyond all reproach. Millions of people would give an arm or a leg to call this country their home.

Only two years before, in nearby Prince William County, another Bolivian man, who had twice been convicted of DUI and was facing deportation and driving drunk, had slammed into a car carrying three Benedictine nuns, killing one and critically injuring the others. The case had made national headlines.[13] What if her father had hit someone? What if he'd hit a child? Hareth shuddered at the thought. Yet in Virginia, a first-time DUI offense received a $250 fine and a year's license suspension. Prosecutors might tack on a minimum of five days in jail if the driver's blood alcohol level was more than .15 percent.

Hareth took stock. It seemed so unfair. They could stay in the country, and her father could help build people's homes and rewire the electrical circuits in their offices. Her mother could raise their children and take care of their grandmothers, and most people would look the other way. But an error that would cost anyone else a couple hundred dollars and the loss of their license would likely mean permanent banishment for her father.

Now, not only could she lose her father, but everything the family had worked for. Her mind began to race. Combined, her parents reported some $50,000 a year in income, with Mario bringing in the majority of the money. Without him, the family would likely lose their apartment. Maybe they could move in with their aunt, though that didn't seem likely to work well. But the younger girls might even end up in the foster care system if Tía Eli didn't take them. Hareth would probably have to drop out of school and work to support her sisters. Without Mario, it was less likely Haziel and Claudia would even make it through high school, let alone college.

Mario's attorney, Vanessa Rodriguez, had come to the United States from Bolivia at age three and had coincidentally been a mentor to Hareth in high school through a Bolivian American youth enrichment program. Only three years out of law school, she didn't look much older than Hareth, and maybe partly because of that, Hareth immediately trusted her. But she also came highly recommended by Dr. Emma. Vanessa shared her small office with her mother's real estate company. She often met with clients on Saturdays, when they were free, padding around in soft bedroom slippers as she reviewed cases.

She was straight with Hareth. They didn't have much of a case. The only chance she saw was prosecutorial discretion, and even then, it was a slim chance. After all, Mario had two strikes against him: he'd come into the country on a visa using his brother's information, and he was facing DUI charges. There were two options, Vanessa advised: either Mario could voluntarily deport himself with the hopes that he might be able to return after a decade, or they could fight the case and spend months of stress and money, likely for the same outcome.

Ten years is not that long, she told Hareth and her mother.

Hareth thought again of the protocol she used with other families. If they kept silent, deportation was all but certain. Going public was a risk, but it might be their only chance. They could quickly get a petition going on Facebook. But Betty refused. What would her friends and family say? She had tried so hard to live an exemplary life in the United States. She had few material things, but she had her pride. Going public with the truth would be an utter humiliation. And it might even put them in more danger. Mixed in with all those concerns was the fury she still felt toward her husband.

"If we fight, we may not win because we are fighting something much bigger," she said to her daughter. The humiliation would be for nothing. "People don't understand about family separation."

But going public might be the only chance of saving her father, Hareth argued back. Maybe they could get a hundred people to sign the petition. It could help. They would need any support they could get to convince immigration officials of three things: that Mario was a valued and upstanding member of the community; that deporting him would significantly affect his family, especially his US-born daughter; and last but not least, that it would be a public relations headache for DHS.

That night, Hareth wrote up a post about her father and sent it to a friend to review. Without telling Hareth, her friend posted it online, and overnight they got 200 signatures. Within days the number reached 1,000. Betty couldn't believe it.

Still the family debated what to do.

Betty was so angry at Mario that she was ready to face separation from him, but ten years was a long time. Hareth realized that if her father left now, he might never come back. She couldn't imagine her family without him. She wanted her sisters to have him in their lives the way she had. Haziel, now in high school, had already missed the early years, and Hareth remembered better than anyone what the nearly four-year separation had meant for them.

True, Haziel and Claudia were both willing to go back if they had to so the family could stay together. But when she thought about it, Hareth knew she was not. She had dreamed of visiting Bolivia, occasionally entertained grandiose fantasies about returning to run for office there. Yet now, as the possibility loomed, she knew—in a way she never had before—that Virginia was her home. She was not prepared to return to a country she hadn't seen since she was eight. She did not want to go back. She did not want to have to choose.

We must fight, she told her mother. Grudgingly at first, Betty agreed.

Hareth's mother had already lost one job when her employers found out she was undocumented. They had helped her find another position, but she worried that publicity would once again render her unemployable. With Mario in detention, she picked up extra hours with the elderly woman she'd long cared for in Georgetown, in addition to her regular nanny shift.

Hareth didn't lie about what had happened, but she didn't shout across virtual media that her father had been arrested for DUI. It had been a traffic stop, she said, unless she had to explain further. The days became a blur of work, shuffling her sisters between home and sports practice, helping her mom pay bills, gathering letters of support from anyone her father knew. At night she couldn't sleep, imagining her father hours away in detention and worrying that immigration officials might come to their home in search of the rest of the family.

A few weeks after her birthday and a month after Mario's arrest, Hareth got good news: her father's case had finally been processed, and he would be released on bond. He would still likely face deportation, but in the meantime he would be home. The moment he walked into the house, his daughters covered him with kisses. He steadied himself and grinned, cracking jokes so as not to weep.

A simple Facebook post was Hareth's only public declaration that day. "Welcome home Dad," she wrote.

MOUNTING PRESSURE

Alex Aldana prepares to meet with his immigration attorney, Berkeley, California, September 2015.

One late night in the fall of his freshman year, Dario hung in the Harvard dorms with a few friends. It was the hour well past any studying when people lingered in rooms, still savoring a schedule that for the first and possibly only time in their lives didn't begin at dawn. They talked home, sports, and weird indie films, the more obscure, the better. One of his dorm mates, the son of a New York banking executive, offered to take them all to a rave in the Netherlands on his father's private plane. Sure, they all laughed, let's do it.

Dario looked over at his roommate, Alex, who was from South Carolina and, like Dario, found the whole New York scene both awe-inspiring and ridiculous. Alex raised an eyebrow. Was this kid serious?

A couple of guys leaned forward, calculating the cost, joking about where they'd stashed their passports. Dario nodded along. Even on a free plane with room and board taken care of, there was no way he'd be able to go. He had no passport. He couldn't leave the country, not if he wanted to ever get back in.

Raves are lame, he scoffed.

Being at Harvard was like that. One minute he was comparing math homework with a friend; the next, someone was talking about hopping over to Europe on his parents' plane. It was insane. Dario loved and hated it. For the first time he was not the smartest, nor nearly the smartest, student in school. Sitting alongside hundreds of other students in the cavernous freshman lecture halls, he could pass. But it didn't come easily. He struggled through classes such as medieval literature and philosophy. He chalked his difficulties up to personal inadequacy, not realizing that many of his classmates, even some from the most exclusive private prep schools, were experiencing similar doubts. He wondered if he belonged. He vowed to fake it if he didn't.

Not long after he arrived, he met a girl. That never took all that long. He hadn't been really single since his sophomore year of high school. She was cool and had gotten him to go to some Latino student events. They even talked, mostly in jest, about getting married so he could adjust his status.

"Dude, why are you getting married?!" Alex yelled when he overheard the plan. "You're eighteen!"

That night Dario told Alex about his immigration status. At first Alex didn't believe him. "I had no idea people who were undocumented could go to college and to Harvard," he later said.

Alex was no stranger to the immigrant story. His father was from Syria, a doctor who had gotten a green card through a visa program for physicians willing to work in underserved communities. His dad had eventually met his mother, a US native, and the two had settled in Greenville, South Carolina. Alex's father spoke sympathetically about the plight of the undocumented mostly farmworkers who increasingly flocked to South Carolina looking for work. His mother, not so much.

Why don't they just do it the right way? he remembered her complaining. *And they don't even pay taxes.*

Dario told Alex that since his father wasn't a doctor, nor did he have a million dollars to invest in a company, there wasn't really a "right way to come." The line for most Mexicans was literally a lifetime long. His parents did pay taxes. Only, unlike Americans, they were unlikely to get back any of the money they put into the system when they retired.

Dario and his girlfriend didn't get married. Instead they broke up. Dario and Alex started hanging around together more. Dario confided in Alex about the film he had started his senior year of high school with other undocumented friends. Alex was fascinated. *You should keep working on it,* he said, and he offered to help. Together they could make a real doc. *Maybe,* said Dario. He'd wanted to come to Harvard precisely so he wouldn't have to think about what his immigration status meant anymore. He joined the Boxing Club. He partied alongside all the other first years.

But still he thought about it—he had to. Not just around crazy stunts like the rave. Many of his friends held odd jobs on or off campus to pay their way or even just for spending money. Dario couldn't get a job, not on the books anyway, although he heard rumors that some undocumented students were able to get jobs cleaning the dorms.

By the fall of his sophomore year in 2012, he applied for a more creative position: sperm donor. There were ads for Harvard students all the time in the campus paper. Who wouldn't want an Ivy League donor? It seemed like a fun way to make a quick buck, and besides, it would make for a good story.

Dario passed the health exams, the drug test, and the interview. He gave a few samples, but ultimately, the clinic rejected his services with no explanation except for a brief sympathetic note from the case manager he'd spoken with. Apparently, even Boston parents desperate enough to pay for a baby weren't inclined to select the offspring of a dark-skinned, six-foot-tall Mexican, he thought bitterly.

Dario knew his dad wanted him to continue his engineering studies, the courses he'd so excelled at in high school, or do law. But increasingly he was drawn back to the camera: the same tool he had turned to so he could document his college application process, the same one his father had so often carried on their family outings to document their lives. With the camera, he could watch the world and have a reason to watch—with a camera he felt safe.

Alex and Dario began to stay up late, drinking beer and mapping out ideas for a film about undocumented students at Harvard. Dario found nearly a dozen, including in the graduate programs, at least as far as he could make out through informal inquiries. It was word of mouth, a friend of a friend who didn't have a driver's license. But few wanted to have their faces on camera. They were scared of the politics and what it would mean for them and for Harvard were they to go public.

Their fears weren't unfounded.

By the fall of 2011, the Obama administration had been on track to deport nearly 400,000 people annually, a record.[1] About half of those sent home had criminal convictions, most commonly immigration violations, drug-related charges, or traffic violations. The number of deported immigrants with criminal convictions would grow to nearly two-thirds of all those deported by 2013, enabling the Obama administration to boast that its priority was now targeting the bad guys. But of those deported criminals, the most serious conviction was generally the misdemeanor of "illegal entry"—the act of living in the United States following a previous deportation.[2] United We Dream had documented dozens of cases of DREAM Act–eligible students who had been detained and put in deportation hearings since 2008. In 2011, young students continued to be among those rounded up. Felipe and other young immigrant leaders struggled to reconcile the president they had campaigned for with Obama's stepped-up deportations, especially since the stricter enforcement hadn't brought Congress any closer to taking action.

The action shifted back to the states. Lawmakers in more than half of the country's fifty states had proposed Arizona-style immigration laws in 2011. Most of the bills went nowhere, but Georgia, South Carolina, Indiana, Utah, and Alabama successfully passed bills on a par with Arizona's, giving law enforcement officials the right to stop and request papers from virtually anyone they suspected of being in the country illegally.

The ACLU, the DOJ, and others immediately sued to block much of that legislation[3] and succeeded in part, mitigating some of the harshest measures. In fact, that year, more pro-immigrant measures than punitive ones passed nationwide.[4] This time around, the business communities took a more aggressive stance against enforcement-only state bills. The immigrant groups were also better organized. Latino groups took out ads against legislation in the swing states of Colorado, Pennsylvania, and Florida. In Utah, even as lawmakers approved tough enforcement measures, they sought to create a local work permit for undocumented immigrants and to discourage local law enforcement agencies from targeting them.[5]

Now, too, the young activists and their allies were loud and unapologetic. In many ways, the failure of the DREAM Act had freed them from the image Congress seemed to demand of them. Presenting the story of the perfect, well-mannered student hadn't worked. Now they could just be human. They took the social media and organizational skills they'd honed during the push for the DREAM Act back to the local fights.

In Florida, students, farmworkers, and other allies spent weeks in Tallahassee holding pray-ins, lobbying lawmakers, and protesting legislation that sought to criminalize those who were in the country without legal status. In Kansas, opponents spread audio clips of state representative Virgil Peck Jr. comparing undocumented immigrants to wild animals.

"Looks like to me, if shooting these immigrating feral hogs works, maybe we have found a [solution] to our illegal immigration problem," he joked during a committee hearing.[6] The public outcry and backlash were loud and swift.

Students were arrested in Atlanta and Indianapolis in protests over measures that aimed to make it harder for undocumented students to attend state colleges. By the end of 2011, some thirteen states offered in-state tuition for students who were in the country without legal immigration status.

Earlier that year, John Morton, now the Immigration and Customs Enforcement director, had issued another memo. This one was more specific. It further laid out the categories for which his agents should use their discretion when it came to deporting an immigrant and was part of the department's effort to focus on those deemed high-priority "aliens."

"ICE is charged with enforcing the nation's civil immigration laws," Morton wrote. "ICE, however, only has resources to remove approximately 400,000 aliens per year, less than 4 percent of the estimated illegal alien population in the United States. In light of the large number of administrative violations the agency is charged with addressing and the limited enforcement resources the agency has available, ICE must prioritize the use of its enforcement personnel, detention space, and removal resources."[7]

In June, he had followed up with still another memo,[8] which explicitly urged care and consideration before detaining young immigrants who had grown up in the United States.

The memo encouraged the officers to take into account the length of time the person had lived in the United States, whether he or she was a child or a teen, his or her level of education or military participation—in other words, many of the same factors listed in the DREAM Act.

The last memo also made clear it was offering no guarantees. "Nothing in this memorandum should be construed to prohibit the apprehension, detention, or removal of any alien unlawfully in the United States,"[9] Morton wrote. But the memorandum showed movement.

About a month after the last Morton memo, the president was scheduled to speak at the National Council of La Raza in Washington, DC. Getting the president was a coup. Leaders from United We Dream had asked NCLR to help broker a meeting with the president, but when it became clear that wouldn't be happening, the young undocumented immigrants took another tactic.

During the luncheon, the president addressed the ballroom filled with a who's who of Hispanic America, reiterating his stance that he could not take unilateral action on immigration. "And I promise you, we are responding to your concerns and working every day to make sure we are enforcing flawed laws in the most humane and best possible way," he told the group, adding, "Now I know some people want me to bypass Congress and change the laws on my own."[10]

Suddenly, a small group of young undocumented activists, let by Felipe Matos, who represented United We Dream's southeast affiliates, stood up, unveiling T-shirts with the slogan "Yes you can!" They began chanting the same words, and to their surprise, for half a minute, many of those seated in the ballroom in their finest evening wear joined in the chanting. It was as if they had finally freed the establishment to let go and to say publicly what so many had been thinking and saying in private.

Obama grimaced but didn't waiver. Soon he had the room back on his side. "The idea of doing things on my own is very tempting. . . . But that's not how our system works, that's not how our democracy functions. That's not how our Constitution is written," he insisted. "I need a dance partner here, and the floor is empty," he said, referring to Congress. "Feel free to keep the heat on me, and keep the heat on Democrats," he continued, but he insisted that whatever he proposed, Republicans would block.

"I need you to keep building a movement for change outside of Washington, one they can't stop, one that's greater than this community. We need a movement that bridges party lines," he added. "And I will be there every step of the way."[11]

Many took him at his word.

Some older groups, such as the National Immigration Forum, had already started campaigns like "Bibles, Badges and Business," reaching out to more conservative religious, law enforcement, and business groups and trying to find common ground, hoping eventually the cultural shift would lead to policy change. Gaby Pacheco would eventually lead a small group of half a dozen young immigrants who opted to canvass Republican lawmakers they thought might be open to learning more about the DREAM Act and even comprehensive reform, in part to pressure Democrats—Obama in particular—to act. Yet there were many other young immigrants who were disillusioned with the Washington lobbying and the painstaking ally building that never seemed to go anywhere, who took up increasingly outside-the-beltway tactics, staking out the homes of lawmakers for protests and ambushing them at campaign events.

The young activists pushed one another to try new tactics. Later, as the 2012 election heated up, they would make national headlines confronting politicians, including GOP presidential candidate Mitt Romney. At a fund-raiser in New York City, a young Peruvian native and United We Dream organizer, Lucia Allain, asked Romney about his dislike of the DREAM Act on camera. It went viral.[12] The young activists could get away with the confrontations precisely because, unlike their parents, they looked young, had no accents, and could often blend into a crowd of political supporters.

In August 2011, DHS Secretary Janet Napolitano had announced the department would review the cases of every immigrant in deportation proceedings individually. It was an extensive task, and while it did help a few dozen young DREAM Act–eligible immigrants whose cases were already in the system obtain deferred action, it didn't do much to allay the fears of thousands of others who at any minute might be picked up and deported.

As the presidential election approached, the activists ratcheted up their efforts. In late January 2012, a few days before the GOP presidential primary, Florida senator Marco Rubio addressed the Republican-backed Hispanic Leadership Network in Miami in his first major speech on immigration, arguing a national consensus existed in favor of helping out young DREAMers. "There is broad bipartisan support for the notion that we should figure out a way to accommodate them," he said of the thousands of young immigrants who had come to the United States as children and were now living in the country illegally.[13]

He urged his fellow Republicans to take action, but not before DREAMers planted in the audience stood up and demanded to know why, despite his rhetoric, he hadn't done more to support the latest version of the DREAM Act in the Senate or taken other steps to help them since moving to Washington. By now Felipe was too well known to gain access. Aides had stopped him at the door, so he helped younger Florida immigrants slip inside.

Outside the conference, Presente.org, the group that had done outreach for the Trail of Dreams, flew a propeller plane over the Doral Golf Resort & Spa (which would be purchased by Donald Trump a month later), where the conference was taking place, protesting Rubio's speech.

Inside, security guards quickly stepped in to escort the protesters out, even as Rubio urged them to let them stay. "They had the bravery and courage to raise their voices," he insisted. He then addressed the students' complaints. Yes, the status quo was unsustainable, Rubio agreed, and consensus to address the problem existed.

"It's not realistic to expect that you're going to deport 11 million people," he continued, but nor could the country legalize 11 million people.

The senator laid blame on conservatives and progressive politicians alike: "We must admit that there are those among us who have used rhetoric that is harsh and intolerable and inexcusable. And we must admit—myself included—that sometimes we've been too slow in condemning that language for what it is." Meanwhile, he added, politicians on the left were guilty of setting unrealistic expectations to win Hispanic votes.[14]

It was a position he would increasingly take, a political jiu-jitsu twist, establishing himself as both compassionate toward immigrants yet wary of comprehensive reform. But without action, it satisfied no one. Two months after the protest, Rubio announced he was working to craft a new version of the DREAM Act, seeking input from advocates such as Cheryl Little and Gaby Pacheco. The bill wasn't likely to go anywhere, and it didn't offer a path to citizenship, but it was enough to make Democrats nervous and the president take notice. Representatives Luis Gutiérrez and Mario Díaz-Balart, who now represented his older brother's former Miami district, kept up the pressure by working together on a House version.

Soon after, United We Dream shifted its strategy from asking the president to "End Our Pain" to a more proactive demand: "Right to DREAM." The new campaign called not only for an end to the deportations, as the "End our Pain" effort had done, but also for temporary legal recognition for the youths so they could go to school and work—a stopgap executive order until Congress took action.

Behind the scenes, the National Immigration Law Center helped put together a legal justification for Obama to take unilateral action. The premise was similar to the idea the Trail of Dreams had pushed for back in 2010. Together with United We Dream and its Los Angeles affiliate, lawyers and advocates worked with UCLA law professor Hiroshi Motomura to draft a framework that would give the president legal cover for going it alone on immigration.

Beyond the legal arguments and the human stories, the immigrant advocates sought out another pressure point, demographics, seven months ahead of the presidential election, and Latino political support for the president was waning.[15] Hispanics had sat out the 2010 election in greater numbers than white or black voters, and the result had been disastrous for the Democrats, who had lost more than fifty House seats as Tea Party candidates swept into Congress. Relentless criticism of Obama by the Spanish-language media for his failure to follow through on immigration reform didn't help.

Most Latinos put education and the economy above immigration on their list of priorities, but comments such as "feral hogs" awoke a deeper response, even in Latino families that didn't have to deal with the immigration system. Obama needed to tap into that response. And he could use the energy of the undocumented youths who, convinced that he would help them, had campaigned their hearts out for him in 2008.

United We Dream threatened the White House it would wait until mid-June of 2012 for action, and then it would, as other undocumented-activist organizations were already doing, take its civil disobedience to a new level with nonstop actions against the administration in Washington and pressure back home in key election states. Internal White House discussions of what was possible within the realm of presidential power began to shift. Since Obama had taken office, constitutional scholars had quietly floated theories that the president had broad authority on immigration. As the call to action built on all sides, top players in the administration began to review their arguments seriously even as publicly the administration continued to maintain that it could not act without the approval of Congress.

OUTSIDE WASHINGTON, young immigrant activists were looking for other ways to keep up the pressure on the Obama administration. For undocumented immigrants with no direct access to politically connected allies, the informal online email groups and burgeoning websites such as DreamActivist.org were a lifeline. Alejandro Aldana, the HIV educator from Mexico, found his way to activism through such email chains and Internet chat rooms.

At first DreamActivist.org was just an informal online resource, allowing anonymous participation and the exchange of tips and ideas among undocumented youth. But it was quickly becoming a coordinating hub for those who wanted to become more actively involved.

Through one posting, Alex found out about a group of activists who were organizing a protest against what they saw as harassment of immigrant college students in San Bernardino County. Alex was among a dozen youths who blocked streets in January 2012 after San Bernardino officers stopped an undocumented student biking on the nearby community college campus at night without headlights, and turned him over to immigration officers. Alex was arrested. It was the second big arrest of young undocumented protesters in less than a year. Both times, the federal government declined to deport the undocumented activists who'd been arrested. Alex took note, and through his work with HIV education he came into contact with even more activists and organizers. A few months later, when a group of students asked him to join a sort of Trail of Dreams 2.0, from San Francisco to Washington, he readily agreed.

From the outset, the Campaign for an American DREAM walk[16] highlighted just how far the youth immigrant movement—and the nation as a whole—had come since the Trail of Dreams, but also how much more the young activists needed to do to win over the rest of the country. For starters, the group quickly realized that they would need to complete a much longer walk this time. Alex and the others planned to walk some three thousand miles, double the distance Felipe and his friends had traversed, arriving in Washington in time for the inauguration. It was more than half a year's commitment. Though few Florida politicians had recognized the Trail early on, Alex and the other half-dozen California walkers received official government support, albeit symbolic, from the get-go. Just a week after they started, the group stopped in Sacramento, spoke before lawmakers on behalf of other undocumented immigrants, and got a standing ovation from the Democratic-led California legislature. The Campaign for an American DREAM walk was also far more spontaneous than the Trail. The sheer distance made extensive planning a daunting task. But the young activists involved were less risk averse. And the Trail's success had already demonstrated that such a walk—even in states seen as less than welcoming to immigrants—was possible.

The California group included more Mexicans than the Trail had, more closely reflecting the nation's Latino and undocumented communities. Nor were they necessarily star students. Alex wasn't a student at all. That was no longer the point. These DREAMers were no longer just the limited group that could qualify for the DREAM Act; they were the undocumented youth of America. They had grown up in this country. They could contribute. They wanted to be heard.

This group was slightly bigger, with members more in flux. Among them was Alex's boyfriend, Nico Gonzalez, a Mexican native from Chicago. Unlike Felipe and Juan, Alex and Nico didn't even try to hide their relationship. None of the so-called UndocuQueer California walkers felt the need to hide their sexual identity.

It wasn't just that they'd embarked on their journey in San Francisco. In the two years since Felipe and Juan had walked across the southern United States and the DREAM Act had failed, not only had Congress repealed "Don't ask, don't tell," but now at least six states had okayed same-sex marriage, with Maine and Maryland about to become the first states in the nation to do so through a direct referendum.* Wisconsin was poised to elect its first openly lesbian senator, and Obama appeared willing to support same-sex marriage at the federal level for the first time.

The display of support across movements—the intersectionality—went beyond the LGBTQ and immigrant communities. In a show of the youth immigrant movement's increasing solidarity with other social justice movements, Alex dedicated much of his April blog to Florida teen Trayvon Martin, the unarmed black teenager who had been fatally shot walking home by a trigger-happy Latino neighbor. "Today I speak truth to those that enforce the law and have the power

---

* Massachusetts, Connecticut, Iowa, Vermont, New Hampshire, New York, and the District of Columbia had previously approved same-sex marriage through the courts, through legislation, or by executive order.

on the streets: our police departments, our department of justice. We will take it to the streets to demand social justice for our brothers and sisters,"[17] Alex wrote. "Today I take a step in unity to bring justice for you, my friend Trayvon. Although we never met, you live in my heart whether immigrant, queer, Muslim or black, our oppressed communities beat as one."

The California group knew earning sustained publicity over such a long trek would be a challenge. By now the National Immigrant Youth Alliance and United We Dream had begun to standardize their advocacy work on behalf of detainees and those facing deportation. Bit by bit they had figured out what worked. It was different each time, but immediate action was what counted: creating a network, building a webpage, seeking donations, and flooding lawmakers' and DHS lines with requests for deferred action were all important. The more noise they generated, the quicker Immigration and Customs Enforcement tended to respond. The trick was to get the ball rolling before the person was physically removed from the country. Once he or she was gone, the game was pretty much over.

Alex and the other activists took their deportation defense work on the road. In each town or city, they highlighted specific cases, collaborating with local nonprofit groups to garner attention for immigrants facing deportation. Yet even as they worked closely with local activists on deportation cases, the group in many ways remained more independent, more self-contained than Felipe, Juan, and the others had been on the Trail of Dreams. They lacked the network support people such as Maria Rodriguez had brought to the Trail. The group relied less on nonprofits for shelter than on their small RV nicknamed "Big Momma."

America's Voice provided some financial support and reposted many of their blogs, but the California crew didn't have the same connections in DC to amplify their message. The belligerent tone of some of their backers, especially Mohammad Abdollahi, didn't help. He had already begun to alienate supporters such as Representative Gutiér-

rez, not only with the sit-ins and the leaked recordings of their conversations but also with snide Facebook and Twitter comments that
veered from the political to the personal.

As the California team made their way across the country, activists
in Washington continued to hammer the administration on executive action. On May 28, some ninety-four immigration law professors
signed a letter based on Hiroshi Motomura's framework, detailing the
precedent for executive action. Immigrant rights groups continued
to pressure the Obama administration directly but also in more subtle ways. They fed both the *New York Times* and the *Washington Post*
enough behind-the-scenes details of the 2010 DREAM Act failure,
and enough anecdotes about current backroom dealings, to give both
outlets juicy page-one stories on the growing call for action. Dozens of
local media outlets began featuring DREAMers. Supportive lawmakers in Washington regularly called DHS. The president could continue
to make the case for only so long that it was Congress's responsibility
to act when it was clear that lawmakers had no intention of doing so.
Esther Olavarria met with undocumented activists and White House
officials including Cecilia Muñoz and Valerie Jarrett to see how the
administration could arrive at an order that would be broad enough
to make a difference to the DREAMers but not so broad as to end up
blocked immediately by the courts.

The Obama administration wanted to have as much support from
within DHS as possible. The department's agents were, in the end,
the ones who would often have to make the call as to whether or not
to detain an individual. But changing long-established practices at a
government agency wasn't easy. "It was a cultural change as much
as anything else," Napolitano later said. "And it meant changing not
only enforcement practices, but training practices, litigation practices,
everything that goes into enforcement."

As DHS secretary, Napolitano had been exploring the possibility
of both broad immigration reform and some kind of executive action for those eligible for the DREAM Act ever since the failed 2010

vote. Now she pressed her staff more urgently to outline a legal frame-work.

Using the White House counsel as their conduit to DHS, Esther and Cecilia also worked to make the case that detaining teens who'd grown up in the country and were contributing to the nation was not the best use of the government's limited resources.

Meanwhile, the National Immigrant Youth Alliance issued a public letter to Obama, urging him to act and threatening more civil dis-obedience if he did not. Far away from the nation's capital, though, Alex and the others were beginning to feel as if no one was listen-ing to them. For many in the media, the Campaign for an American DREAM walk did seem like something of a replay, a "been there, done that." Early on, the group had given access to young filmmakers who were interested in the effort, but they needed to generate more imme-diate publicity to have an impact. They needed to do something even bigger. In early June, three months and 1,256 miles into the walk, they reached Denver and found that something.

Colorado was a key presidential battleground state. Its Latino com-munity had grown by more than 40 percent over the decade[18] and now made up a fifth of the population. The place seemed ripe for action, and one of Alex's fellow walkers, Javier Hernandez, had spent some time organizing there.

They considered infiltrating a nearby detention center or sitting in in the offices of Denver state officials, but they quickly learned the Democratic-leaning local politicians were unlikely to press charges against them or have them deported, meaning they'd get little atten-tion. They brainstormed in Big Momma, deciding that they would need to go after something or someone who would react. Obama needed the state's Latino voters. He could little afford to have dozens of young Latino immigrants protesting against him. Maybe someone from their group could do a sit-in at his state campaign headquarters.

"Do you expect this person to be arrested?" asked Veronica Gomez, a recent college graduate from California State University, East Bay, and one of the walkers.

"Yes," answered Nico, the group's de facto political organizer.

"How long would they sit in?" Veronica asked.[19]

They debated who should do the sit-in and for how long. Alex had already been arrested in Los Angeles, and besides, since he didn't qualify for the DREAM Act, he wasn't the best representative of the cause. The group also needed people like Alex on the outside to drum up community support. They considered the others. Veronica hesitated. Over the next few days, she thought back to her college graduation, how proud her parents had been, snapping crazy photos, yet how much despair she had felt even at that moment, knowing the only job she had been able to line up was a babysitting gig.

That night she and Javier agreed to do the sit-in. They talked strategy with some of the more experienced young protesters, who suggested they pretend to volunteer so they could scope out the office. The worker who greeted them on their first visit to the Obama campaign office was nice enough, a skinny guy with glasses who looked barely out of his teens. He showed them around, and the group did volunteer work for an hour or so as they took in the lay of the land. Alex and the others felt bad for him but pressed ahead.

After the initial tour, they spent the next four days walking through possible scenarios, including what it would mean if both Veronica and Javier ended up in detention. They began making signs and painted a giant cloth with Obama's image in red, white, blue, and black and the words "Stop Deporting Dreamers."

Then, on June 5, the team returned to Obama headquarters, accompanied by a group of local TV reporters. Veronica sported a maroon mortarboard; Javier, a blue one. He delivered a petition to the same worker who had welcomed them days before, with signatures from thousands of people urging the president to put forth an executive action to protect undocumented youths from deportation.

"We are actually not going to leave this establishment until we hear action from President Obama," the nervous Javier told the young campaign worker.

The campaign staff, a mix of young, old, black, and white women and men, looked on somewhat dumbfounded, nervous but polite as Veronica and Javier locked arms and refused to move. A placard in the floor-to-ceiling front window read "Latinos for Obama."

"We're gonna be here as long as we have to be here," Javier said.

At first the Obama staffers were friendly, but as the afternoon wore on and a bigger crowd gathered, banging drums and chanting, they frantically called Chicago and Washington for guidance. They tried to ignore the protesters, going about their regular business, ringing a celebratory bell whenever they signed up new volunteers.

Outside, Alex had reached out to local religious, immigrant, and civil rights groups for solidarity. From his experience with the protests in Southern California, he knew that if they wanted to keep the media's attention on the sit-in, they would have to offer a scene outside every day, rain or shine. Soon dozens of protesters showed up, chanting. A band replete with accordion and tuba serenaded the Obama staffers and protesters with Mexican rancheras. He was exhausted yet had never felt more energized.

The campaign workers taped paper across the office's front windows to block the view, carefully making sure not to cover the "Latinos for Obama" sign.

Eventually, the Obama campaign was forced to issue a statement: "We deeply respect the commitment and courage of these young people, and completely agree that Dreamers who serve in the military or go to college should become citizens and be allowed to contribute to our country, but the only permanent solution is to change the law. . . ."

By evening, a handful of police officers arrived and met with staff in the back. The protesters prepared to be arrested.

Nothing happened. The Obama campaign said the protesters were not trespassing, and the police left. The protesters were flummoxed. Now that they weren't going to be detained, they had to figure out their next move. Late on the night of June 5, in response to one reporter, Veronica blurted out that she and Javier would begin a liquid-only hunger fast. Once more, they upped the ante. Lots of immigrants had done fasts, but not in a campaign office of the president of the United States of America.

What the protesters didn't know was that back east the administration, poised to take some sort of executive action, had turned to other immigrant advocates for help. The other Washington-based immigrant advocate groups could have promoted the protest, urging their journalist contacts to write about it, but they mostly kept silent. America's Voice would post a blog on June 7, two days after the sit-in started, then nothing until well after it had ended. The Washington advocates had mixed feelings about the California walkers. Some worried about the unpredictability of the maverick organizers and feared occupation of the campaign office would alienate the administration enough to torpedo any plans the president had to take executive action.

But others saw a larger strategy, in which helping Obama respond to the occupations also played into a good-cop, bad-cop dynamic, where both were essential. Just as during the 1960s, Malcom X and eventually Stokely Carmichael provided a counterpoint to leaders like Martin Luther King Jr. and groups like the NAACP, the fasters made the Washington-focused immigration groups look like a more rational and attractive alternative to engage with. Gaby Pacheco offered suggestions. Any arrests would only garner more attention and turn the group into martyrs, she warned. "If any of the protesters do leave, they should not get to come back," she added.

Veronica and Javier were totally unprepared for a hunger fast. The first two days were fun. More media arrived. The protesters slept on the floor on blankets, and the office staff carefully stepped around them. Soon, though, they switched from Gatorade and water to Pedialyte, and the fast began to take its toll. Alex wondered how long they could keep it up. He continued to organize vigils several nights in a row outside. People huddled in sleeping bags under a tarp through a massive June thunderstorm. Denver immigrants stood outside and began to share their stories.

Even without much national coverage in the mainstream media, the protest began to have an effect. Two days in, and the Metropolitan State College of Denver announced it would lower the tuition rate for undocumented students. Activists in other cities, seeing they would not be arrested, began staging similar actions. Some occupied the Obama campaign office in Oakland. Young immigrants staged protests outside his offices in Cincinnati, Detroit, and Dearborn, Michigan, and planned ones for Charlotte, where the Democratic National Convention was scheduled for later that summer. Then the campaign got wise and started closing offices before the protesters arrived.

Veronica and Javier lasted six days. On Monday, June 11, they finally called off the fast. As they left, unsteady on their feet and in need of an escort outside for a press conference, Alex and the rest of the group felt a sense of victory. They were already discussing their next stop: Chicago, the heart and headquarters of Obama campaign land.

For the president, under pressure from all sides, doing nothing was no longer an option. The day after the fast ended, Cecilia Muñoz and other White House aides were scurrying to prepare for the president's announcement, checking and reviewing again and again the proposal, the speech, the talking points to the media, to Congress, to immigrant groups and other stakeholders, revising up to the last minute, trying to avoid leaks. There was no room for error.

As she was going over documents, Cecilia got a call from her husband's office. He was being sent to the hospital with chest pains. She was frantic, but there was so much at stake for so many. He spent the night alone and was released the next day. Cecilia sent him home in a taxi so she could focus on ensuring the executive order was properly rolled out.

White House staff began to give the heads-up to veteran immigration reporters, then eventually to activists and congressional staff, whom they knew were far less likely to adhere to the news embargo and might leak too much before the president made his announcement. Cecilia called journalist Jose Antonio Vargas personally to tell him he would not be covered by the order because he was over the age cutoff. She called veteran activists such as Frank Sharry to share the news. He sat listening silently, stunned. It was finally happening.

Felipe and the other activists were told to get prepared. He began dialing his network, once again organizing watch parties, just as he had for the 2010 DREAM Act vote. Still, the activists got only the bare outline. They had no clear idea of what the president would say or how many people the executive order would cover.

THE MORNING OF June 15, 2012, the president strode out onto the steps of the White House and into the Rose Garden, where he unveiled the most dramatic immigration reform program the United States had seen in nearly three decades: Deferred Action for Childhood Arrivals. Obama explained that the Department of Homeland Security initiative would cover young people who had come to the United States before the age of sixteen and were age thirty or younger; who had been physically present in the country for the past five years; who were in school, or had graduated from high school, or had joined the military. They would be allowed to stay in the United States for two years and to renew their status at the end of that time. The result: they would be eligible to work, in many states to drive, and they would no longer have to fear that any interaction with police could lead to deportation.

"These are young people who study in our schools. They play in our neighborhoods. They're friends with our kids. They pledge allegiance to our flag. They are American in their heart, in their minds, in every single way but one: on paper," the president said as he unveiled the program that would soon be better known by its acronym DACA.

Exercising his oratorical gifts, the president urged Americans to empathize with the plight of those very different from themselves: "Put yourself in their shoes. Imagine you've done everything right your entire life—studied hard, worked hard, maybe even graduated at the top of your class—only to suddenly face the threat of deportation to a country that you know nothing about, with a language that you may not even speak."[20]

The Washington-based nonprofit Migration Policy Institute had estimated that more than 1 million people would be affected by the order and later increased that number to 1.7 million.[21] The president then added an economic argument to the moral one: "It makes no sense to expel talented young people, who, for all intents and purposes, are Americans—they've been raised as Americans; understand themselves to be part of this country—to expel these young people who want to staff our labs, or start new businesses, or defend our country simply because of the actions of their parents—or because of the inaction of politicians."[22]

But those words also underscored the clear line of separation: the kids were blameless; their parents were not. As Marie Gonzalez watched the announcement from afar, her stomach rolled over. She thought of her mother alone in Costa Rica. It had been seven years since Marina had left Missouri. Three more years, and then the decade-long ban against her mother's return would be up. *Soon, soon, Mami,* she promised silently. *Soon.*

As the president turned back in to the White House, Neil Munro, then a reporter with the conservative *Daily Caller,* again yelled out, "What about American workers who are unemployed while you import foreign workers?"

Questioning unfair competition from low-wage foreign workers was more than fair. Many conservatives who opposed more immigration argued the practice of bringing in cheap farmhands and seasonal hotel workers had spread to importing lower-wage nurses and basic tech workers and was hurting middle-class Americans.[23]

In this case, though, the "foreign" workers he was referring to were U.S.-raised. Unlike the thousands of "foreign" workers brought over every year on temporary visas by farms, hotels, and tech companies, and unlike the thousands more who crossed the border without a visa or overstayed their tourist visas to look for work, these young immigrants had been brought up to expect the same wages and conditions as their classmates and peers. By giving them status, Obama was ensuring many could demand better wages.

Although Obama made the announcement, the administration was careful that the actual regulations came from the agency in charge of such matters, DHS. And the president emphasized the measure was not a permanent fix.

"This is not a path to citizenship," he said. Ultimately Congress would have to pass a law to make the protections permanent, providing the president some cover against the argument that he was usurping congressional power. The temporary nature of DACA could also create a concrete incentive to help keep a sympathetic leader in the White House, one who could be counted on to renew the order when it ran out.

In Long Beach, Dario's mother shrieked from the living room and ran to wake her son, who as home from college and sleeping late. Dario sat up. His first thought: "Thank God I didn't get married." His mind flashed to all the things he wanted to do: get a driver's license, find a job to help his parents, maybe study abroad.

Hareth heard the news in Los Angeles during a protest in front of the downtown immigrant detention facility. She and dozens of other young activists had returned for the second year of Dream Summer at UCLA. They stopped chanting, stopped waving their signs, and stood in a circle holding hands, for just a few quiet minutes savoring the unexpected victory.

In Miami, Felipe Matos stared at the television. Around him, some forty activists—a few of whom had walked part of the way with him to Washington, had protested in congressional offices, or had stood with him outside detention centers—shouted and danced. *We did it!*

Even though Felipe had known something was coming, he hadn't imagined the president would go so far. The president was in fact doing just what Felipe and Juan had asked two years before.

"And most people think without a vote you can't do anything," Felipe said.

His hands were sweaty. His cell phone wouldn't stop ringing. But he wasn't thinking about school or getting a driver's license or even a job. He wasn't even thinking about his sister, who wouldn't be eligible for the protection because she'd come as an adult. He was thinking about the secret wish he'd been afraid to say aloud while his future hung in the balance. Maybe now one day he and Juan would finally have enough stability to create a family of their own.

Cecilia Muñoz spent all day and the next fielding calls and interviews. It wasn't until she drove home from the gym on Saturday and heard radio interviews with DACA eligible immigrants that the scope of what the administration had done finally hit her. Cecilia parked in front of her house, walked inside in her workout clothes, and sat down on the couch and cried.

Alex Aldana heard the news in Denver after a dinner at the home of one of their regional supporters. It had been an evening of devouring heaping plates of food and laughing raucously to help Veronica and Javier recover from their fast—and to prepare for the next leg of their journey to Chicago. He reread the DACA rules, hoping, even though he knew better, that he'd missed some clause that would include him. His stomach dropped. He had not. It was the same story. He'd arrived too late. It wasn't enough. There were so many deserving people who were not included. Everyone else was cheering. Alex stood to the side. Many of his fellow marchers, including Veronica and Javier, wanted to return home and finally get their much coveted driver's licenses. Some wanted to apply to college or graduate school. Alex wondered if they would come back, wondered what the march was about now. In the back of his mind he kept asking himself, *If we could accomplish this much, what more can we do?*

10

AFTER DACA

Dario waits to speak publicly for the first time at Harvard University about being undocumented, Cambridge, Massachusetts, April 2013.

The DREAMers had gone mainstream. Hollywood stars such as Rosario Dawson and *Desperate Housewives* star Eva Longoria became outspoken public champions. Donors who had previously funneled money through organizations such as America's Voice or the National Immigration Law Center now began channeling grants directly to United We Dream. The group, which had operated on a shoestring budget out of borrowed offices at the National Immigration Forum, finally had a room of its own.

Much of the money flowed in specifically to help educate young immigrants about how to apply for DACA. Thousands of teens were poring over old Facebook posts, high school transcripts, family photo albums, anything to prove their constant presence in the United States over the past five years. It was an arduous process. Students without social media profiles worried how they could prove that they'd lived in the country that long. Those who'd moved struggled to get records from their former schools. Spanish-language media issued warnings about unscrupulous notaries posing as immigration lawyers and charging large sums to help fill out the paperwork. Around 550,000 applied for DACA during the first year.

In June 2012, *Time* magazine published a stark cover of thirty-five young, undocumented immigrants from fifteen countries under the headline "We Are Americans*/*Just not legally." The group stared out from the black background. Front and center stood Jose Antonio Vargas, the former *Washington Post* reporter who had come out about his own undocumented status the year before. Inside was a story Jose Antonio had written on the them and their future in America.

Other immigrant groups increasingly adopted their strategies and even borrowed some of their leaders. The National Day Laborer Organizing Network invoked the young activists in a months-long cross-country tour from Phoenix, Arizona, to Charlotte, North Carolina, timing their arrival to coincide with the Democratic National Convention that September. The group hired Tania Unzueta to help coordinate the media outreach for the tour, which it called the "'No Papers, No Fear' Ride for Justice."

"Actions by undocumented students, such as coming out of the shadows, civil disobedience, and occupations of electoral offices have shown what happens when our community acts for itself," the group said in a statement, "it changes everything."[1]

As the election approached, many of the young activists refocused their energies. Alex Aldana peeled off from the California team weeks after Obama's Rose Garden announcement, joining hundreds of other immigrants who now turned their attention from protesting against the president to getting him and local candidates elected. If the president wasn't going to give him DACA, *at least he is providing me a job,* Alex thought. He joined Nico Gonzalez in Albuquerque and worked with a grassroots immigrant rights group on local campaigns, volunteering in a community garden in exchange for room and board. He felt at home organizing, working to get people out to the polls, especially in the LGBTQ and Latino communities. It wasn't really about Obama. It was about getting ordinary people to take advantage of the privileges that Alex so desperately desired. He canvassed to help elect local officials, including the state's first gay Latino state senator, Jacob Candelaria.

New Mexico was a purple state, a swing state, where Latinos made up 46 percent of the population and were also among the most likely to cast their votes across party lines.[2] They were far less likely to be immigrants than in places such as California and Florida, and as Alex knocked on their doors, he began to understand their history. Some told him they'd become Republicans after getting amnesty from the 1986 immigration reform law passed under Ronald Reagan.

Over the years, they had begun to lean blue, but not consistently. They had thrown support to Bill Clinton in the 1990s and to Obama, but in between, they had backed George W. Bush's 2004 reelection campaign.

Alex found the hours long. Dogs chased him. Plenty of doors slammed in his face. The heat was unbearable many days. Still, it was a welcome change from the daily sixteen-plus-mile walks. And going door to door was definitely easier than finishing high school by day while working full-time washing dishes at night.

A few dogs, he could handle.

SINCE HER FATHER'S death, Marie Gonzalez had taken a further step back from activism. In the fall of 2012, she and Chapin flew with his parents to Costa Rica to surprise Marie's mother on her fiftieth birthday. Marina had begun to remake her life in Puntarenas, and for the first time, the family enjoyed a tourist-style trip, spending the weekend in the cloud forest of Monteverde. They rode zip lines and drank copious amounts of local coffee and rum. It was the best vacation Marie could remember, the first time she hadn't been dealing with immigration papers or helping clean out her father's belongings. They gorged themselves on local seafood, and only a day or so after Marie returned did she remember that she had long since lost her native stomach for local Costa Rican food. As soon as they returned, Chapin was immediately sent to handle claims for the insurance company where he still worked. Marie weathered the illness alone. She watched the election returns in between running to the bathroom, so sick she could barely get to work. It felt like the worst flu she could remember. A friend at work suggested she get a pregnancy test. *No way am I pregnant*, Marie insisted—until the little pink plus sign appeared in the window of the plastic wand.

Marie wanted to feel elated, but she was terrified. What would a baby do to her and Chapin? He had always kept her feet on the ground, had kept her from falling apart after her parents left, had offered his parents as surrogates when she couldn't embrace her own. He was a writer at heart, played guitar, too. He had stayed with the insurance job to support them despite his musical interests, hadn't complained, just did it. He was big, blond, and goofy, almost the opposite of Marie in so many ways. And just when things were finally getting a little easier, a little more predictable, this. . . . She wondered how kids would affect their relationship, frightened about not being able to just blow off steam with Chapin over a few beers. And what if one day she were separated from her baby as her parents had been from her? But she could see Chapin as a dad. Yeah, she could definitely see him doing this. She dialed Chapin's cell, a grin on her face. "Hey, so how do you feel about being a dad?"

ON NOVEMBER 6, 2012, Obama captured 71 percent of Hispanic votes, a result second only to that of Bill Clinton's reelection. New Mexicans were hardly the only Latinos who came out in force for the president. Obama won wide margins in swing states such as Colorado, Virginia, and Florida.

DACA had barely begun to roll out, but the cushion of safety the order would soon provide so many young immigrants was already taking effect. Now that those with DACA could work, many organizations and even politicians were tapping them for their skills. Representative Luis Gutiérrez hired the first undocumented youth to work in his office. The activist Erika Andiola,[3] from Arizona, joined the community outreach team for the campaign of a Democratic politician, Kyrsten Sinema, who that fall won her first US House election.

Life had changed overnight for those with DACA, but not for many of their loved ones. In the fall of 2012, an officer stopped Erika's mother, Maria Minerva Guadalupe Arreola, for allegedly speeding. It was hard for Erika to believe. Her mother had always been terrified of being pulled over, a fear only magnified after Joe Arpaio's 2008 raids of the Arizona water parks, where she had worked. But SB 1070 also allowed local officers to pull over anyone whom they might suspect of being in the country unlawfully. The officer had run Maria's name through the system, and that was when the traffic stop became more than a traffic stop because Maria's name was already in the system. About fifteen years before, she had brought the then eleven-year-old Erika across the Mexican border. The first time she crossed, Maria had been caught and sent back. The second time they made it, but by crossing again she had violated Title 8, US Code § 1326, and committed the felony crime of reentry into the United States following a deportation. Punishment was up to two years of prison, followed by an expedited removal order. Now, if her information from the traffic stop was turned over to DHS, immigration officers might come looking for her.

And they did. Around 9 p.m. on Thursday, January 10, 2013, the agents hammered on the door of Erika's home. The agents asked her mother and brother to come outside. Minutes later Erika posted what had happened on Facebook: "My house just got raided by ICE and they took my mom and my brother. They had no reason to do this!"

Like Hareth, Erika had worked enough cases through the immigrant networks to know time was against her. The faster she acted, the more likely she was to save her mother. Unlike Hareth, Erika was defiant from the start.

"This is real!" she cried, her voice catching between sobs. "I need everybody to stop pretending nothing is wrong, to stop pretending that we are just living normal lives, because we're not."

The next day, Erika spoke with her brother, who was eventually released from detention, and learned her mother would soon be deported. She raced to the Immigration and Customs Enforcement office, only to learn her mother was already on a bus to the border. Within hours, she put her activism to work for her family. She was on a conference call with ten different immigrant organizations, brainstorming about a campaign to save Maria. They put out urgent calls to their social networks across the country, and Arizona's lawmakers, as well as the White House, were flooded with calls to save Maria. Suddenly, officials reversed course. The driver of Maria's bus got word around 9 a.m. Friday as he was driving his group of detainees to the border. He took the call and pulled over. Shortly after he hung up, he turned the bus back around. The order had gone out; Erika's mom would not be deported that day. News of their victory raced across the young undocumented networks. It was empowering but also chilling. They might be safe for the moment, but it was a reminder of just how vulnerable their parents and siblings remained.

By 2013, Silicon Valley also threw its support behind the DREAMers. Facebook's Mark Zuckerberg teamed up with tech leaders, including the cofounders of Dropbox and LinkedIn, to create the bipartisan lobbying group FWD.us, focused primarily on broader immigration reform. The group often used the DREAM Act–eligible immigrants as the face and raison d'être of the campaign. It began offering hackathons in places such as Cambridge and Miami, empowering the activists with twenty-first-century tech tools.

Many Silicon Valley leaders were immigrants or the children of immigrants and felt a natural affinity with the undocumented students they met, who tended to be the high-achieving public faces of the movement. They also couldn't stand the idea of wasted young potential. And they were often more familiar with the issue by virtue of being based in California than many other Americans because of the sheer number of immigrants in the state.

But the tech titans also saw the potential for allies in their own efforts to streamline the immigration process for the world's best, and least expensive, engineers, software developers, and also increasingly lower-level analysts, web developers, and other potential employees. An immigration policy that combined their desire for a more updated foreign worker visa program with the DREAM Act or an even broader comprehensive immigration policy might also protect them from pushback over the outsourcing of white-collar jobs.

Laurene Powell Jobs had founded a nonprofit mentoring group for first-generation college-bound students and said it was there she had learned that a number of participants were undocumented. In 2013, she broke her nearly two-year public silence following the death of her husband, Apple cofounder Steve Jobs, to advocate for the DREAM Act.

"I think there's been a great realization over the last several years that, in fact we do not wish to punish the children because of any actions from their parents," she said during an interview with NBC's Brian Williams.[4]

She helped produce a half-hour film by Davis Guggenheim about the DREAMers and a website to share their stories. She founded the Emerson Collective, a nonprofit that would champion DACA and the DREAM Act, among other issues.

Silicon Valley's support was much welcomed, but some young activists were once again split. Should they push again for a stand-alone DREAM Act, taking Silicon Valley's backing and running with it? Or now that they had some modicum of safety, should they return to fighting for broader immigration reform that would include their parents and older siblings?

The debate wasn't limited to what kind of legislation they should push for in Washington. Some young activists, including Tania Unzueta and many in the National Immigrant Youth Alliance, wondered whether they should be focusing on a bill at all, given how many people were being detained. They had little hope Congress would pass beneficial legislation anytime soon and believed they could have more impact by using their limited resources to reduce immediate suffering by fighting the Obama administration's expanded deportation policy. These activists began to turn their attention back to the border. During the summer of 2012, a small group of young undocumented activists had infiltrated the same Broward Transitional Center where Juan had helped the youths plan the desks-and-chairs protest back in the fall of 2009. Their dispatches from inside upped the ante for what daring action would be taken next. Activists moved their sit-ins from congressional offices to the roads outside immigrant detention facilities, blocking the departure of buses like the one Erika's mom had rode in to the border.

The young activists' parents were also emboldened. Like Hareth's mother, Betty, who joined the Dream Project, and through campaigns such as the "No Papers, No Fear" Ride for Justice, they had begun to share their stories publicly. Now they joined their children in getting arrested while stopping buses headed across the border.

HER FATHER'S ARREST spurred Hareth to expand her role in the movement. It felt selfish to focus only on her own family's troubles. During the summer of 2012, she made public service announcements to encourage other teens to register for DACA and expanded her work with the DREAMers of Virginia. And she began to think about comprehensive immigration reform that would go beyond those eligible for DACA.

Hareth attended her third Dream Summer program in 2013. This time, she was placed at an even bigger organization, the AFL-CIO. The subway ride each morning from Arlington to the McPherson Square subway stop only blocks from the White House transported her across a distance far greater than just the Potomac River. At the AFL-CIO, she was part of a much broader conversation about the future of America than she had been even at United We Dream.

It had been more than a year since her father's detention. Mario had completed his alcohol education classes and paid his fines. But as the next immigration hearing approached that fall, the family's attorney, Vanessa Rodriguez, once more warned them about getting their hopes up. Now she advised them to at least consider voluntary departure, and they trusted her enough to take her advice seriously.

Had Mario been in the United States for a decade before being arrested, he might have had a better chance of staying. A decade of good citizenship was worth something in the eyes of the Department of Homeland Security under President Obama, but Mario had been two years shy of that marker. He wasn't a college student with a clean record. The family could fight the case for another year or so against what was an all but inevitable outcome, or he could start ticking off years on the ten-year ban and come back sooner, Vanessa told them.

Once again Hareth's parents looked to their eldest daughter for the final say.

We fight, she said.

Earlier that year, Hareth had met Erika Andiola at an organizing training and learned firsthand about the online petition and the videos Erika had created for her mother. Hareth decided to create a similar campaign for Mario, spreading the word about his case throughout the national immigrant networks. On her long subway ride home from work, she racked her brain for people she'd forgotten to reach out to and the small, neglected details about her father that she could add to the page to help his case. One afternoon she began writing a few free-form lines in her notebook. The words began to shape themselves into thoughts, ideas she was too shy to share. It felt good to write. Hareth leaned back against the vinyl seats of the air-conditioned subway train, and for a few minutes she felt free.

At first she kept her father's case quiet at work, some days not speaking to anyone. But she confided in her supervisor, Ana Avendaño, the union's longtime immigration policy coordinator. And over time, her colleagues began to learn her story.

"The AFL-CIO takes care of its own" had long been a union staple. But Ana put a different spin on the words. "We take care of each other," she told Hareth. Don't give up.

In September, a month before her father's hearing, the AFL-CIO offered Hareth a speaker's spot at its national convention in Los Angeles. The union had promoted a pro-immigrant platform since 1999. But Hareth's speech came as the union announced it would include more low-wage nonunionized labor, even undocumented immigrants, in its organizing efforts. Now more than ever, the union sought to bridge the native/immigrant labor divide as states across the country sought to copy a 2011 Wisconsin law that had significantly weakened union influence.

At the convention that year, the AFL-CIO issued resolutions to support citizenship drives; a push for comprehensive immigration reform; and the creation of low-interest loans and other union benefits even for those who weren't able to join the union.[5]

Many of the proposals the organization announced weren't new, but that year they were updated with input from groups such as United We Dream and the National Day Laborer Organizing Network. The largest federation of unions in the United States of America was no longer paying lip service to the importance of immigration reform. It was looking to become a lead partner in the fight.

President Obama was set to address the convention the same day as Hareth was scheduled to talk, and Hareth planned out in her head how she would wait for him offstage and beseech him to help save her father. Ana Avendaño warned her how hard it would be to just "grab" the president, but she couldn't bring herself to dampen Hareth's determination. Hareth was almost giddy. If anyone could help, it would be the president.

Then, at the last minute, Obama didn't come. Hareth was crushed. The morning of her speech, she stepped outside to the parking lot for a few minutes to collect herself. It was the day before her father's birthday. What exactly could she say to these men and women to convince them her family's plight was worth their time? She called her friend Carolina Canizales, the national deportation defense coordinator at United We Dream.

Carolina had been cheerleading for Hareth throughout that year. Even if they couldn't save Mario, even if he was deported, they would keep fighting to get him back, she'd insisted. *Don't give up hope*, she'd admonish Hareth from time to time. Hareth had to keep her father's spirits up as well. Now once again Carolina offered advice. *Tell them to stand up*, she suggested. The physical act of moving, getting up out of a chair, literally standing up for something, was a long-standing organizing tactic. It would send a powerful message of solidarity to anyone watching and would create energy in the room, she promised.

Suddenly Hareth began receiving urgent texts. The schedule had been changed again. Her turn was almost up. She needed to get back into the convention center.

She made it to the stage just in time. Richard Trumka, the AFL-CIO president, gave a brief introduction and description of her family's case, then Hareth stepped up.

"Hi, everybody, how are we doing?" she called out. The crowd murmured in response.

She squared her shoulders, smoothed the black blazer she wore over her red-and-pink flowered dress, and looked out at a sea of gray-haired, mostly pale men in suits and polo shirts. She exhaled. "I know we can do better than that," she said, her nervous laugh echoing. Louder shouts.

She pushed ahead. She reminded herself she had little to lose. She told the crowd how she'd hoped to see the president and tell him about her father and how disappointed she was that that wasn't going to happen.

Backstage Ana and the schedulers looked at each other. Hareth was supposed to read a poem she'd written, not improvise.

Hareth continued. Maybe, she said, since she wasn't going to speak to the president, they could all send a message to the president together. "If you want to tell President Obama to stop my dad's deportation, please stand up," she said. Ana held her breath. She peeked out from the side of the stage. It was difficult to see the faces on the darkened convention floor.

Ana heard the shuffle of chairs and feet. First from the front, then slowly a wave moving toward the back, the cavernous room thundering with applause as hundreds of union members rose to their feet.

Hareth clasped her hands and stepped back up the broad blue-carpeted steps of the convention stage. She turned to survey the crowd, a timid smile spreading across her face. Only then did she launch into the words she had first sketched out on those long metro rides, words that over time she had polished into a poem:

AMERICA, WE NEED TO TALK!

Don't be afraid, and stand because we believe this is the year, the year
*   that the dreams of my parents will be realized*
And the dreams of millions who came and crossed borders
Unimaginable to reach the land of opportunities
. . .
Let's go on and tell them,
While they who have the power sit
Separating us as they see fit
While my father's hands blister from work all day
And he doesn't feel like he has a say.

Her voice cracked. Yes, she was talking about immigrants, even those in the country who had taken union construction jobs. Yet her audience wasn't turning on her. They, too, were fathers and daughters.

They seemed to understand she was speaking about them, too, and about a system that each year seemed to provide ever-growing rewards for an ever-shrinking number of people.

America, we are liberated by the pain
So let's talk, because
America is home
A land of dreams for all dreamers.

Once more the audience stood and applauded.

By October, Hareth had generated more than 8,000 signatures in support of prosecutorial relief for her dad. As she collected letters and cards in support of Mario from those who knew him, she also began to pay more attention to her parents' lives. She'd known about their sacrifices, of course, but it was one thing to hear her father complain about back pain at night or tell little Claudia he was too tired to shoot hoops; it was another to go to see one of the buildings he was working on, hear how it had been nearly destroyed, see how he was slowly and carefully reattaching cables, see the crawl spaces he had to contort his body into so as to install electrical wiring and the heights he had to climb, sometimes without a harness, to install the cables.

As a teen, she had turned to her mother, confided in her, shared jokes, romantic woes, and even tears over her father's drinking. Sometimes Mario seemed almost an enigma. Hareth was amazed at how quickly his colleagues rallied to offer their support, how the team showed up to finish the job when he was in detention, how they deferred to him on the more complex jobs, how much they seemed to admire and trust him. Some days, she felt as if she were seeing her father for the first time.

She brought dozens of supporters to his immigration hearing. It was a five-minute event to turn in her father's file, but even the presiding judge asked Mario's attorney, Vanessa, why so many people were packing the courtroom and the outside hallway. "They're here in support of my client," Vanessa responded.

A few weeks after the AFL-CIO convention, Ana Avendaño received a call from the National Day Laborer Organizing Network. Leaders at the network had seen Hareth speak. They wanted her for a music video up-and-coming artist Aloe Blacc was filming. Hareth was at a United We Dream national training for DREAMer moms when she got the invitation. Days later, she found herself in a studio near Hollywood, California, appearing in a video for an acoustic version of Blacc's hit song "Wake Me Up." The electronic dance mix version with Swedish DJ Avicii had already topped the global charts.

The video told the story of a young girl taken from her mother by a border patrol officer as the woman attempted to cross the border. The young girl grew up to be an immigration activist, and Hareth played her as an adult. Many of the actors in the video were undocumented immigrants as well.

Hareth insisted on wearing her own T-shirt, a Dream Project shirt, in honor of her friends back home in Virginia. The video garnered more than 19 million views, not even close to the EDM version's success but enough to get media attention. People Hareth didn't know approached her, telling her she'd brought them to tears.

At a United We Dream national summit that year, people treated her like a celebrity, and she began to hear through the grapevine that some were too intimidated to talk to her. Her own shyness among her peers didn't help things. She ached a bit for her anonymity. In December, her internship ended, and life returned to something resembling her version of normal. She had been working with fellow students to successfully push for in-state tuition in neighboring Maryland, less successfully in Virginia. Now she joined Gaby Pacheco's new Bridge Project, which had begun lobbying Republicans on immigration reform. The small group of undocumented youths put into practice the president's call at the National Council of La Raza to build a movement that bridged party lines. Gaby and the others at the Bridge Project believed they could no longer rely on Democrats to move forward on legislation. If they wanted to get a bill passed, they would have to make a better case to the Republican lawmakers who led Congress.

By now Hareth was used to telling her story to friendly lawmakers. They might hedge their bets politically, but personally they often seemed to agree that the country was benefiting from the labor of people like her parents and that the government had tacitly allowed them to live in the United States while denying them most civil rights and protections. She was used to telling her story to people who believed the situation left these immigrants vulnerable, while creating unfair competition for legal immigrants and US citizens, and that the best solution was to create some kind of process to allow them to work legally.

With the Bridge Project she was quickly jolted awake to a parallel reality. She spent her days talking to people who, instead of seeing citizenship as the answer, felt that Hareth and millions like her must leave. Otherwise, they reasoned, it would set a precedent for future groups of undocumented immigrants to ask for the next amnesty, and the next.

Away from the cocoon of sympathetic lawmakers, Hareth quickly realized that just telling their stories was not enough. Slowly she began to learn the grunt work of lobbying: building relationships, listening to the other side, talking baseball when necessary, trying to figure out what the undocumented immigrants could offer that the lawmakers with whom they spoke needed.

The veteran Mexican American Legal Defense and Educational Fund had agreed to sponsor the group, helping open congressional doors and giving it some political cover and gravitas. Hareth soon realized lawmakers and their staff sometimes didn't even realize she and her colleagues were undocumented. Some days she felt like a spy on a reconnaissance mission to discover which lawmakers would support a comprehensive immigration reform bill if it came to the floor; which lawmakers were willing to learn more; which might not support the bill but also wouldn't oppose it; and which were quietly working on their own legislation.

Some days it was exciting. But every morning she felt as though she were walking into the lion's den. For a while, things seemed to be looking up in Congress. Polls showed Republicans were supportive of some kind of broad reform.[6] Senator Marco Rubio had finally signed on to the idea, helping lead the so-called Gang of Eight, four Republicans and four Democrats, who negotiated a compromise bill. Once again John McCain, Jeff Flake, Lindsey Graham, Chuck Schumer, Dick Durbin, Bob Menendez, and now Democrat Michael Bennet of Colorado hashed out a compromise that included a path to citizenship. So much had changed since the 2010 DREAM Act vote. Now it was the Senate pushing for reform as the Tea Party–infused House backed away.

LIKE THOUSANDS of other undocumented immigrants, life in Cambridge had changed in subtle and not so subtle ways for Dario after DACA. He stopped looking for obscure part-time jobs and landed a position at a campus-affiliated bar. He joined the Boxing Club and began to take part in more of the privileges of school, even a party at the Delphic Club, one of Harvard's exclusive Finals Clubs.

He began to delve more seriously into film. He moved from the bar gig to a job in Widener Library's audiovisual department, watching all the obscure and classic movies he could get his hands on in his spare time. He immersed himself in film-related classes. Armed with DACA, the other undocumented students on campus became more willing to talk to him. Dario and his freshman roommate, Alex, sought a grant from Harvard Law School's Immigration and Refugee Clinic to restart their project.

But even with this new freedom, or maybe in part because of it, he also headed for a sophomore slump. Dario joined the Latino Men's Collective and earned a less-than-stellar reputation among his Latina classmates for having a few too many one-night stands and contributing to the group's spreadsheet, which listed many of the women by "hotness" and physical attributes. He got drunk enough one night while walking home from a party at MIT to slam his face into the side-walk and break two teeth. He wondered how it was that everyone else seemed to have it together.

A few months after the Boston Marathon bombing, Dario made a short film in which he pulled out the rest of a broken tooth on camera and had Alex, wearing an actual Boston Marathon number, stand on the rail of Weeks Bridge and appear to contemplate jumping into the Charles River. His dean hauled him into his office for a chat. That spring his low grades landed him on academic probation. Dario feared that he might fail out of Harvard, and for the first time in his nineteen years, he wondered if he might also be failing at life.

It was Dario's father who came up with the idea of a road trip, some-thing to provide perspective and freshen his mind. Maybe he thought it might jolt his son back to reality. Dario loved the idea. He and Alex decided to drive to the California-Mexico border over spring break to film scenes for their documentary on Harvard's undocumented stu-dents. He still couldn't cross it without additional permission, and he hadn't been anywhere close since he and his family had crossed nearly two decades before, but he was fascinated by the power that mysterious line had over his life. His father encouraged him despite his mother's misgivings about their taking the Mustang. *Go to the border and see for yourself the difference between the countries,* Dario Sr. encouraged. *See what it means to cross.* DACA would protect him, and the Mustang was the perfect road-trip car.

Alex flew out to Dario's home in Carson. They left early in the morn-ing, along with Dario's younger brother, Fer, and another friend from home. Dario drove more than two hours, elated to be back behind the wheel of the Mustang, legally at last. The Argentinean group Los Fab-ulosos Cadillacs blasted them down the freeway. It seemed only fitting to play his father's favorite rock en español band. Dario took the Exit 1A, San Ysidro Boulevard, the last exit before the border. Adrenaline pumped through him as if he were headed into the boxing ring. He drove along the main drag looking for parking. Giant palms lined the streets. Men with backpacks hanging across their shoulders sat with women and kids in Burger King. They passed strip malls galore. They were still in the United States. Every sign was in English, yet it was as if someone had switched out all the actors. Dario glanced at Alex, wondering if he noticed he was the only white guy around.

Above the roofs of the check-cashing joints, banks, and vitamin supplement stores, Dario could see the hills rising on the other side of the line, the brush dry and untamed. That was Mexico, but the neighborhood of San Ysidro where he stood didn't feel all that much different. He wasn't even sure where the border was. What if they accidentally crossed?

Now that they had arrived, he wondered if his mom might have been right about the car. He'd heard enough about the gangbangers and the narcos along the border. He wondered if he and Alex looked like easy marks.

They found a parking spot. Dario grabbed the video camera and tripod and set out for a bridge along the main entry into and out of Tijuana. So much security on one side, long lines of cars, and only turnstiles on the other. They watched those headed back to Mexico: men dressed in jeans, T-shirts, and work boots, some as if they'd just come off a morning of hard labor, women with groceries, families with luggage.

It didn't take more than a few minutes for the officers to approach the boys. They wanted to know what Dario and Alex were filming and whether they had permits.

"We're just filming for a school project," Alex said. Dario tried to emulate his friend's confidence. Never act like you don't belong, like you shouldn't just be there. They flashed their school IDs, and Dario was glad he was wearing his Harvard Boxing Club T-shirt.

The officers told them they couldn't film the border due to DHS security regulations and shooed them away. The officers didn't appear to be armed, and, all things being equal, they seemed pretty cool, Dario thought, just doing their jobs, though he wondered how they would have been treated if he hadn't been wearing his Harvard T-shirt. As they walked away, Dario's mind flashed back to the year before, when he'd gotten a speeding ticket while driving in the Mustang. After he'd flashed his Harvard ID, it hadn't even occurred to the officer he was undocumented.

"You should know better, you go to Harvard," the officer had commented while writing up his ticket.

Dario knew sometimes Alex and his friends scratched their heads about his careless attitude. He knew the risks. He knew he had to be safer, more cautious—always.

Dario couldn't answer why he did some of the "stupid shit," at least not an answer his friends would accept. In so many aspects of his life he *was* careful. He'd always been a top student, at least until college. He helped his parents, looked out for Fer and Andrea. Sometimes he just didn't want to be reminded it was more dangerous for him to mess up than for any other American teen; he didn't want to think about how much he had to fear.

They decided to drive someplace where they could get a clearer shot of the border for the film, something more explicit. They decided on the beach. At Border Field State Park they all got out and walked down the dirt path toward the sand. The place smelled like dusty sage. In the distance they could see the wall or the fence or whatever it was called. On the other side of the fence, sloping up into the hills, the houses were jumbled concrete rectangles, all on top of one another. As they finally hit the beach, the smell of sage turned to the stink of sewage.

The metal pilings stretched out maybe a hundred feet into the Pacific, creating a border well into the sea. Despite the "Danger," signs, Dario wondered if people ever just swam around them but decided it couldn't be *that* easy. The poles on the beach were two stories high but far enough apart that small children could squeeze between them. But again, Dario didn't see anyone try. By now clouds had covered up most of the sun. It was cold, and the water was dark. Save for a Border Patrol agent sitting on his ATV on the dune above them, the US side of the beach was empty.

On the Mexican side, there was a full-on fiesta. Small kids kicked a worn soccer ball back and forth, running up and down the beach in too-short pants, T-shirts half falling off them. The kids playing soccer ran up to the pilings to get a closer look at Dario, his friends, and their camera.

The wind picked up, blowing sand into their eyes. The group was hungry. They headed back to the car. They'd gotten the footage they needed. It was time to go home.

As they drove north, Dario thought about how to work the shots he'd captured of the kids playing soccer into the film. He thought about the fence. He knew the stats, knew thousands crossed every day, yet, seeing it up close, the barrier felt so final, so official. This here, folks, is the end of your ride.

They made it back to Dario's house by dark. That night, as he lay in bed, Dario kept thinking about the kids playing soccer, how happy they had been, wondered if that was what life had been like for his cousins growing up in Mexico. Had they been that poor? He wondered if he could have been happy, too, playing soccer if his parents had never left. Except they had. He didn't want to be on the other side. Sure, he spoke the language more or less, but Mexico was not home.

His dad had been right. The trip to the border cleared Dario's head, at least somewhat. By the end of sophomore year, he began to try to mend fences on campus. On the last day of Harvard University's Arts First weekend, hundreds of students and their parents strolled beneath the lush elms and towering oaks of the Yard. They snapped pictures of the statue of John Harvard and the majestic Widener Library. Few noticed the crowd gathering across the green, atop the marble steps of Memorial Church. Some fifty students were huddled together, not the descendants of the Winthrops or the Quincys but the sons and daughters of recent immigrants, many of them immigrants themselves. While the rest of the campus took in the annual festival's jazz ensembles, symphonies, and Bhangra dances, these students geared up to present their own quiet show, their own coming-out. And for the first time, Dario joined them.

As he waited for the event to start, he sat apart from the other students, scrolling through his speech on his iPhone. Many of the others had already practiced telling their stories, shared them in small groups or even to an occasional journalist, and were able to explain the duality of living in the country illegally, fearing deportation, yet being a privileged Harvard undergrad. Dario had rarely spoken publicly about his family's history.

On the steps of Memorial Church, the spiritual and physical heart of the university, the students began to speak. One senior recalled how his mother had died while he was in high school and how a teacher volunteered to take him in. He spoke of how his scholarship to Harvard wasn't enough to pay for his books or toiletries and how his sophomore year he danced in an all-male club because his illegal status prohibited him from getting a work-study position on campus.

Another woman stood up, a friend and mentor who had avoided Dario of late, frustrated by what she viewed as his "bro" attitude. She told the group about how her father had never hit her growing up because any mark could trigger a visit from child services—which in turn might prompt a visit from immigration officials. "But my mom was fair game," she added.

Dario sank lower in his seat. There was nothing so tragic about his life. His dad had spent so many years telling him not to worry about money, even buying him that crazy Mustang. Jesus, he was an ungrateful ass.

Finally his name was called. He stepped up to the microphone. The wind was picking up. People were getting tired of sitting. He regretted not printing out his speech, too hard to read from the iPhone.

"Some of my worst memories of childhood were when I went to work with my dad. He'd wake me up at six in the morning on weekends . . . and drive me half asleep to construction sites in Beverly Hills or Palos Verdes or Bel Air," he began.

"*No quiero que crezcas sin saber hacer obra de mano*. No son of mine is growing up without knowing what manual labor is," Dario Sr. had told him.

The crowd laughed with recognition.

His parents had encouraged him to stick to the books only when they realized how bad he was with a wrench, Dario continued. He recalled his little sister asking why their dad made beautiful houses for people in Beverly Hills and Palos Verdes but couldn't fix their old bathroom. He remembered telling his little sister that their dad had been laid off during the recession, with few protections because of his immigration status, and that he was now cleaning more houses than building them.

That time no one laughed.

"That just killed me," he said quietly. Dario began to ramble about not wanting to ask his parents for more money, about looking for a gig as a sperm donor.

"He did *not* say that!" a friend yelled out, laughing at Dario's admission.

"The downside is, I'm close to failing all my classes," Dario continued, as if telling the punch line. The group was silent.

"But I have to give a fuck," Dario quickly added. The organizers exchanged more looks, wondering if they'd made a mistake letting him speak.

Then he stopped. He looked out at the students, at the handful of professors and other friends, as if seeing them for the first time.

"I don't know," he said. "I just feel happy that you guys are here. A lot of you don't have to care. Or you could be on the other side of the debate. And things being the way they are, the other students and myself who are up here really don't have much we can do to change it—but thanks anyways," he finished, and stepped off the stage.

That summer, Dario returned home, and at the start of his junior year he moved off campus to avoid some of the distractions that had hurt his studies the previous semesters and to take advantage of the cheaper rent. Over his father's objections, he officially declared visual arts as his major. He became a leader of the Latino Men's Collective and the Boxing Club.

In late fall, he received a call from his father. His mother was sick. It was likely cancer. He shouldn't worry. They would beat it. But by January, doctors had confirmed the disease had established a stronghold in her kidneys. Dario took a leave of absence from Harvard and flew home.

MARIE WAS SICK through most of her pregnancy. Finally, in March, she and Chapin decided she should quit her job and spend a few months with her mother in Costa Rica. If Marina wasn't allowed to be there in Missouri when the baby came, at the very least she could pamper her daughter beforehand and allow Marie's grandmother to do the same. It was the most time mother and daughter had spent together in seven years. Marina became acquainted with the adult version of the nineteen-year-old she had left behind, and for the first time, Marie began to see her mom as a woman in her own right. "That's how I made peace with the fact she wasn't going to be there at the birth," she said. She ate fresh fruit every day, and for the first time in years, she let others take care of her.

Araceli was born in Kansas City, Missouri, in July 2014. Secretly, Marie had wished for a blond Missouri-looking baby, hoping her daughter's citizenship would never be questioned. But she fell in love the moment she saw the dark curls on the baby's head. Celi, as they would call her, came out with a feisty cry, full of fight, "just like her mom," Marie joked.

As she held her daughter, Marie ached to have her own mother with her, to share her pride in the life she had just created. The nurse took the baby over to Chapin, and Marie watched him, the person whom she had leaned on, her cheerleader and partner through so many ups and downs, as he cradled the baby in his arms, his eyes wide, taking in every part of the tiny new creature. Marie leaned back against her hospital bed pillows and rested.

11

THE NEXT BATTLE

Isabel and Felipe Sousa-Rodriguez take a day off at the Magic Kingdom Theme Park in Orlando, Florida, April 2017. (COURTESY OF ISABEL SOUSA-RODRIGUEZ)

In early June 2013, Juan Rodriguez turned in his application for US citizenship. He also requested a name change.

Ever since he was a kid, Juan had wanted a different name, something more sophisticated, a pseudonym like that of the great authors. It wasn't just the fact that his name was so common, though; Juan, like its English version, John, symbolized to him the most classic of male names, the most classic male identity.

He'd grown up with a male role model, his father, who had almost never expressed weakness, tenderness, or even sadness. If that was what it meant to be masculine, Juan wanted to run in the opposite direction.

He wanted to challenge how men defined themselves, starting with their names. Increasingly, he wondered if he even met the definition of a man. What if inside were more a mix of the feminine and the masculine. And what if sometimes he felt much more feminine inside, what if sometimes he felt more like a woman? Juan, who questioned everything, began to talk more openly with Felipe, wondering why he had to choose this binary way of being. He wanted a name that reflected all this. He chose his mother's name: Isabel.

The year Juan officially became Isabel, Caitlyn Jenner had yet to come out, gendered bathrooms had yet to become a topic of controversy on the nightly news. Isabel downplayed the name change at first. It was too complicated to explain to anyone beyond the most inner circle. Isabel began to use the pronoun "they" to describe themselves, a recognition of both the feminine and masculine sides of their nature, a separate, nonbinary category. Many days, they still dressed more like a man. Friends were confused at first: "they," meaning Isabel and Felipe or just Isabel? But slowly the new name and Isabel's new identity began to sit more comfortably and the confusions diminished, were more easily laughed at. Coming out as a queer man had been easier for Isabel than for Felipe, and Isabel had been patient. Now Felipe could hardly begrudge his partner's new journey.

Miguel Flores, the immigration agent who sat across from Isabel and reviewed their application for citizenship, didn't seem particularly fazed by the name change. In fact, he perked up to hear that Isabel had married a Brazilian. He, too, loved Brazilian culture. Apologetically, though, he told Isabel he would have to make a correction, changing Isabel's marital status to single. Regardless of whether the state of Massachusetts recognized the wedding vows between two men, the federal government did not—meaning that Felipe would remain an "illegal alien."

Their timing was terrible. On June 26, 2013, just days after Isabel submitted their citizenship application, the Supreme Court overturned the Defense of Marriage Act, which defined marriage as an act between a man and a woman. The Court sidestepped the fundamental issue of whether same-sex marriage was protected by the US Constitution, but the 5–4 decision meant the Obama administration was free to recognize state-approved unions and to grant them the same federal rights and privileges given to men and women who wed.

Had Isabel requested citizenship a month later, they would have automatically been able to petition for Felipe. Now Isabel and Felipe celebrated the bittersweet news at home. Isabel would finally be able to petition for Felipe's citizenship but would have to file an entirely separate application for Felipe, a process that could take years longer.

Felipe attended Isabel's naturalization ceremony with mixed emotions. He was thrilled for Isabel to finally receive a full-bodied bear hug from the United States of America, and he was happy to see Isabel's name change, knowing how much it meant to his spouse. Yet once again he was left on the sidelines.

Felipe watched the group of forty immigrants, many Latinos, one woman in a hijab, a few from Canada, when they stood to recite the Pledge of Allegiance. Lee Greenwood's "Proud to Be an American," blasted from the speakers as a video of America's mountains, beaches, and heartlands filled the room with inescapable Olympic-style patriotism.

The judge who administered the citizenship oath surprised Felipe, speaking at length of his pride in being the grandson of Italian immigrants and cautioning them not to lose their history and languages. The judge lamented that his own grandfather had spoken only English to his children, ensuring they would be monolingual. *Speak your native language*, he urged. *What makes this country special is what we bring to it.*

After the music and the speeches ended, Isabel ran over to Felipe and embraced him. Together they pulled out the new citizenship certificate. "Look! Look!" Isabel pointed to the paper. Printed across the left-hand side, in elegant script, was the word "Married."

Isabel and Felipe would never know for sure, but they wanted to believe that it had been the sympathetic agent, Flores, who had gone back and amended the application and, in one fell swoop, recognized Felipe's right to marry the person he loved and put him on the path to becoming a US citizen. Felipe and Isabel immediately set about filing for Felipe's residency.

ELSEWHERE AMONG the immigrant activists, joy over the DACA victory was fading. The Gang of Eight's comprehensive reform bill passed the Senate in June.[1] Among its requirements: a more than decade-long path to citizenship for millions of immigrants; mandatory workplace checks of employment eligibility; increased border security; and more visas for temporary workers. It also shifted the immigration priorities away from the family-based focus established in 1965 to the prioritization of certain skills.

Still, Tea Party Republicans saw no benefit to supporting a bill their constituencies wouldn't embrace. They questioned the message amnesty would send to those still considering whether to cross illegally or to come and overstay a visa. Speaker of the House John Boehner refused to bring the vote to the floor. Marco Rubio backed off from his own proposal. The Democrats didn't seem to be in a tremendous hurry, either. Anger over Republican stalling on immigration might not hurt them in the midterm elections with most voters, while a vote in favor of comprehensive reform could put them at risk with others.

Felipe and Isabel moved to Central Florida, where Isabel helped to expand the Florida Immigrant Coalition's work with young students and other activists in and around Tampa. Once more they began lobbying for the in-state tuition bill, first floated in Tallahassee a decade before. Felipe took a job with GetEQUAL, the group behind the military veterans who had chained themselves to the White House fence. It seemed like the perfect fit, an LGBTQ organization looking for alliances with other grassroots groups.

One fall afternoon, the organization sent him to the house of two burgeoning activists named Kimmy and Barb to provide them training. Inspired by the immigrant movement, the couple had recently gotten themselves arrested outside Senator Rubio's Central Florida office to demand that he support a bill banning workplace discrimination based on sexual orientation. But they hadn't known what to do after that.

Felipe unpacked his poster pad and Magic Markers. With his preppy orange polo shirt, khaki pants, sandals, and black-framed glasses, Felipe gave off more the impression of an intellectual Abercrombie & Fitch model than a radical agent of change.

"Your goal cannot be to change the infrastructure of the country," he said as the women sipped beers and shared their couches with their small barkless Basenji dogs. "It has to be concrete."

He wrote "Theory of change" in big letters on his pad. "It's really important to figure out who has the power to give you what you want," he said. "What do I have that, if I take it away, they [will] do what I want?" he added. "How many days left in Congress?" The women didn't know.

"There are fifty days. So, if your campaign lasts sixty days?" Felipe paused, all sweetness and light. The woman looked at him, unsure.

"We lose," he said. "That's why you need a plan."

For more than an hour, Felipe gave the women the tough lessons he'd distilled from his more than six years in the trenches. He worked them on the difference between strategy and tactics. Tactics alone—a sit-in, a letter-writing campaign—didn't generally achieve much, he explained. To make change, they would need a broader strategy.

They discussed putting the pressure back on Florida Democratic senator Bill Nelson, who had recently announced his support for same-sex marriage but still wouldn't back the antidiscrimination bill.

What resources could they take away? How much money was Nelson getting from LGBTQ donors? The activists worried not enough people would follow through. After a march to which 250 people showed up, only 10 had come to a follow-up meeting. Each action has to bring in more people, Felipe told them, creating a "snowball effect." But even for economically comfortable US citizens, it was tough to tell people to take off a day of work.

Kimmy jumped to her feet as the session ended. "I feel so motivated now," she said. "We had just stopped after our first effort."

Felipe grinned.

Like many Americans, Barb and Kimmy had never really known someone living in the country illegally. They'd hired undocumented workers for jobs, maybe, passed them in the street, but they'd never broken bread or shared a beer with one and certainly never taken a crash course on social change theory from one.

But if immigrants were to have any hope of succeeding, these were allies Felipe was convinced they needed.

ANOTHER BIG FIGHT was brewing in Washington. Activists were asking the president to expand DACA to include young immigrants such as Alex who hadn't made the original cut and even the parents of US citizens and those with DACA, such as Dario Guerrero Sr. and Hareth's mother, Betty Ayala. It was a bold request, they knew. Yet if the House refused to take up the Senate bill, they saw few other options. Once again the president insisted he had no authority to take action without Congress.

Outside Washington, other activists were increasingly convinced that the sit-ins, and now even the more brazen Washington protests, were becoming passé. With each new action the ante was upped, until that new action became the norm, and the media and the public became inured to its impact.

They needed to raise the stakes once more. In July 2013, three young immigrant activists, including Lizbeth Mateo of the National

Immigrant Youth Alliance, who'd protested in John McCain's office with Tania Unzueta back in 2010, flew to Mexico to reunite with family members they hadn't seen in decades. There they began to stage one of the most audacious immigrant actions they had ever carried out.

The small group joined half a dozen DREAMers who had weighed their prospects in the United States and mostly self-deported after high school, in one case only days before DACA was announced. Such cases weren't common but weren't unheard of, either. Some had been unable to find jobs or go on to college in the United States. Others had already lost family to deportation and opted to rejoin them, or were simply tired and fearful of the constant uncertainty. So they had left. Now, though, they wanted to be considered for DACA retroactively.

Together the group dressed in the seemingly requisite caps and gowns, locked arms and turned themselves in at the Nogales, Arizona, port of entry, seeking asylum in the United States. For so long, immigrant activists had focused on keeping people from being deported. Now they were shifting the lens to the forgotten families that had already been split up. And they were testing the government's willingness to recognize a broader category of so-called DREAMers, young immigrants who'd come of age in the United States, regardless of whether they were officially eligible for the DREAM Act or even DACA. The media dubbed the group DREAM 9. The activists called their action the "Bring Them Home" campaign. The US government refused the precedent-setting request for humanitarian parole and placed the border crossers in detention, where most spent more than two weeks as they applied for asylum.

Just as she had done for her mother, Arizona activist Erika Andiola joined other activists across the country creating petitions for each border crosser, encouraging her networks to flood Immigration and Customs Enforcement and local lawmakers with calls and emails, lining up attorneys, and working contacts in Washington. At the AFL-CIO, Hareth advocated for support of the DREAM 9. She and another intern monitored the situation each day. Some at the AFL-CIO questioned whether the DREAM 9 had gone too far. During one discussion, veteran labor leaders worried their action was too radical. The group at the border was trying to challenge the very idea of borders. Hareth and her fellow intern looked at each other.

"No, this isn't radical. This is cool!" they responded.

Those who had crossed into Mexico for the action and then tried to return to the United States, such as Lizbeth Mateo, put their DACA applications in jeopardy. Yet all nine were eventually allowed back in, at least temporarily, until their cases were settled. Capitalizing on what they viewed as a success, in September the National Immigrant Youth Alliance organized a larger group dubbed DREAM 30. This time, though, only those who'd been deported or self-deported—those who had little to lose—participated.

The next wave of crossing garnered more attention and controversy. House Judiciary Committee Chairman Bob Goodlatte (R-VA) called the actions immigration fraud and highlighted the "stunts" as another reason to clamp down on border security. Besides, he argued, wasn't self-deportation the whole point? Talented youths who couldn't find jobs should return and contribute to their home countries, regardless of whether they spoke the language or ever remembered living there.

But it wasn't just those opposed to comprehensive immigration reform who took issue with the actions. The campaign once more brought to the surface long-simmering tensions over strategy within the movement. Respected immigration advocates, such as David Leopold, the former president of the American Immigration Lawyers Association, denounced the protests as irresponsible publicity stunts that distracted from the effort to achieve lasting immigration reform. Some lawyers worried those who had crossed into Mexico only to come back hadn't been adequately advised about the legal risks they faced, and they feared the border actions would make the movement look too extreme, scaring off potential allies. Others worried that the mass requests for asylum would hurt the chances of those for whom winning asylum was literally a question of life or death.

The Alliance's Mohammad Abdollahi responded that no one should speak for the nation's 11 million undocumented immigrants but the immigrants themselves. Waiting on allies and trying not to scare them off hadn't gotten them very far, he insisted. The exchanges quickly got ugly and personal, and they were available for all to see across the internet.

Shortly after Representative Luis Gutiérrez helped release one of the DREAM 30 from detention, activists held a sit-in at his office, refusing to leave until the congressman talked to the president about freeing more of the detainees. As they had during the 2010 battle, they surreptitiously taped and aired conversations with the congressman. Gutiérrez announced that he was done dealing with the National Immigrant Youth Alliance and urged families not to participate in the border crossings. The group would soon find itself sidelined.

But others would continue the in-your-face actions against their allies and even the president. In November of 2013, Ju Hong, a twenty-four-year-old UC Berkeley graduate and an undocumented activist from Korea, interrupted Obama during a rally in San Francisco.

"You have the power to stop all deportations—" he shouted over the president.

"Actually I don't," the president replied, waving away Secret Service agents ready to remove Ju and others from the event. Once more, Obama reminded the activists that their only permanent protection lay with Congress.

"That's part of our tradition. And so, the easy way out is try to yell and pretend like I can do something by violating our laws, and what I'm proposing is the harder path, which is to use our democratic processes to achieve the same goal that you want to achieve, but it won't be as easy as just shouting," he warned. "It requires us lobbying, and getting it done."

Alex Aldana was inspired by Ju, and by the Bring Them Home campaign. He was also increasingly concerned about what he wasn't seeing in the news: the unofficial reports that more young teens, sometimes kids, who were arriving in the United States alone or with only their mothers. Through his outreach work, he had met some of them, kids fleeing abuse and gangs back home, and kids simply seeking a better life. He couldn't help but identify with them, and lately there seemed to be more and more arriving.

He was right. In the summer of 2013, Joseph Langlois, an associated director for refugee, asylum, and international operations of the US Citizenship and Immigration Services, provided drafted comments for a congressional hearing to Alicia Caldwell of the Associated Press, noting that asylum requests, most of them from Central America, had nearly quadrupled since 2009, with more than 12,000 requests in south Texas alone. Many were young people coming alone, officially described as unaccompanied minors.[2] Still, most major outlets had yet to pick up on the impending Central American migrant crisis.

Alex felt helpless when it came to these kids, and he felt stuck on so many fronts. As he coordinated media support for the California participants in the DREAM 9 and the DREAM 30, he began to wonder whether he shouldn't throw it all to the wind and go back to Mexico himself. Life remained uncertain without DACA. He couldn't advance with the nonprofit work without proper identification. Every day he feared he'd lose his job. He and Nico had parted ways.

When his paternal grandmother became ill in the fall of 2013, Alex opted to return to Mexico. It was a good time to go as he had been invited to talk about his activism at the prestigious international art conference 89+ Americas Marathon[3] in Mexico City. In late December, he crossed the border and took a bus to Guadalajara to care for her. He hadn't seen her in a decade, and he'd already lost one grandmother without saying good-bye. He knew he might not be able to get back to the United States. But he felt he had nothing to lose.

IN FEBRUARY 2014, Hareth's father had his final immigration hearing. A crowd of supporters joined them in the court. Hareth sat on the wooden benches with her father, mother, and sisters. As the judge called out the name of each immigrant on the docket, she wondered whether they had family helping them, whether they had come to the United States alone. She remembered back to the first day her father arrived in the United States and how she had not recognized him. In recent months he'd spoken about his case and about others at local churches. They had collected so many letters of support. Vanessa had gotten a call from the judge's chambers. Things looked good, but Vanessa was afraid to get her clients' hopes up. As Hareth glanced over at her father, her heart sank. So much depended on the judge.

It seemed as though the judge would never get to Mario. Finally the bailiff called his name. Friends and supporters waved American flags. Mario stood up.

If the judge isn't in a good mood today, Hareth thought, *it's not going to be a good day for us either.*

She nearly missed the judge's ruling.

"Administrative closure."

What? At first Hareth didn't even know what it meant. But everyone was cheering. She felt faint. For practical purposes, the case against her father was closed. Immigration and Customs Enforcement could reopen it, but even Vanessa was now optimistic that at least under President Obama, it was unlikely anyone would go after Mario again— unless, of course, he went looking for trouble. A story of family separation and victory like hers didn't happen very often, Hareth knew, and she said a silent prayer of thanks.

Mario's case was done. So was Hareth's body. A month later, exhausted, sick, and with terrible stomach pain, she was rushed to the emergency room in the middle of the night.

"My body has officially given out," Hareth wrote on her Facebook page in February. Doctors ran tests but came up with very little besides stress. When she was released twenty-four hours later, she was afraid to tell many of her friends and fellow activists the conclusion she'd come to: she wasn't sure she could continue the fight. In the cold gray of winter, she dreamed of leaving the movement behind, fleeing the responsibilities of family and work, and running off to Florida to finish college by the sea. It was a crazy idea, but she'd learned about Miami Dade College through Gaby Pacheco, and it sounded to Hareth like paradise.

In the next few months, as Hareth's health improved, her friends convinced her to stay in Virginia, and she returned to Capitol Hill with the Bridge Project, but her heart wasn't in it. She applied for a scholarship to finish her international relations degree at the small, all-women Trinity College in Washington, DC, whose alumnae included House Minority Leader Nancy Pelosi and Hillary Clinton's 2008 presidential campaign manager, Maggie Williams. When she was accepted for the fall, Hareth danced for joy. For the first time in four years, she would simply be a student—free to work, dance with friends, go to the gym, go out to eat, enjoy the small pleasures in life she had so often missed. She couldn't wait to start.

HARETH WAS hardly the only activist exhausted and wondering whether there were a way forward. Even the veteran advocates were frustrated and in some cases burned out.

"I never thought I'd still be doing this so many years out. I imagined myself doing a lot of other things," Frank Sharry said quietly during a break at an immigration conference in late 2013.

John Boehner was still refusing to bring the comprehensive immigration bill to the floor for a vote. When House Majority Leader Eric Cantor, a Republican whom activists had viewed as more sympathetic to the bill, lost his Virginia primary in a surprise upset by a candidate with a strong anti-immigrant platform, any chance of the House taking up the bill evaporated.

Meanwhile, the number of deportations and unofficial returns on Obama's watch inched its way up to 2 million. Prodded by the DREAMers, even the National Council of La Raza, one of the few veteran groups that had remained at least outwardly steadfast in its support of the White House, publicly drew a line in the sand. On March 4, the organization's president, Janet Murguía, called the president "Deporter in Chief" and demanded he stop the stepped-up deportations. Gutiérrez took to the House floor and repeated the demand.

But the president truly still believed Congress was the correct body to tackle the issue, Cecilia Muñoz insisted. And unlike some of the young activists, he very much believed in the concept of national borders. During one meeting with DREAMers and veteran immigration advocates about the growing number of unaccompanied minors crossing the border, Obama told them he hadn't slept well the night before.

I'm not just worried about these kids but also in Sudan and other places, Cecilia Muñoz recalled him saying. *It's very unfair that kids in El Salvador live in a very different situation than a kid born in the United States. [But] we live in a world with borders. And I'm president of a country with one, and I need to enforce these borders.*

But it wasn't all up to the president. The Department of Homeland Security was supposed to detain those crossing the border illegally. And if that meant mothers with children because they were the ones crossing, then so be it, was essentially the agency's view.

Cecilia worked with others over the summer to provide better shelters for the children who were coming in increasing numbers, but that didn't mean they would all be allowed to stay. Sometimes she grew exasperated with her former colleagues. Even as she knew how frustrated they were with the logjam in Congress and the years of inaction, they had become so focused on the issue of deportation that they no longer seemed to be pushing lawmakers to act, focusing instead all their ire on the president.

To those behind the Bring Them Home campaign, the success of the first two events and the increasingly strong words from Washington allies signified one thing: it was time for one more, even bigger border crossing.

"The participants in this third border-crossing were deported or forced to leave the United States because of programs supported by the Obama Administration," the organizers said in their statement. ". . . State laws denying immigrants access to a college education, jobs, or housing also made life incredibly difficult. Some were just tired of living in fear, and returned. However, upon leaving their homes, they found life even more difficult. . . . No one should be forced to stay away from their children; no one should be forced to live in a country they barely remember."[4]

ALEX HADN'T RETURNED to Mexico just to see his grandmother or even attend the conference. He'd also hoped to use the techniques he had learned helping with the DREAM 9 and DREAM 30 to bring back his older brother, Carlos, who had self-deported to Mexico after a bad breakup. Once he was there, though, the activist in him couldn't help but also get involved in LGBTQ and other organizing events, including attending the first official lesbian wedding in Guadalajara. But Carlos didn't want to go back. And in the barrio where he lived, Alex was often singled out by locals for the patterned shirts he wore, the way he walked. Not long after he arrived, he was jumped by a few men on his way home from a club. Alex was ready to go home.

He had been in touch with Lizbeth Mateo, and as he learned about plans for a third border crossing, he reached out to help. He was afraid to stay with his brother any longer, and he hated the idea of returning to his undocumented life. This time he would request asylum based on credible fear of homophobia in Mexico. The organizers told Alex they would attempt to bring back 150 people this round, not just DREAMers but adults, too, families, and a couple of unaccompanied minors. This time they would challenge the entire immigration deportation system and force the media and activists to recognize more than just the immigrants in caps and gowns. Alex had already walked more than a thousand miles across the United States. He'd lived in a shelter with his mother. He figured he could survive detention, especially if it would get him home.

The plan was to turn themselves in at the border in Tijuana and once more seek asylum. They would literally and visibly overwhelm a system they already deemed broken. But what Gutiérrez and others had been trying to tell the young activists was that getting asylum wasn't easy: you had to be able to document credible fear of persecution by your own government or a well-founded fear of persecution on account of race, religion, nationality, membership in a particular social group, or political opinion that your own government failed to protect you from. And just who won asylum often depended on the jurisdiction and on what judge heard the case. Approval rates varied wildly.[5] In Arlington, Virginia, for example, where Hareth lived, judges approved more than 70 percent of the cases they decided between 2009 and 2014. But in San Diego during that same time, approval rates ranged from less than 10 percent to more than 60 percent, depending on the judge.

But to Alex, the persecution he would face as a gay man in Mexico seemed clear, especially as an outspoken activist. He wasn't worried, not for himself anyway. The National Immigrant Youth Alliance organizers were also confident. Most of the DREAM 30 had been allowed to wait out their cases in the United States. They might lose, but at least they could buy time, maybe until comprehensive immigration reform passed.

As the day for the return drew near, Alex began to feel more uneasy. He had little interaction with the national nonprofits, but he'd begun to hear some of them were strongly discouraging the actions. And when two young girls who had traveled across Mexico to cross the border joined the group, he wondered if it might be better for him to remain behind and help them in case they were turned back. Still, he listened to those who insisted that when so many people were actually detained, advocates would have to step forward and defend them.

Days after Murguía called the president "Deporter in Chief," more than 150 people showed up at Otay Mesa Port of Entry on the San Diego border.[6] On Monday, the first day of the action, nearly 30 DREAMers turned themselves in. Many had self-deported like the previous groups—some days or weeks before Obama had announced DACA. One twenty-year-old, Jaren Rodriguez Orellana, had recently returned to Honduras after his older sister had been deported.[7] He described being stabbed by local gang members at 10 a.m. one day after he had refused to pay their "protection" fee.

The rest of the week brought parents, sometimes with small children, who were often hoping to reunite with their US-born sons and daughters. A small group of people, including Alex, were seeking asylum based on their LGBTQ status. A handful more tagged along on the off chance their cases could be resolved. Alex tried to keep a spreadsheet of everyone. He tallied about twenty-five families, thirty-five DREAMers, and ten LGBTQ activists.

The returning immigrants came in waves across the same entry point that Dario had visited the year before and each time requested either humanitarian parole (which allowed them to enter legally but did not grant permanent residence nor necessarily a work permit) or asylum. They were quickly detained at the border and taken to the Otay Mesa Detention Center, which had a mostly open floor plan, with pods around a center area filled with metal cafeteria-style tables and seats. At night their cells were locked, as well as several times during the day at "check-in." But otherwise they could circulate in the common area or visit the library, which was also in a small cell-like room. Officers housed the gay detainees in cells in the center of the long wall, two to a room. To Alex, it felt like being forced onto center stage.

At Otay, Alex met detainees from around the world. One twenty-year-old man was fleeing Afghanistan and hated loud noise. "But the Nigerian folks, the black folks, the Mexican folks, everyone [was] watching telenovelas, and they put him right there, and it must have been driving him crazy, all this noise, and one day he snapped and smashed the TV," Alex said. The Afghani was taken to solitary confinement as punishment.

Psychologists came and talked with the detainees for a few minutes and listened. They'd give them ibuprofen but not much else, Alex said.

The ACLU would later call for closure of the Otay Mesa Detention Center, run by the Corrections Corporation of America, following reports from nonprofits of several serious complaints, including sexual assault, harassment, and neglect.[8]

By then Gutiérrez was refusing to work with the organizers. Hareth was no longer working at the AFL-CIO, which had also pulled the plug on its support of the border crossers. The nonprofits had helped provide bond for the few dozen youths who'd previously crossed, but they didn't have endless funds, nor were they willing to spend a lot of resources on a form of protest they hadn't been consulted on and didn't support. Many other advocates were pouring all their energy into getting Obama to expand his earlier executive action.

Alex had helped organize for the DREAM 9 and the DREAM 30. Alex thought he knew what to expect. But there were so many people who needed his help, and this time he was on the inside. Each day it felt like *The Hunger Games*. Nobody knew who would be chosen for deportation, who would be allowed into the United States. DREAMers who assumed they'd have a chance to be released into the United States and make their appeal got a rude awakening.

I'm going back because I have a degree and I don't speak with an accent, Alex remembered one young man with DACA telling another immigrant who had a minor criminal conviction. Both men were sent back across the border to Mexico.

The DREAM 9 had left detention after less than a month. Most of those in the DREAM 30 group had also been released, in large part because outside groups had agreed to pay their bond. Now the numbers overwhelmed even those nonprofits that did try to help. This last group, the DREAM 150, had to hustle to get their families to raise the roughly $7,500 to pay the bond so they could fight their cases from outside of detention.

To Alex, the saddest cases he saw at Otay Mesa were the indigenous women arriving from Chiapas. Many hadn't come with his group and had little support. They often struggled just to make themselves understood. Many couldn't read, and although their first language might be Kanjobal or Tzotzil, they had to explain their cases in Spanish or English, often without a translator. They would be asked over and over about the traumas they had faced, domestic violence, gangs, military assaults. Each time they had to relive the trauma, sometimes breaking into sobs as they met with immigration officials.

People looked to Alex for guidance and advice, calling him "lawyer" and jokingly nicknaming him "messiah." When he couldn't help them, they also blamed him.

You lied to me! You said you were going to help me!

At first Alex and many others refused to pay the high bond fee.

We are not going to pay anything. We aren't criminals, we shouldn't have to pay to get out of jail, he insisted. Alex appealed the cost of his bail three times. Some in the group conducted hunger strikes, but many of the participants did eventually get some outside support from family, friends, and even a few nonprofits, and posted bond. By late April, more than a month after he had been detained, Alex was among the last of the 150 still at Otay. He began to worry he would never get out. He had applied for asylum based on the harassment he faced in Mexico, but there'd been errors in the application that had delayed processing. He'd visited Vera Cruz, but officials marked that he'd lived there. The first day he was interviewed, he'd given conflicting dates for the beating he'd received in his brother's neighborhood.

His mother made videos pleading for help for Alex.

But when he spoke to her on the phone, she rebuked him. *I don't have the money for bail, hijo,* she sobbed. *Why, why did you want to leave?*

Finally, Alex received the green light to apply for asylum due to a credible fear based on being an LGBTQ activist, and he grudgingly asked friends to raise the bail money as a loan. After his initial petition for asylum was accepted, he posted bail while he waited for the case to make its way through the courts. Ironically, his sexual orientation, which had always made him feel vulnerable, now might save him.

Alex left Otay the first week in May. There were no cameras, no huge celebrations. Friends gave him a ride back to San Francisco, where he'd lived before his departure. It was a relief to be there as the city had become a sanctuary for LGBTQ refugees. He was not alone. The process was glacially slow. The immigration courts were woefully backed up. It might be years before a final decision was made in his case. Meanwhile, he could buy time and gather evidence. His asylum hearing was pushed back until December 2017.

He was done with big protests. He wanted to go back to doing work he knew would have a direct effect, rather than waiting years for politicians to move. He owed thousands of dollars for the bond. He slept on friends' couches, taking odd jobs until he could get his temporary work permit reinstated. Eventually he returned to his work in HIV prevention, helping researchers study health care outcomes for those most at risk in the LGBTQ community. Enclosed spaces and white rooms now terrified him. At night, when he closed his eyes, he heard the sobbing of the women and men he had not been able to help. Still, he knew he was better off than many. If his petition was approved, he would be on his way to US citizenship. And either way, for now, he was free.

A MONTH AFTER Alex's release, in June 2014, President Obama publicly stated that he would go it alone on immigration if House Republicans refused to bring the Senate bill up for a vote.

Activists eagerly awaited the president's next move, preparing for a summer of outreach around executive-branch immigration relief, just as they had done for DACA back in 2012. But once again outside events intervened. Roughly 60,000 unaccompanied children and teens, mostly from Central America, had come across the border in the last year. Many mistakenly believed they would be able to take advantage of any new proposed legislative or executive changes to the nation's immigration rules, or they and their families feared it would be even harder to cross after. The crisis Alex had seen coming, the one USCIS officials had testified to Congress about the previous year, finally made the front page.

Obama delayed executive action on immigration as the administration tried to reduce the flow across the border. But now congressional Democrats from swing states were nervous about how such an announcement would affect their campaigns. They urged the president to hold off until after the November midterm elections.

IN LATE JUNE, USCIS called Isabel and Felipe in for their interview, the so-called marriage test, the last hurdle to Felipe's getting a green card. Felipe was terrified. What if they got a homophobic officer? After all, it was Florida, where gay marriage would remain illegal until January of the following year.

But in the end, the only problem with the application was that Felipe's doctor had forgotten to sign a page, which they quickly remedied in a frantic rush to his office across town. Once more, they opted for a name change, this time to combine Felipe's mother's surname with that of Isabel's father, becoming the Sousa-Rodriguez household.

They celebrated Felipe's legal status on July 4, but the reality of his new life didn't sink in until he got his work permit in the mail. That night, he sent a photo to his mother. She told him she was both laughing and crying. She might not approve of his marriage to Isabel, but at least she could appreciate the vast difference this one piece of paper would make because of it.

Earlier in May, Florida had finally passed in-state tuition for undocumented youths, thanks in no small part to months of lobbying and organizing by Isabel. The win buoyed the spirits of state and national activists. Seeing their success, Felipe, too, was moved. Inspired by Isabel's work and refreshed by a couple of years away from the fiery heart of the battle, Felipe left GetEQUAL and rejoined United We Dream, this time directing strategy from Washington, splitting time between the nation's capital and Florida.

Almost immediately, though, he put to work his experience at GetEQUAL. When the Obama administration announced workplace protections against discrimination based on sexual orientation, United We Dream put out a press release congratulating its LGBTQ brothers and sisters on the executive order. Felipe was back but bringing in new allies from his time away.

DARIO SPENT the summer of 2014 focused on a different kind of documentation: medical insurance, doctors' orders, prescriptions. He'd come home telling himself it would be a break from the stress at school, a vacation. But he knew from the beginning that the odds of beating renal cancer weren't good. By May, the chemo wasn't working. Rocio's legs were thinner than those of his eight-year-old sister Andrea. She lay most days unable to move on the hospital bed in their living room, soft casts keeping the muscles in her calves from atrophying. Andrea spent hours by her side.

It fell to Dario to translate what the doctors were saying. It wasn't the language exactly. His dad was surprisingly fluent in English after so many years working for and with Americans. It was more what wasn't being said, the tone, the scientific language. They had known they might have only a few years. Now the doctors were giving Rocio only a few months.

Dario and his father sat down at night and filled out insurance form after insurance form. For years Dario's father had been using his old Social Security number to pay taxes, and through it he had acquired medical coverage for the family. They would not have to rush to the emergency room and wait long hours for what would essentially be free treatment. But the out-of-pocket expenses burned through their savings. The insurance company sent back their claims. It wanted to know if Rocio could eat solids and walk twenty paces before it would pay.

"People should really be worrying about their health and not all this bullshit," Dario groused.

Rocio's family flew in to see her, the first visit in years, and she seemed to realize the significance of such a gesture. Still, Dario wasn't sure his mother understood how rapidly she was deteriorating. The doctors didn't seem to want to say it in front of her, and he wasn't sure how much his father was telling her, either.

Dario tried not to respond "with overtly emotional distress," as he put it to adults who asked how he was doing. He owed that much to his sister and brother. But sometimes he worried his outward lack of emotion made his mother think he didn't care.

Dario began filming Rocio, getting her to tell stories about her childhood and her arrival in the United States. It distracted them both. And he began using his university-level research skills to find alternative cures. He started with diet. He tore up the family's traditional menu of meat, rice, and a few veggies on the side. He began to cook organic, vegetable-laden meals. He invested in an industrial-strength blender, filming the day it arrived, as orange carrot juice went flying into his hair.[9]

"The first to vomit loses!" they joked after Dario whipped up his first cleanser and mother and son lifted and clinked their glasses. Dario Sr. hated the ever-present camera. But Rocio insisted. Let him film, she said. Her husband was powerless to say no. Eventually the family got used to the little red light and the glass eye constantly trained on them. And, after a few weeks of the health diet, Rocio could walk again. She had more energy. One afternoon, as she sat in the living room, she heard a loud crash from the kitchen.

"*Hijo*, be careful of your toes!" she called.

"How do you even know what happened?" Dario yelled back.

Was he using a big knife?

Uh, yeah.

Did it fall on the ground and almost land on his foot?

Uh, yeah.

"I know these things because I'm your mother," she yelled back. Rocio was still in charge. Everyone breathed a bit easier. Dario began thinking about how he could use the film back at college in the fall. They waited eagerly for the latest results from the doctors.

But the tumor had continued to grow. *There is nothing more that can be done*, the doctors told Dario and his father.

They were afraid to share the news with Rocio. Dario stepped up his Google research. He ordered $200 herbal remedies from Mexico. He learned about experimental treatments outside the United States.

He found dozens of advertisements online for holistic and alternative healing centers in Mexico that Americans were flocking to. There was one not so far away in northern Baja that boasted advanced immunotherapies. Maybe, just maybe, he could take her there.

Dario Sr. stalled, fearing Rocio might not be able to get back into the United States. She began to lose energy again. Dario insisted, "We have to even if it's against her wishes."

His father acquiesced. After all, his son was a student at Harvard. He knew much more about these things, and living far away from his own family, Dario Sr. didn't know who else to consult. If he did nothing, he would feel guilty. And they had little to lose. Since Dario had DACA, he could request permission to leave the country and accompany Rocio. Fernando, a U.S.-born citizen, could visit her there. Dario Sr. would stay behind with Andrea.

At night Dario Sr. curled up onto the edge of the hospital bed next to his wife and fell asleep to the sound of her breathing. They hadn't slept apart in decades. He couldn't imagine being separated even for a night.

Dario applied for fast-track permission to leave the United States and waited. Those with DACA were at the mercy of US Citizenship and Immigration Services as to whether they could leave the country. The process was still new, and it was not uncommon for their applications to visit ailing relatives outside the country to be rejected.

The government responded quickly. It didn't deny his request, but DHS wanted more evidence to show the dire need for Dario's departure. Afraid of calling too much attention to his mother's status, he had also mentioned an ailing aunt back in Mexico. Now he would have to go into the DHS office and make his case. All he could think about was how little time his mother might have left. They had to leave, he decided. Dario figured his dad could send the necessary documentation while he was in Mexico. He knew it was reckless to leave without permission, but he'd watched on TV as the DREAM 30, and many in the DREAM 150, had made it back, from what he could tell. If they could do it, so could he.

On the day Dario and his godparents were to drive across the border, Rocio refused to get out of bed. She didn't want to go. She didn't want to leave her younger children.

Andrea sat next to her mother. "When will I see you again? Are you coming back?"

Dario Sr. begged her to get up, and when that didn't work, he began yelling. "You think I *want* you to go? You think I'm happy about this? You have to get up. You have to do this," he said, his voice breaking.[10]

Rocio turned her face to the wall.

But later that morning, Dario and his mom eased into the back seat of his godparents' minivan. It would all be fine, he told himself. He was at Harvard. They would work it out once his mom got the treatments.

The alternative treatments didn't work. After a couple of weeks, Dario took his mother to the home of her parents in Guanajuato, Mexico. Fernando flew down to join them. On the night of August 13, 2014, Dario Sr. spoke to Rocio. *Take care of the children*, she told him. *Not yet*, he protested.

The next day, Rocio Meneses closed her eyes for the last time. She was surrounded that afternoon by her two sons, her parents, and her siblings. The man she had shared her life with for almost a quarter of a century, the man with whom she had raised her children, fought and flirted, cried and danced with, was not by her side. He couldn't risk leaving the United States. Fernando and Dario were old enough to fend for themselves if he couldn't get back in, but not Andrea.

Shortly after his wife's death, Dario Sr. received a letter from the US Government. His son's request for advance parole, the required permission needed to leave the country, had been denied because his son had failed to supply the additional evidence requested.

After his mother's death, Dario went to visit his father's family on the outskirts of Mexico City. He contacted a lawyer, Alan Klein, recommended by his friend Oscar. He asked what he needed to do to get home.

It's not that simple, his new attorney explained. Dario had likely lost his protected DACA status by leaving the country without government permission. In the eyes of the government, he had self-deported. He was going to need special humanitarian parole.

Dario's uncles said he should just walk across the border with a bunch of other college kids and no one would notice. He could risk going to the border and turning himself in like the DREAM 150, the lawyer agreed, but he discouraged that tactic unless Dario was ready to spend weeks or even months in detention. Dario didn't feel quite as brave as he had driving down to Tijuana from the other side of the border. He decided instead to wait out the process at his grandparents' home. He contacted Harvard, and the school's attorneys and lobbyists in Washington put in a good word for him, but the November elections were coming up, and no one seemed in any hurry to give a relatively privileged Ivy League DREAMer a break.

At first Dario passed the time with the cousins he'd never known, going to clubs with them, learning about Mexico. But his cousins worked, and they soon returned to classes. Dario began sleeping till noon in the tiny basement room of his grandparents' home. He was embarrassed to admit that he was often afraid to walk around the neighborhood, of getting jumped by the local gang.

Down the road from his grandparents' house was a garage and, next to it, at the bus stop, a liquor store. It closed early but kept a window open for those in need, often for workers getting off late. Dario took to waiting for his cousin in the afternoons as she got off the bus, so she wouldn't be harassed.

He thought about his cousin earning 10 pesos an hour, about 50 cents.

Fuck no. Fuck no, he declared silently.

He stayed up till 4 a.m. writing music and free verse. He couldn't sleep anyway. He joked to friends that it was Emma Watson that kept him going, inspiring him to fight to return to the United States and win an Oscar so she would notice him. He told himself it would all eventually make for a good film. He tried to sound chill when his friends called or when the dean checked on him. This was his semester abroad. He'd be back by Christmas.

He wore his mother's rosary and kept her ashes in a box near his bed. At night, when he couldn't sleep, Dario had to admit to himself that as much as he had wanted to pretend otherwise, his life was still governed by the one piece of paper he did not have. Yet during those sleepless nights, the realization that truly made his heart pound had nothing to do with his immigration status. It was simply this: "I don't have a mom anymore."

12

NEW ALLIANCES

Immigrant activists await oral arguments in U.S. v. Texas *at the Supreme Court, Washington, DC, April 18, 2016.*

As immigrant groups waited for Obama to make his next announcement, another domestic crisis was brewing. Shortly after noon on August 9, 2014, a young man named Michael Brown was shot at least seven times by a police officer in Ferguson, Missouri. Michael Brown was black, the officer was white, and African Americans in Ferguson spilled out onto the streets to protest, quickly joined by supporters across the country. Local residents' anger stemmed from more than the fatal shooting of the teen; it came from years of living under a police department that the US Justice Department would later describe as having a pattern of unconstitutional policing. As one subsection of the Justice Department review put it: "Ferguson Law Enforcement Practices Disproportionately Harm Ferguson's African-American Residents and Are Driven in Part by Racial Bias."[1] The August uprising gave new life to the Black Lives Matter movement and reignited national discussions about race, justice, and the very definition of the word *criminal*.

Obama weighed in on the controversy in November, linking the protests to the immigration movement. "I've never seen a civil rights law, or a health care bill, or an immigration bill result because a car got burned," he said. "It happened because people vote. It happened because people mobilize. It happened because people organize. It happens because people look at what are the best policies to solve the problem. That's how you actually move something forward."[2]

The president's words were both true and not true. What he asked of the young people, both the black Americans demanding change from police and the immigrants seeking to stop the deportations, many could not do. Nearly one out of thirteen adult black citizens had lost their right to vote due to having a criminal record, according to the nonprofit Sentencing Project.[3] In some states, such as Florida, the number was much higher. There, more than a fifth of black adult citizens were unable to cast a ballot because of the arduous process of regaining that right. The vote was, of course, similarly out of reach for millions of undocumented immigrants. But people were paying attention to those demonstrating in the streets of Ferguson and to their issues, just as they were paying attention to the immigrants stopping buses at the border and chaining themselves to the fences around federal buildings. These young people were mobilizing and changing the conversation on social media and beyond.

Yet the president was right about the legislation. That would continue to require painstaking organizing, lobbying, and votes. It would also require more allies. Solidarity among immigrants, US-born Latinos, and black Americans was hardly new. When a group of Southern California parents had turned to the courts in 1946 to end public school segregation for Mexicans and Mexican American children, the NAACP's Thurgood Marshall had worked on the case, honing the arguments he'd make before the Supreme Court in *Brown v. Board of Education of Topeka* less than a decade later.[4] Martin Luther King Jr. sent a telegram of support for Cesar Chavez's fast on behalf of farmworkers. And in the early 1970s, the more radical Chicano Brown Berets and the Puerto Rican Young Lords modeled themselves after, and worked with, the Black Panthers, creating breakfast programs for kids and a neighborhood health clinic in Chicago. But by the millennium, much of that unity had fallen out of the public narrative.[5] Stories about tensions between those living in traditionally African American neighborhoods and the Latino and Asian immigrants moving into these communities, more often dominated headlines.

As many young immigrant activists refocused their efforts on fighting detentions and deportations, the natural overlap between their campaigns and the fight to reduce the incarceration rates of black Americans came into focus. Donors saw this, too, and by 2009, they had already begun funding bridge-building retreats between young African American and immigrant rights activists. Trayvon Martin's death had been a key moment for activists like Felipe and Alex Aldana. But Ferguson made those connections feel more urgent, with the immigrant activists retweeting messages from Black Lives Matter activists and livestreaming video from the protests.

DARIO WATCHED the Ferguson protests from his room on the outskirts of Mexico City. Alan Klein had told him to sit tight. He had left the United States without permission, but he had been desperate, the lawyer reasoned and was optimistic they would eventually get things sorted out. Dario took the advice and tried to view his time as extended vacation.

But the government denied Dario's initial request for parole back into the country. As October began to fly by and it was clear Dario would miss another semester, his confidence began to crumble. He considered telling his story to the media, but his lawyer worried that any publicity would hurt his case with officials in Washington. Dario, meanwhile, wondered whether anticipation over Obama's next announcement on immigration might make officials reluctant to intervene. Since the president's June promise to take action if Congress didn't pass immigration reform, the flood of immigrants from Central America had slowed. Direct pressure from the United States on the Central American governments had begun to take effect. So, too, had pressure from the United States on Mexico, which in turn began its own immigration crackdown along its southern border to keep Central Americans from passing through on their way north.

Now that the immediate crisis was beginning to recede, immigration advocates demanded to know when the president would make good on his offer. Yet once again, Democrats running in tight congressional races feared a backlash and urged the president not to act before the election. Obama bided his time.

Alan Klein submitted another request for Dario, and they waited for the government's answer. Weeks went by. Alan finally agreed to let him speak to the media on the record. A few days after that, AP reporters spent a day with Dario at his grandparents' home in the suburbs of Mexico City.[6] The story went live on the afternoon of October 14. Two hours later, Dario's attorney announced the government would allow him to come home. Dario received word he had been given humanitarian parole. Records obtained under a FOIA request showed that DHS officials had already been working to get Dario his humanitarian parole, thanks in large part to intervention by both Harvard and Senator Durbin's office. Still, it was unclear how much longer the process would have dragged on, nor whether it would have happened at all, had it not been for the media coverage.

After that, Dario's life became surreal. Reporters staked out his family's home back in Carson. Media in Spanish and English wanted interviews. A week later, Dario arrived at the San Ysidro border, dressed in a stylish blue oxford, jeans, and glasses. He carried his mother's ashes as he crossed the same border he and his friends had visited the year before. He grinned and held up his passport as he walked out of the Border Patrol office and into the fall sun. A gaggle of reporters and cameras followed him. On his passport were printed the words: "Not a visa. Holder has been granted parole authorization for up to two years."

"I can't believe I'm home," Dario told the reporters. "In just a few hours I'll be home with my parents"—he stopped—"with my dad."

On the drive home, Dario couldn't help but notice that people used their turn signals, that there was so little trash along the road. Since TV cameras were still parked outside his father's home, Dario met his father and brother at the home of one of his dad's clients. Andrea had stayed behind with family friends.

They pulled into the garage, and Dario waited nervously for his father.

"*Hijo!*" Dario Sr.'s hands trembled slightly in front of him as he ached to reach out to his son. Instead he rubbed his stomach nervously as he slowly strode toward Dario.

"Wassup?" Dario asked.

That was all it took. Dario Sr.'s hands instantly flew around his son, squeezing him so hard that Dario let out a groan. Fernando joined in, and Dario closed his eyes, exhaling between brother and father.

LESS THAN A MONTH after Dario's return, President Obama stepped up to the microphone to announce his most audacious immigration policy change yet. Behind the scenes, Esther Olavarria had again worked to pack as much into the proposal as possible. This might be the last chance to produce something out of the years she had dedicated to reimagining the US immigration system. Labor unions wanted farm-

workers to get protected status. Activists such as Erika Andiola wanted
to see the parents of all DREAMers covered. Other young undocumented immigrants wanted the arrival cutoff age to include those
who had entered at sixteen. The administration lawyers kept pushing
back. Whatever the president did, it needed to be limited to hold up
in court and in the court of public opinion. The debates within the
White House continued. Up until hours before the announcement,
few activists knew who would be covered and who would once again
be left out.

On November 20, Obama spoke directly to the US audience. This
time, he did not choose a Rose Garden ceremony, where reporters
might interrupt. Instead, he made the announcement on a Thursday
night during prime time. ABC declined to interrupt its Shondaland
lineup for the speech. None of the other major English-language
networks aired it live, either. But the Spanish-language channels carried the president's words uninterrupted. The speech was timed to
air before Univision's prime-time presentation of the Latin Grammy
Awards, meaning millions of Latinos across the country had their TV
sets primed and waiting.

In Arlington, Hareth watched Obama's speech at home with her
parents. They were joined by their friend Ingrid Vaca, a fellow Bolivian and single mom who cleaned houses to support her young sons.
A reporter from The Guardian camped out with the group as they
sprawled across the living room in front of the TV with pizza.[7]

They listened to the Spanish translation as the president spoke. It
was time to step up security at the border, said Obama. DHS planned
to increase funding for surveillance and apprehension, especially for
new arrivals. The administration would also make it easier for high-
tech workers and students to stay in the country. But few in Hareth's
living room were interested in any of that.

Finally the president got down to it. DHS, he said, would expand
temporary protection to cover young people who had been living in
the United States since 2010, rather than the original date of 2007.
The order would keep the cutoff age at time of entry at younger than

sixteen, but it would no longer matter how old DACA recipients were when they submitted an application. The Department of Homeland Security would also issue deferred action to the parents of US-born citizens and legal residents who had been in the country since 2010. The order was again meant to be a stopgap measure, Obama stressed. It had been nearly eighteen months since the Senate had passed the last version of a comprehensive immigration bill, and Speaker John Boehner still refused to bring it to the House floor.

For those in Congress who questioned his authority, "I have one answer," Obama told congressional leaders. "Pass a bill."

As the president spoke, Hareth stared at the television, stunned. She glanced at her mother. Betty didn't know whether to laugh or cry. She and Hareth's father would be legal for the first time in a decade, would not have the threat of deportation hanging over their every move.

The expansion of executive-branch protection for a broad class of immigrants was not unprecedented. But the scope in terms of actual numbers made it the most expansive in US history. Still, as ever, the president had to draw a line. And this time, that line cut right across Hareth's living room.

Her parents looked over at their friend Ingrid. Like the Andrades, Ingrid had entered the United States at least a decade before Obama's announcement and had two nearly grown children. She had been a leader among the DREAMer mothers, encouraging Betty and others to speak up. But because, unlike Betty, she had not given birth to a child in the United States, she would be left out of the president's largess.

Betty's mind was already racing toward the future. Maybe Mario could go back to working as an architect instead of contorting himself into crawl spaces to fix electrical wiring. Maybe she could return to work as an accountant or even go back to school herself. But first she wanted to visit her father, who had suffered a stroke a few years before. It had been a decade since she'd seen him. A few days later she let her employers know she would need time off to travel to Bolivia as soon as the regulations were put into place. She would take the time unpaid. It didn't matter.

That night at the Latin Grammys in Las Vegas, Enrique Iglesias won Song of the Year for "Bailando," and in his acceptance speech he recognized the president's announcement. "Tonight is not only an historic night for all Latino artists, but for all Latinos who live in the United States," the pop star told the crowd via video link from Paris. The Colombian singer-songwriter Carlos Vives dedicated his award to President Obama.[8]

A day later, Obama repeated the announcement before a friendly audience at a high school in Nevada. Undocumented immigrants made up more than 7 percent of the state's residents, the largest population share in the country.[9] In the audience stood veteran farmworker advocate Dolores Huerta, Senator Bob Menendez, Representative Luis Gutiérrez, and dozens of immigrants and their families.

Astrid Silva, the young woman from Las Vegas who had gotten Senator Harry Reid's attention in 2010, introduced the president. Now her father faced possible deportation. "I cannot imagine my life without him. There are so many families in the same situation and thanks to President Obama's action, they will go to bed without the fear of being awoken by a knock at the door,"[10] she said.

The new regulations wouldn't help everyone, she realized. But Astrid and others like her had privately concluded this was the best they could get. And something was better than nothing. "I know our community and the president will keep fighting for comprehensive immigration reform," she added.

Backers of the DHS order estimated it would affect some 5 million immigrants, nearly half the nation's undocumented population. Privately, they knew the number could be even higher. Still many immigrant activists had hoped the president would go bigger. Even up to the night before the announcement, they had lobbied and prayed the president would include all parents of DACA-eligible immigrants, not just those whose children were permanent residents or citizens.

Their logic: since Republicans were likely to challenge in court whatever the president did, he had nothing to lose by casting the net as wide as possible. Some activists were so disappointed by the final proposal that they declined to attend the Nevada speech, fearing their presence would appear to be a stamp of approval on a policy that still left so many of their friends and community in limbo.

Days later in Chicago, hecklers interrupted the president during a speech, demanding an end to the detentions and criticizing him for not going further. "I understand why you might have yelled at me a month ago," Obama retorted. ". . . It doesn't make much sense to yell at me right now when we're making changes."[11]

Overall, the announcement was celebrated within the immigrant community, even as it reinforced what Hareth saw as a false divide. In Nevada, Obama had spoken of "exceptional people like Astrid,"[12] a comment that seemed to exclude the millions of workers who weren't going to fancy colleges or standing before the AFL-CIO. Once again, the administration was emphasizing the need to deport felons, not families. Hareth thought of her father and his DUI and how slippery the line between the two could be.

Still, she printed out all the requirements and posted them on the fridge. Betty and Mario organized their documents to be ready at the first chance. Mario's immigration case was closed, at least for now. They saw no reason why he wouldn't qualify.

AS PART OF THE CHANGES, the administration would also end Secure Communities, the program that required local law enforcement to automatically run fingerprints of those arrested, even for traffic stops, through the DHS database. For the rest of Obama's time in office, such searches would go back to being at officers' discretion. It was the third incarnation of the federal government's effort to better coordinate between local and national authorities, balancing the government's need to know who was in the country with local law enforcement agencies' need to build trust in their communities. The program was facing constitutional challenges, too. Citing Fourth Amendment protections against unreasonable seizure, a growing number of law enforcement agencies pushed back against DHS immigration detainers.[13] These were the requests that police and sheriff departments hold immigrants who were arrested for up to forty-eight hours after they would otherwise be released, to give Immigration and Customs Enforcement agents time to come get them.[14]

Felipe and Isabel were dubious about the Secure Communities changes, but they were elated by the expanded protections. Felipe's sister would finally be able to come out of the shadows and drive her children to soccer practice without fear.

"The bottom line is, mass amnesty would be unfair. But mass deportation would be both impossible and contrary to our country's character," the president said.

In his Nevada speech, Obama acknowledged the pushback he would receive from ordinary Americans over the new regulations. "I want everybody here to understand, there are folks who are good, decent people who are worried about immigration. They're worried that it changes the fabric of our country. They're worried about whether immigrants take jobs from hardworking Americans. And they're worried because they're feeling a lot of economic stress, and they feel as if maybe they're the ones paying taxes and nobody else is taking responsibility. So they've urged me not to act," he said.

"And I hear them. And I understand them. But you know, I've also got a lot of letters and emails reminding me why we had to act—from American family members of hardworking immigrants who feared their families could be torn apart; from DREAMers who had proudly stepped out of the shadows and were willing to live without fear, even though it was a big risk for them; from Republicans who don't agree with me on everything, but are tired of their party refusing to vote on reform. . . ."

What few people focused on in his speeches was the stick that came along with the carrot: "If you plan to enter the United States illegally, your chances of getting caught and sent back are going up."[15]

Both Hillary Clinton and Bernie Sanders[16] came out in support of the new directive.[17]

On the Republican side, the reaction was even swifter. John Boehner accused the president of acting like "an emperor." Michael McCaul, the chairman of the House Homeland Security Committee, called the plan "a threat to our democracy."[18] They also noted that mass amnesty wasn't even necessary. If people got the idea that it was tougher to enter and live and work illegally in the United States, more would leave on their own accord. Even Senator Lindsey Graham, part of the Gang of Eight that had crafted the 2013 legislative reform, threatened to defund the effort.[19]

Yet it soon became clear Obama had put Republican lawmakers in Washington in a bind. Shutting down the government hadn't gone well for them in the past. Impeaching the last Democratic president hadn't worked either, and they were unlikely to pass a veto-proof bill to stop the order. Besides, DHS's US Citizenship and Immigration Services, in charge of processing immigrants, was almost entirely self-funded through application fees—including fees for the very types of applications Obama was proposing. The immigrants would pay their own way for the new Deferred Action for Parents of Americans and Lawful Permanent Residents program.

State politicians, however, had more leeway in challenging the president. Leading the charge was Texas attorney general Greg Abbott, who had just won the governor's race with a "get tough" border policy platform. On December 3, 2014, Texas sought an emergency injunction to preemptively stop DHS from moving forward with applications until the full case could be heard in court.

Some twenty-five other states joined the lawsuit. Many of the states, including Texas, Florida, and Georgia, were among those with the largest number of undocumented immigrants and thus potentially among the most burdened by the requirements of the new measure. But they were also among the states that had most benefited from the labor in construction, hospitality, and of course agriculture that those same immigrants provided. Others, such as Nebraska and North Dakota, had relatively few undocumented immigrants. But, like Florida and Texas, they were led by conservative GOP legislatures and governors who opposed the order on principle. They threw Obama's own words back to him, emphasizing that to go beyond the original DACA order would be beyond the scope of his powers.

"This lawsuit is not about immigration. It is about the rule of law, presidential power and the structural limits of the U.S. Constitution," they wrote in their complaint.[20]

To bring their lawsuit, though, the states had first to show that they had standing, meaning that they would be directly affected by the change and had a right to sue. For Texas, the question came down to driver's licenses. Texas subsidized its licenses by more than $100 per person, and Abbott argued that even modest estimates would put the cost at "several million dollars."

In his speeches on the new proposals, Obama had alluded to precedents for this "deferred action," set by Republican presidents. In 1990, President George H. W. Bush had given the deferment protection to the spouses and children of undocumented immigrants eligible for citizenship under Reagan's 1986 amnesty. His administration had issued the order so that husbands, wives, and children who would eventually be eligible for citizenship, some 1.5 million people, couldn't be deported while their family members prepared to petition for them, and he'd done it only after Congress had refused to take action.[21]

Shortly after Hurricane Katrina, President George W. Bush's administration issued a similar order on behalf of roughly 5,500 foreign students, allowing them to stay and work temporarily in the country even if they had come in on a study-only visa.[22]

But Texas argued that the scale was different this time. Under the Obama administration order, a minimum of roughly 4 million, and possibly many more, people might be eligible. Also, the previous examples had affected immigrants who had a very good chance of eventually getting legal status (for example, a spouse or child of a US citizen). In the case of the Katrina students, they had previously enjoyed legal status as students and faced losing that status as a result of a natural disaster, not through any action of their own.

Texas district court judge Andrew Hanen sided with Abbott and the other plaintiffs.[23] In February, he issued an injunction, a more than one-hundred-page treatise designed to withstand appellate review. Since Texas provided driver's licenses to everyone with official legal presence in the state, Hanen agreed that it had standing, and that was enough for the case to go forward. Outlining more of his own views on the matter, Hanen added that Texas and the other states were likely to have additional reasons to weigh in, including the cost of educating undocumented children, which the state put at more than $9,000 per student, and more than $700,000 in uncompensated medical care for undocumented immigrants.[*] But courts had already ruled that states needed to cover their education, and the potential for an additional future burden was too speculative to rule on so early in the case, Hanen noted, so for now his ruling focused on the driver's licenses.

Hanen also chided the Obama administration for failing to follow proper rule-making procedures before announcing the plan, noting that "once those services are provided, there will be no effective way of putting toothpaste back in the tube."

The twenty-six states that filed the complaint could not have picked a better judge for their case. Hanen was the same Texas judge whom California attorney and dentist Orly Taitz, one of the originators of the Obama birther conspiracy, had chosen when she had filed a lawsuit accusing Obama of "trafficking illegal aliens." The lawsuit had

---

[*] But Hanen also went above and beyond, ruling that the states were likely to be able to show that the federal government had all but abdicated its responsibility to carry out Congress's directive to deport millions of people by officially allowing them to stay and thus had a right to step in. He concluded that Obama had likely violated the so-called take care clause of the Constitution, which requires the president to "take Care that the Laws be faithfully executed," by seeking to give status (albeit temporary and with limitations) to such a wide swath of people.

eventually been thrown out, but not before Hanen required federal agents and officials to submit testimony showing they were *not*, in fact, in the business of "illegal alien" trafficking.

Immigration advocates across the country, and even the Justice Department, at first seemed undaunted by Hanen's ruling and continued to push forward, providing information about the new order.* Then, in May, a three-judge appellate panel in New Orleans denied the federal government's request to throw out the injunction and eventually reaffirmed Hanen's order.²⁴ Hareth's parents quietly put the documents they had prepared back into their file cabinets. Betty didn't talk about going to Bolivia anymore.

Exactly one year after Obama made his historic immigration announcement, his administration asked the Supreme Court to intervene in the Texas case. It was an effort to both move the case out of Hanen's hands and settle it more quickly once and for all. Justice Department lawyers made a simple argument: "Nothing in the [deferred action policy] affects Texas's freedom to alter or eliminate its subsidy at any time. Any 'pressure' here is thus self-created." Texas could easily charge the undocumented immigrants for the licenses, they argued. And ensuring that those immigrants, who were in fact already living in Texas, had the right to work would actually reduce the strain on the state because they could be more self-sufficient, they added.

IN JUNE 2015, billionaire developer and reality show host Donald Trump threw his hat into the ring for president, descending an escalator at Trump Tower in New York City and giving a speech in which he accused Mexican undocumented immigrants of being Americans' worst nightmare. His entry into the presidential campaign completely

---

* At first the Justice Department seemed to flout his order, sending out three-year work permits to thousands of undocumented immigrants, a move it later claimed had been a mistake. When Hanen threatened to hold DHS secretary Jeh Johnson in contempt, it reversed course and professed contrition.

upended American politics and political debate in many ways, but perhaps most startling was the talk about immigration.

"The U.S. has become a dumping ground for everybody else's problems," he told the crowd gathered before him. " . . . When Mexico sends its people, they're not sending their best. They're not sending you. They're not sending you. They're sending people that have lots of problems, and they're bringing those problems with [them]. They're bringing drugs. They're bringing crime. They're rapists. And some, I assume, are good people."[25]

Along with announcing his candidacy, Trump promised to build a massive wall along the border and make Mexico pay for it. He soon also called for a ban on Muslim immigrants.[26]

In a country where it increasingly seemed as if only a relative few people could still get ahead, now Americans had someone voicing on a national stage the fears some quietly harbored about their lack of advancement in the face of so many newcomers.

Although national surveys showed most Americans supported immigration reform, Trump seemed to embolden those who not only sought a reduction in illegal immigration but also feared the changing demographics of the nation or, to put it starkly, the so-called browning of America. Not long after his announcement, former KKK leader David Duke decided it was the time to relaunch his long-dormant political career and run for the open US Senate seat in Louisiana. Duke would lose, but the reentry of groups such as the KKK into public view and the proliferation of the online white supremacy groups that Felipe had been wary of was just beginning.

For the most part, the major media outlets initially treated Trump's entrée into the race as a sideshow. But in the Spanish-language media, Trump's line about rapists was radioactive. Univision dropped the Spanish-language simulcast of Trump's Miss USA and Miss Universe pageants, prompting him to sue. NBC, which owns Univision's Spanish-language rival Telemundo, ended its English-language contract for the pageants.

In the midst of the feud, Univision anchor Jorge Ramos sought an interview with the candidate. He sent a handwritten request, as he often did for big interviews, and included his cell phone number so they could discuss it more. Trump did not pick up the phone to call. Instead, he posted Ramos's cell phone on social media. Ramos discovered a few million people had access to his cell phone number only after landing from a flight and finding his voice mailbox full of obscene messages.

Ramos remained dogged in his pursuit of Trump, now albeit with less diplomacy. He was determined to get the candidate to explain just how he planned to build a wall across the southern border and deport 11 million people. On August 25, during a Trump news conference in Iowa, Ramos stood up. As was his custom, he didn't begin his question with a question; he began with a statement. Trump tried to ignore him, but Ramos, known for both his charm and his determination, refused to sit down.

"I have the right to ask a question," Ramos insisted.

"No, you don't. You haven't been called," Trump replied. "Go back to Univision." For the millions of Univision viewers who would later watch the clip dubbed in Spanish, as well as those who watched on Univision's English-language TV network Fusion, he might as well have said "Go back to Mexico," where Ramos had been born and had gotten his start in journalism.

As Ramos continued to press Trump on how he could deport 11 million people and build a wall across the southern border, Trump looked over toward his security guards. A moment later, a guard with a buzz cut, who was a head taller than Ramos, pushed him out.

"Don't touch me," Ramos insisted. "I have the right to ask a question."

Outside, in the lobby, a Trump supporter confronted Ramos. "Get out of my country," the man growled, perhaps unaware that Ramos had become a US citizen in 2008.

Back inside, ABC's Tom Llamas and MSNBC's Kasie Hunt asked about Ramos. First Trump insisted he didn't know Ramos, who only a few months before had graced the cover of *Time* and whose private phone number Trump had shared with the world. Then he seemed to backtrack, saying he'd be happy to have the Univision anchor return.

After being escorted back in, Ramos again began his question with a statement. "You cannot deny citizenship to children in this country," he told Trump, referring to proposals to bar from automatic citizenship the U.S.-born children of undocumented immigrants. "You cannot—"

"Why do you say that?" Trump interrupted.

"Because you cannot do that . . . You'd have to change the Constitution to do that—"

"Well . . . no, excuse me," Trump retorted, talking over Ramos. "A lot of people think that's not right."

When at last Ramos got to his original question about how Trump planned to build the wall, the candidate's response was simple: "Very easy, I'm a builder."

In the coverage of the incident that day, much of the mainstream media focused on whether Trump was too thin-skinned, whether Ramos was an objective journalist or an advocate, and whether by making a statement before his question, he had been grandstanding. In fact, he would later say it was the undocumented activists who had influenced him to speak up and not back down.

"In Iowa, I was thinking what would a DREAMER do with Donald Trump?" Ramos said. "I decided to stand up because they wouldn't be seated. I decided to keep talking because they wouldn't keep silent."

Following the Ramos-Trump exchange, few media pundits focused on how after years of internal and external analysis in which the Republican Party had concluded it needed to do a better job reaching out to Latinos and other immigrants, the party's new mantra seemed simply to be "Let's build a wall."

United We Dream couldn't get involved directly in politics due to its status as a 501(c)(3) nonprofit. But now it decided that staying out of the election altogether could have devastating effects for millions of young undocumented immigrants and their families. It created a new arm, United We Dream Action, which, as a separate 501(c)(4) group, could get involved in limited political activity.

Top young immigrant activists had already begun lining up with the candidates. United We Dream's director of advocacy and policy, Lorella Praeli, who had taken over from Gaby Pacheco, joined Hillary Clinton's campaign in May. Erika Andiola signed up for Bernie Sanders's campaign that fall.

Hareth thought about joining one or the other, but she held back. In part, after three years of activism and fighting for her father while trying to finish school, she wanted to focus on her studies. Also, neither of the candidates inspired her. In 2014, during the unaccompanied-minor crisis, Hillary Clinton had echoed the Obama administration's stance that children who crossed the border should be sent back as quickly as possible to their families in Central America.

In many ways, it was a practical statement. "Just because your child gets across the border, that doesn't mean the child gets to stay. So, we don't want to send a message that is contrary to our laws or will encourage more children to make that dangerous journey," she said.

Her views were nuanced, but she made clear that children who could be returned to family members in their home countries should be: "They should be sent back as soon as it can be determined who the responsible adults in their families are."[27]

For Hareth, the notion that children fleeing gang violence, abuse, dire poverty, or all of the above should be sent back as quickly as possible was heartbreaking.

Then, in the winter of 2015, she was one of several young immigrants invited to a roundtable with Sanders. She liked his talking points about helping unaccompanied minors, ending mass detention, and pushing for executive action and reform, ideas she imagined Erika and other immigration activists working with his team had encouraged. But after the cameras stopped rolling, the candidate didn't seem much interested in talking with her and the other young immigrants. He seemed tired.

Hareth wasn't the only one on the fence. The members of United

We Dream Action, like those of many progressive organizations, were split over whether to take direct action in favor of Clinton or Sanders or stay neutral.

In mid-January, the Supreme Court announced it would accept the Obama administration's appeal against Texas, a signal that the nation's top justices believed it was time to weigh in on both immigration and Obama's efforts to expand the powers of the presidency. More than three hundred civil rights, social groups, and labor organizations signed an amicus brief, urging the court to end the injunction and allow the program to move forward. Law enforcement agencies from Los Angeles County, Boston, El Paso, Salt Lake City, and Dearborn, Michigan, as well as local representatives from a hundred cities and counties, also weighed in, supporting the measure.

With the court's conservative majority likely to favor states' rights as well as a tough stance on illegal immigration, the top immigrant activists and their fellow advocates didn't hold out much hope. Then the day before Valentine's Day, Supreme Court justice Antonin Scalia died, leaving the court with only eight justices and a roughly even ideological split. That changed things. But the Republican-led Senate refused to hold a hearing to consider Obama's pick to replace Scalia, throwing off all bets as to what the court might do.

By early 2016, it also became apparent that the fast-track deportations Obama had promised back in 2014, when he had first announced the expansion of DACA, were in full swing. Immigration and Customs Enforcement officials acknowledged the stepped-up efforts in January.

"This past weekend, Immigration and Customs Enforcement (ICE) engaged in concerted, nationwide enforcement operations to take into custody and return at a greater rate adults who entered this country illegally with children," DHS secretary Jeh Johnson said a statement. "This should come as no surprise. I have said publicly for months that individuals who constitute enforcement priorities, including families and unaccompanied children, will be removed."[28]

The young activists awaited the Court's ruling as the presidential race heated up.

IN THE FALL of 2015, Isabel won a scholarship to the City University of New York's PhD program to study sociology. Felipe was worn out by commuting between Tampa and Washington, DC, for his work with United We Dream, and by the separation from Isabel. They also needed money now that Isabel was going back to school. Felipe took a job at a tech company seeking to expand its philanthropic arm, where he was paid to look at struggles around the globe, including education reform efforts in his native Brazil.

In Brazil, he saw a different kind of activism, one based on collective storytelling rather than that of the individual. "They talk about 'This happened to our village. Then the military came,' and they tell their personal stories, but it's about the larger community," he said. "We've been telling our individual stories first, in order to get at the community."

Maybe, he thought, the immigrant rights activists needed to better explain how their individual stories fit within the larger narrative of the country. The collective story was hardly a new form of activism—it had been the bedrock of the 1960s civil rights movement—but it was one that the DREAMers had often rejected in lieu of the Horatio Alger–style American success story. The image of individual young undocumented immigrants who through hard work could successfully pursue the American dream had been effective in capturing the nation's attention. But Felipe wondered if new tactics were now needed.

Something else happened when he started visiting Brazil. Much to his amazement, his extended family welcomed Isabel, with trepidation at first but eventually with open, if slightly bewildered, arms. Felipe's mother still refused to recognize Isabel, let alone Felipe's marriage. Yet Felipe no longer spoke of her rejection with the pained longing of a child but rather with the cool detachment of an adult.

"That's how she feels. It's the Evangelical Church she belongs to," he said.

He and Isabel moved into the basement of a house in Queens, which they shared with friends and called Casa Mariposa, a nod to the adopted immigrant symbol of the butterfly. Felipe kept their fridge stocked with milk and cheese—just because he could. Having cheese in the house was still his daily reminder: "I'm okay. I have enough."

In March 2016, they threw a housewarming and thirtieth birthday party for Felipe, turning it into a fund-raiser for his old group GetEQUAL.

They invited friends from across their lives: LGBTQ and Black Lives Matter activists and members of United We Dream. Laura Figueroa, Felipe's old high school confidante who'd invited him to the church, came, as did Monona Yin of the Four Freedoms Fund, a champion of the Florida Immigrant Coalition, where Felipe and Isabel had met. One friend brought a cake, a sloping, teetering mass of spongy blocks frosted in bright colors in homage to the *favelas* (shantytowns) near Rio, where Felipe had grown up.

Felipe dressed up, sporting a blue button-down shirt. Isabel chose a short red dress with lipstick and heels to match. Felipe grinned as Isabel descended the stairs. As Isabel increasingly defied gender labels, he'd wondered if he'd still be as attracted to the person he'd fallen so hard for back in 2008. Turned out the answer was a resounding yes. Isabel's fierce independence, whether it took the form of walking to Washington, refusing to shake the president's hand, or putting on a little red dress, was part of what attracted Felipe to his husband. But it was what Isabel's evolving identity said about his own self that gave Felipe pause. He'd spent so many years fighting with his family and the world to be recognized as a proud gay man, an "UndocuQueer." He was no longer undocumented, but he was a staunch member of the LGBTQ community. Yet now, if strangers asked the name of his partner, more than likely they would assume he had a wife. If Isabel identified more as a woman, Felipe wondered if he could still claim his identity as a queer man.

But as Felipe watched his naturally introverted husband making an effort to be social that night, escaping only occasionally to refill the bowls of white beans and plates of ham, French macaroons and empanadas, he thought once more of his secret wish. What he wanted, maybe not for this birthday, but someday soon, was to become a father. Isabel was still unsure, wondering if they could swing it between their jobs and educational responsibilities. They needed to save more money, too. Unsaid were the other concerns: they likely couldn't afford private adoption, and they wondered if they would be approved through the state-run process. *Someday*, thought Felipe.

Later in the evening, friends offered toasts. Isabel reached over to gently tug Felipe's ear and thanked everyone for coming, for being part of their adopted family. Then they turned and wrapped their arms round Felipe. "Felipe is like the greatest thing that has ever happened to me, and I adore him and I worship him—" Isabel blushed happily.

Finally Felipe spoke. He'd written a poem for the occasion, imagining all he'd ever wanted to tell his mother and all he'd ever wanted to tell the world. It was, as always, a grand and dramatic flourish:

"Meu Filho [my son], the moon shined on you. That's how my mother recounts the night I was born. . . . In a world where you are nothing but an illegal, in a world where you are reduced to just a faggot. In a world where you are mostly broke. I understood. I understood my canvas was rained with blood and strife. Ten thousand, nine hundred and fifty-eight days later I'm still here, for reasons still unknown to me. . . . I am the green grass outside the Miami airport. I reek of the open sewer in Duque de Caxias. I am the Cristo Redentor in Río. I am the best and worst, I'm still living a dream. But if you ask me really, I'm nothing but my mother's son."

ONE MONTH LATER, the Supreme Court heard oral arguments in the Texas case. On April 17, the night before the justices would hear the case, a group from DREAMer Mothers in Action, middle-aged women wearing hot pink T-shirts, huddled under a makeshift tarp on the wide stairs of the Supreme Court building. So much had changed since their children had first come out publicly as undocumented immigrants. Now these women, inspired by their sons and daughters, regularly attended protests and kept up their own steady stream of social media. That night they kept vigil so the younger activists could get sleep for the morning. Nearby candles encircled a poster that demonstrators had left a few hours before with the photos of hundreds of people: mothers, fathers, and children—some who had already been deported, some whose fate could soon be decided by the Court.

Already a line of several dozen people snaked around the building as activists on both sides sought the few coveted spots available to hear the arguments. It was easy to tell who was there representing each side of the debate. Those who favored the president's actions seemed cautiously optimistic and chatted freely.

Near the front of the line, roughly a dozen people sat comfortably in chairs, smartly dressed in warm parkas against the cold midnight winds. They didn't seem to know much about the case but appeared to be hired to hold places for others, a common practice before big Supreme Court cases.

A few seats down from them, an older man in glasses and a New York Yankees cap piped up as one journalist began chatting with those at the front of the line. "You don't have an opinion," he spat out to the group of men and women serving as place holders, "at least not while I'm paying you." The man declined to identify himself nor comment on which side he was representing, though it seemed clear he had not come with the immigrants.

Above, in the quiet of the night, American flags whipped in the breeze, clanking against the poles, as if to shout, "*This* is America! *This* is America!"

By the next morning, the Supreme Court steps were filled mostly with immigrants and their advocates. Senator Dick Durbin and Representatives Luis Gutiérrez and Zoe Lofgren, a Democrat from California, mingled with activists before entering the court. Josh Bernstein had come as well. A smaller contingent supporting the states' case also gathered, but their chants were generally drowned out by the larger pro-immigrant crowd.* The demonstrators held signs and chanted but were careful not to provoke the authorities. United We Dream and the veteran organizers wanted no arrests that day, nothing that could hurt their legal case. Most notable, though, was not so much who was standing outside the court, but who was allowed in. Gaby Pacheco, along with journalist turned advocate Jose Antonio Vargas, had been invited to attend the hearing. No longer were the DREAMers looking down from the marble gallery at those in power. No longer were they simply shouting from the outside. Now they were invited inside those marble halls to address the nation's most powerful judicial body.

---

* It wasn't the only demonstration that morning. Across the street, on the Capitol grounds, hundreds of activists showed up to demonstrate against corporate donations to political campaigns. Ben Cohen and Jerry Greenfield, the founders of Ben & Jerry's ice cream, were among three hundred protesters arrested for unlawful demonstration activities on federal grounds. That mostly white, union-backed protest stood in stark contrast to the mostly Latino demonstrators across NE First Street, but eventually they came over and offered their support. (Diane Ruggiero and Daniella Diaz, "Co-founders of Ben & Jerry's Arrested at Capitol," CNN, April 19, 2016. http://www.cnn.com/2016/04/18/politics/ben-jerry-democracy-awakens/.)

13

GRADUATION

Hareth Andrade-Ayala shows off her diploma at her home in Arlington, Virginia, May 2016.

Dario tossed sneakers, cologne, Clorox wipes, and books by C. S. Lewis and Junot Díaz into the boxes strewn around his bed. He stripped off his T-shirt and wiped sweat from his face. His cramped attic room in Harvard's Leverett House was cozy in the winter, but with no air-conditioning, the early-May heat wave had turned the room into a dry sauna. Hard to believe that nearly two years before he'd been packing his clothes in another cramped room in Mexico. And now he was graduating. He looked out over the house master's second-story balcony and the green quadrangle below, the site of spring lectures and tomorrow's ceremony. Beyond, rowers cut through the surface of the Charles River in smooth, confident strokes.

He'd missed many house events, preoccupied with his mom, his classes, girls . . . too often girls. He shrugged. Too late to worry about that now.

Since returning to school in January 2015, he'd moved back on campus and tried to stay out of trouble. He'd slimmed down, become captain of the Boxing Club, and cut down on his drinking. He'd begun mentoring younger Latino students, although in reality that often meant letting them tag along with him to parties.

Dario figured as long as nothing too horrible happened, those were the requisite crazy nights you were supposed to experience at least once at college, nights too many undocumented immigrants shied away from for fear of disappointing their parents or making one false move.

He set one of the boxes on the bed and carefully added his parents' wedding video, along with blown-up photos of his mother. He would leave the silver box next to his computer, the one that held his mother's wedding ring and crucifix, for last. Dario tossed into a box the negative results from an HIV test he'd recently taken, unsure of how much health care coverage he'd have after leaving college but presuming it would be good to have. In went the "Thanks, but no thanks" letter from the sperm donor office, his awards, his DACA file, papers, sweaters, a soccer ball.

Downstairs, families buzzed into and out of the dorm, women with elegant bobs, men in navy blue sports jackets who smiled benignly while somehow still making clear they owned the world. Dario avoided the scene and finished packing. He would miss the afternoon pregraduation speaker, Steven Spielberg. Although he had grown up binge watching *Jaws*, *Raiders of the Lost Ark*, and the like, now it felt like a point of pride as a film student to say he found them too predictable. You could time to the minute when a plot turn was likely to happen.

His own film was coming along: the story of his mother's decline, his experience in Mexico, his parents' history, all set against the Aztec creation myth. He'd turned in the first half as his senior thesis and received top honors. His dad wanted to see it, but he refused to show it to him. If his dad didn't like it, Dario wasn't sure he could bring himself to finish it.

Soon his friend Oscar Velazquez would arrive. The two had gone to high school together, both taking buses across the city to attend their magnet high school. Oscar had studied microbiology at Cornell University and now worked at a Columbia University research lab in Manhattan. He, too, was undocumented. A third high school buddy, Daniel Artiga, was also graduating from Harvard and would join them for the festivities. Dario would spend his last couple of nights with these high school friends and other undocumented and immigrant Harvard youths. He'd spent his early years running to and away from this group, but he no longer feared being associated with them. Besides, he now realized he didn't have a choice. They were linked, and they understood one another.

Dario wondered what it would be like in the fall without his crew. He'd gotten a small fellowship to work on the film and planned to spend the summer in Boston doing just that. For the fall, he'd lined up an internship at the Dumbarton Oaks Research Library and Collection in Washington, DC. The Harvard Trustee–run institution had a pre-Columbian collection that might be relevant to the film. He still couldn't believe it: a year in Washington, in Georgetown, no less, getting to learn about his own history, ancient as it was. He was still waiting for his DACA application to be reinstated, his official identity and the necessary paper to finalize the internship, but at least for now he had the humanitarian parole.

He carefully laid out his clothes for the next day's official graduation festivities. He glanced over at his wallet on the desk, and he smiled, reminded of the vending machine heist.

A week or so before, Dario and his friends had hijacked the experimental art project of a fellow student who had put the entire contents of his wallet into a school vending machine—an exploration of how commercialized human identity had become.

Dario had heard about the project and had been both captivated and irritated at how much privilege it required to renounce the very documents he so desperately needed. Dario, too, wanted to shout to the world that his identity, the value of his self, was far more than a piece of paper, a driver's license, but that was a luxury he couldn't afford.

Instead, he and several other undocumented friends had gotten the rolls of quarters the old-fashioned machine required and bought the entire contents of the wallet. Then they had put up an anonymous ransom note: they would return the items in the wallet only if their classmate could verifiably demonstrate his identity with transcripts, a birth certificate, a personal letter from the young man's mother, and enough social media posts to prove he'd been in the country for the last five years—a nod to all the requirements they'd had to complete for the Deferred Action for Childhood Arrivals program. To their surprise, the student agreed. A few exchanges later, and he submitted to a fake "DHS" interview led by a friend of Dario's pretending to be an immigration officer. The prank ended with a few shared drinks and the return of the wallet and its original contents: credit cards, cash, and a meal plan card, which turned out to be the most essential item in the billfold.

Dario finished the afternoon packing. He wasn't going to miss all the events. After a quick shower, he donned a crisp white oxford-cloth shirt, jeans, and shiny caramel-colored loafers and galloped down the stairs to join the cocktail already under way in the Leverett quad.

Dario's trip to Mexico had turned him into a minor celebrity in his dorm. He made the rounds with the assistant deans and professors, but he spent little time with his fellow graduates. Since he'd missed a year of school, this wasn't his original class, and he'd kept more to himself since his return. He chatted in the shade with the older ladies from the cafeteria staff, who fussed over him in Spanish in between refilling pitchers and tidying tables.

A variety of languages and dialects floated across the green from around the world, as parents ordered their children in near-universal tones to stand up straighter, not to stain their good shirts, to enjoy one of their last afternoons at this hallowed place. Many of the parents had been born outside the United States, but it seemed to Dario that most of the families were important elsewhere. A father might be wearing a kurta instead of a blazer, but in his measured confidence he was the same. They still operated in a different world, and Dario looked on enviously. One day he would no longer have to fake it, either.

Later they packed their boxes into Daniel's family's van. Daniel and his father would drive back to California with the graduates' belongings. Dario's father had flown in using his driver's license as ID thanks to a 2015 state law that allowed California to issue licenses to undocumented immigrants. That night the young men went to pick up Dario's grandfather and uncle from the airport. Dario hadn't seen either man since he'd left Mexico. He bent down and hugged his grandfather, nearly crushing the small man in the leather jacket and black fedora.

The next day, at the Leverett House graduation ceremony, Dario stood in line on the grass in his black mortarboard and gown, sporting dark sunglasses, and waiting for his name to be called.

"Darrrrrrghio Guerrero," the faculty dean and physics professor, Howard Georgi, called out, rolling the Spanish "r" with a guttural Russian-like twist, a gesture at once earnest and a reminder of how foreign his name still sounded rolling off the lips of Harvard faculty. Dario didn't care. As he walked up to receive his diploma, he shook Georgi's hand, then impulsively hugged him, flashing a peace sign to his family.

"¡Ay güey!" Dario's father called out, falling back on the all-purpose

Mexican equivalent of "dude!" and clapping his son on the back after the ceremony. Andrea leaned against her older brother as he proudly displayed his diploma. Dario tousled her hair as he answered questions from a Telemundo reporter who'd covered his return from Mexico. What would he tell other young immigrants in the country who thought Harvard was out of reach?

It took Dario three tries and a bit of coaching to say what he wanted to in Spanish. "For undocumented immigrants who think this is impossible, they have to visualize their goals, work hard, and they will accomplish it. It might take time, but it's possible. Anything's possible!" he said giddily. And in that moment he believed it.

As they headed back to the dorms, women from the janitorial staff stopped Dario, seeking photos with him as if he were a movie star.

"*Félicitaciones, hijo!*" they cried.

That night, the family went to the Harvard Club for dinner along with hundreds of other proud families. It was their first real reunion without Rocio. There was no empty seat at the table. And yet there was. Dario and his siblings sat at a table against the dark wood-paneled wall and ate mostly in silence, looking around at the other families chatting animatedly, at home there. It was Dario Sr. who had wanted to splurge on the night, but now he wondered if they wouldn't have had a better time elsewhere. Andrea spilled a cup of water, and her eyes darted nervously to her brother.

"It's okay," he said gently and reached over to help her cut her steak. He looked over at his brother and ribbed him about using the appetizer plate for the main buffet. Everyone started complaining about having way too many plates and forks, cracking one another up as they dug into their desserts.

A WEEK BEFORE, Hareth had donned her own cap and black gown, kicking off her sneakers in the car and pulling on her heels just as she arrived at school. She drove alone, ahead of her parents. Hareth knew they would likely be late, maybe arguing, and she didn't need more stress.

Her graduation from Trinity Washington University in DC, just a few miles from the Capitol, was a more low-key affair. But the button-bursting parental pride emanating from the parents and the nervous smiles of the soon-to-be graduates were the same.

Homemade gold letters on one mortarboard spelled out "WE MADE IT" and spoke for many others. Unlike at Harvard, where graduation seemed all but guaranteed, many of the African American and Latina students alongside Hareth were among the first in their family to receive a college diploma in the United States—or anywhere.

Trinity had once been a popular school among strong, independent white Catholic women from the Northeast looking to come to Washington. But after Georgetown University and other local schools had opened their doors to women, its population had plummeted until the school had begun to recruit minority youths. Now its reputation as an affordable alternative in the nation's capital was on the rise, its classes once again full.

The changes, which reflected the broader demographic shifts under way across the country, had made some alumnae uncomfortable. Many of the graduates that day had worked full-time as they earned their degrees or managed families. Trinity didn't "look like" the school these alumnae remembered.

A few years before, President Patricia McGuire had finally called them out: "Just beyond our front gates, there are countless women in the city, nation and world who still can reap great benefits from an educational paradigm focused on their success," she said in a 2008 interview with the local *Georgetown Voice*. "The fact that the majority of these women happen to be African American and Latina today does not mean that our mission has changed, as some have asked."[1]

The Andrades arrived just before the ceremony began. Haziel sat between her parents, holding the slender, elegant hand of her mother and the thick, rough fingers of her father. Claudia was at her national middle school basketball tournament, and Betty discreetly followed the game via WhatsApp even as she listened to the speakers.

Trinity alumna and former Bryn Mawr College president Dr. Jane Dammen McAuliffe gave the keynote speech, recognizing the global threats facing the next generation of graduates while condemning Trump's December 2015 call for "a total and complete shutdown of Muslims entering the United States until our country's representatives can figure out what the hell is going on."[2]

McAuliffe told the graduates that yes, war and savagery were committed in the name of Islam, but, she added, "that does not warrant a situation in which Muslim American kids start asking their parents if it's safe here, if they're really welcome, if they're really American." She closed by urging the students to get out and vote.

Betty's thoughts stretched back to Hareth's first day of kindergarten. She had been so worried her daughter would dissolve into tears, but she hadn't, and when Hareth came home at the end of the day, pigtails askew, stockings ripped and stained, she was grinning, eyes sparkling, thrilled with her new adventure.

Betty reached further back to her own years in school. She had dropped out of university to support Mario so he could finish his degree. She'd always wanted to return, but there had never been time or money. Now at least her eldest daughter had fulfilled her dream, and Haziel, too, would be leaving home soon for her own adventure, the first in the family to go away to college. Betty had wished for Hareth to have that freedom but was happy to keep her close to home at least for a little longer as Hareth sorted out her future.

After the ceremony, Mario embraced his daughter under drizzling rain, brushing away tears. Hareth had wanted to celebrate at a restaurant, as many of her friends had, but there were too many people who wanted to join them, and it was too expensive. So Tía Eli had offered to prepare the feast.

She and Hareth rarely talked now about the years when the girls had lived with her. Hareth sometimes worried it would hurt her mother to be reminded of that time. In any event, Eliana was the type to move forward, not look back. As Hareth stepped through the front door, once again in her sneakers, and saw the living room decked out with white-clothed tables, fluted glasses with folded gold confetti napkins, and centerpieces of spring violets, she sucked in her breath at the transformation. Once again, her aunt had come through for her.

More guests arrived that night: Ana Avendaño from the AFL-CIO; former school board member Emma Violand-Sanchez, Hareth's long-time Bolivian mentor; even "Mr. Monopoly," her former high school adviser, Robert Garcia. Claudia arrived, still wearing her number 24 basketball shirt. The team had won, and now they were headed to the national finals in Myrtle Beach, South Carolina. Betty hugged her daughter and immediately began to worry whether she and Mario would be able to attend, whether it would be safe for them to travel. But she tucked those fears away. Now there was something else to celebrate.

As they took their seats at the table, Mario addressed the group in Spanish. "I am so happy, so content with my daughter who has given us so much happiness today, well, really every day," he said. "Thank you to you all for collaborating with Hareth. Maybe without your help and support we wouldn't be here today—" He paused, waiting for Hareth to translate, as was the family custom.

She blushed but did her job.

"We are so proud of you," he said, turning to his daughter. "Continue forward, always with the same enthusiasm—"

Hareth stopped translating. "I've already forgotten the rest," she said quickly, looking at the floor.

"I am so happy tonight," Betty joined her husband, speaking in clear English. "There are—there are no words to express how happy I am."

Claudia gave her eldest sister a hug. Everyone was graduating, she noted: Hareth from college, Haziel to college. "I'm the only one who will be left in the house," she said sadly.

Hareth thought about Haziel leaving, leapfrogging ahead of her to be the first in the family to attend a residential college at the Virginia Commonwealth University in Richmond. She would be left behind for the first time.

Finally, it was Hareth's turn to speak.

She pointed over to her aunt. "I don't get to thank her a lot, so, *gracias*, Tía, for making this possible." She stopped and took a deep breath before saying, for once, the unsaid: "She loves me so much, and she was there for me when my parents weren't able to be."

Hareth lifted her glass to the rest of the room. "There was a time when I was so confused. I didn't know if I was going to be able to finish," she said, "but obviously with all your friendship and mentoring and calls and the family, going through the tough times we've gone through, I can say it was definitely worth it."

IN THE SPRING of 2016, after more than a decade in exile, Marie Gonzalez's mother, Marina Morales Moreno, was finally able to request permanent residency in the United States. The ten-year ban had run out, and now Marie petitioned for her mother's green card. Starting over in Costa Rica had been difficult enough, but without Marvin, Marina had little to keep her there. She wouldn't have minded splitting her time between the two countries, but she was afraid DHS might revoke her visa once again. Better to be safe and make a permanent move. Marie and Chapin had just moved to New Mexico for his work, and she'd given birth to baby Lorena the previous summer. With two babies under age three, having her mother there would be a godsend.

Once more, though, government bureaucracy seemed to be playing a cruel game with their lives. The green card was approved but did not appear. USCIS officials couldn't seem to locate it. Later, they told Marie there had been a card production error. A dozen calls and email chains later, Marina finally received the paper that would allow her to call the United States home. Summer rolled around, and Marie's girls were old enough to be in school and day care. Marina could also watch them, and for the first time, Marie felt overwhelmed by the choices ahead of her. New Mexico was more expensive than Missouri. She needed to work.

"I just don't know where I'm supposed to be," she said one afternoon as she gently bounced her youngest daughter on her lap. "So many times, I've had to wait for someone other than me, but now it's up to me, and it's hard because I've gotten into this comfort zone."

She considered paralegal work. Once she had wanted to be a lawmaker or a lawyer. She thought of all the people who had to fill out legal forms, immigration related or otherwise, without the help she'd received over the years. It was all so damn confusing, and she was fluent in English. She could help those who weren't. Yet she struggled to make the numbers add up between the cost of advanced education, the nonprofit world, and child care. The separation from her own parents, even as a young adult, still tore at her. She wanted to be there for Araceli and Lorena, as well as for Chapin, who had supported her for so long. No matter what she decided, she would be letting someone down.

"Early on, people had projected so much success onto me," she mused. "And I didn't really live up to that. I have these degrees, and I have this ability. People are like 'You are a stay-at-home mom? What are you going to do?'"

It was no longer an undocumented immigrant or even an immigrant dilemma, yet the pressure of the DREAMer identity to always represent well, to give back, hung over Marie. And then fate interceded in her favor. She found a job through a small employment firm that allowed her to work part-time. It was a low-level government job, but it required a security clearance, and, unlike her father, Marie didn't have to worry about what a background check would turn up. Friends told her half jokingly she should consider running for office. As she watched the presidential campaign, Marie, less than half jokingly, said she would think about it.

EARLY ON in her presidential campaign, Hillary Clinton promised once again to introduce a bill for comprehensive immigration reform within the first hundred days of being in office. Her Democratic rival, Senator Bernie Sanders, was an unknown among most Latinos, and he had to play catch-up. Sanders had arrived in the US Senate in 2007, just in time for the last major push for a compromise immigration bill, and had sided with the AFL-CIO against the bill over its lenient guest worker provisions. By the time the 2013 Gang of Eight bill had come to a vote, Sanders had changed his mind. Something, he felt, was better than nothing, and he had backed the comprehensive immigration legislation, guest worker provisions and all. Still, immigration was not a hot topic in Vermont, and it was not among his best talking points.

Hiring Erika Andiola and a young charismatic immigrant activist and attorney named César Vargas for his campaign began to turn things around. They helped arrange for Sanders to visit the Arizona border in March and speak about immigration reform. But Sanders did more than focus on deportations and the border; he linked the stepped-up incarceration of immigrants to the broader US prison system that had made the United States—home to only 4 percent of the world's population—responsible for nearly 22 percent of the world's known prison population.[3] And he reminded his audiences that black Americans made up nearly half of those prisoners.

For Erika, it was clear the immigration movement had a lot to learn from the Black Lives Matter activists. They had forced open the conversation about race and the US justice system that went beyond passing any specific law, to the fundamental American ideals of equality laid out in the Constitution. So much of the immigration movement had been wrapped around legislation, around citizenship, essentially focused on changing the law. Now Erika and many others increasingly focused on the need to change the perception of the immigration system itself—a system that increasingly criminalized thousands of undocumented immigrants.

More and more, the young activists were taking what they learned and branching out with new organizations. Tania Unzueta, the Chicago advocate, helped found the Chicago-based Mijente (My People), whose mission was to support low-income communities of color.[4] One of the first Mijente actions was a peaceful mass protest with local black youth activist groups at the 2015 International Association of Chiefs of Police conference held in Chicago. Carlos Saavedra from Boston worked on another new group called Cosecha (Harvest), which encouraged immigrants to participate in mass work stoppages to highlight the nation's reliance on their labor.

Changes were evident at United We Dream during its annual retreat in June 2016. Following the DACA and DAPA orders, the group had taken more than a year to step back, look at its accomplishments, and assess its future direction. It had grown so much in such a short time. The old structure had become unwieldy and even counterproductive.

"It was the first time we'd had the time and breathing room to take stock," United We Dream cofounder and executive director Cristina Jiménez said of the review. What Cristina and others at United We Dream realized was that they still needed to change hearts and minds, but they weren't going to get anywhere without a bigger coalition. "Many people in our movement have stopped talking to [those outside], and we're just talking to ourselves," she said. "We need to push ourselves to be in uncomfortable places and have uncomfortable conversations."

Cristina and the other youth leaders also now understood that citizenship on its own hadn't protected poor black Americans, Muslim Americans, and Latinos from racial profiling, nor did it necessarily provide a living wage for many white Americans. If they truly wanted to help their members, they could not stop at the issue of legalization. In its strategic plan for 2020, the coalition recommitted itself to promoting "womxn's rights" and to working beyond the Latinx communities, using gender neutral terms for both groups for the first time. The organization also promised additional nonviolence and grassroots training for up-and-coming leaders, and it committed to fighting more local battles to build up a stronger grassroots national movement— the same tactic organizers had used more than a decade before with the in-state tuition fights.

The UWD artwork reflected the shift. A new logo depicted immigrants in a range of colors and included one woman with a hijab. At United We Dream's first congress in 2009, all the participants had fit into one classroom. Now, as its annual conference approached, organizers scrambled to find hotel space for the thousands of participants headed to Houston. The event's sponsors had expanded as well and now included Planned Parenthood, SEIU, and other unions, as well as the Ford Foundation. Participants came from as far as Great Britain, where they had begun their own undocumented immigrant coalition modeled on the efforts of UWD.

This time the black immigrant coalition UndocuBlack Network made its voice heard at the conference, calling out the organizers when speakers' Spanish phrases or jokes weren't quickly translated into English for the non-Spanish-speaking immigrants, even at one point challenging the keynote speaker, Jorge Ramos. When he repeated the common refrain that immigrants were not criminals, several black immigrants pushed back.

"What is this racial dynamic when we say that we are not criminals? What is the subtext with this? The subtext is that the black people are criminal," they argued. Ramos, they said, should call out the unjust laws that turned poor and desperate people, regardless of their nationality, into criminals—rather than perpetuate this false distinction.

Ramos was gracious. He listened. He didn't have a quick answer, and he didn't pretend otherwise. This was new territory for him, too. It was an argument the young undocumented activists would increasingly put forward. No longer did they want to be used as the counterpoint to criminals, be it their own parents or anyone else. And, like Hareth, they questioned the easy distinction in the catchphrase "families, not felons."

Many of the older leaders like Felipe, Tania, and Marie did not attend the gathering. Nor did Gaby Pacheco, who was now helping run a nonprofit scholarship program for undocumented students cofounded by former *Washington Post* publisher Donald Graham.

But Hareth, still enjoying postgraduation freedom, booked a flight at the last minute. No longer was she the minor celebrity from the Aloe Blacc video or the AFL-CIO speech. Now she sat quietly in the massive hall, enjoying lunch while catching up with old friends about their lives, marriages, new jobs, recounting relatives who had been deported. She marveled at how young some of the participants seemed. Many of those attending were first-timers. Hareth had been considered a baby activist when she went public with her immigration status as a senior in high school. Now some high school sophomores had traveled across the country to attend the congress with their teachers.

Organizers had planned a march for the following day at Houston's massive downtown jail complex, where law enforcement officials had partnered with the federal government to check inmates' immigration status. An up-and-coming UWD leader from Connecticut, Tashi Sanchez-Llaury, gave the crowd some lighthearted practical advice. "I know us girls look really good in heels," she told the crowd of newbie activists, "but tomorrow is *not* the day." Then she got serious. Above all: the participants were to remain orderly and nonviolent. UWD was straddling unchartered space, gaining permission from, and working closely with, law enforcement on a march that would protest law enforcement.

Some younger activists saw it as a cop-out. Others saw it as the necessary compromise for a grassroots organization that also held a seat at the table during White House meetings. The group's leadership, now paid, included some activists who were the oldest in the movement and now long undocumented themselves. Occasionally young activists groused about their earning salaries to advocate for undocumented youth. Others saw the United We Dream staff as providing necessary access, continuity, and stability—key players needed to balance the even more confrontational wings of the movement, and to educate newly out undocumented teens about their broader history.

The changes at United We Dream reflected the demographic changes of the movement. Like Marie and Felipe, like Erika and Dario and Alex, many young undocumented immigrants were no longer limited to working as activists. They were out of school. They had loans to repay and families to support, and they could fill out W-2s. They were increasingly part of the US economy.

"We are infiltrating," United We Dream advocacy director Greisa Martinez told the conference participants. "They just don't know it. We are already in health care, government, business."

Overlooked by many during the conference were Jorge Ramos's more sobering words. At the end of his talk, he urged the teens and young adults to understand and respect why their parents had remained silent for so many years.

"Your parents had to fight in a completely different way," he reminded them. "The fact that you are here right now means that your parents were right. . . . They needed to be silent."

The parents of those at the conference were part of a generation that had sacrificed it all for their children, Ramos told them. They were in a sense a lost generation. Even if their parents did eventually adjust their status, people like Betty and Mario, Dario Sr., and Marina would have spent the better part of their lives to a degree invisible and in fear.

"It doesn't matter what happens," he continued, referring to the Supreme Court's pending decision on whether to expand temporary protection to millions more undocumented immigrants but also more subtly to the presidential election. "You're gonna keep fighting," he said. It was both a statement and a demand. "We cannot lose another generation."

ON JUNE 23, 2016, the Supreme Court issued its ruling on the administration's expanded DACA order. It was one line: "The judgment is affirmed by an equally divided Court."

There was no accompanying opinion, no tea leaves to examine. For now the case was done, the expanded legal protection Obama had announced in 2014 on indefinite hold. Millions of immigrants would remain in the shadows as they had for decades, working and driving illegally, unable to obtain medical insurance, and fearful of reporting criminal abuse, lest they be deported. It was a blow for the young activists and their advocates, who knew the order could easily disappear altogether under the next administration. For Cecilia Muñoz, it was also a chilling predictor of what might happen to DACA. A successful challenge to one part of the program could lay the groundwork for successful challenges to the rest of it. How the lawsuits fared could depend on how strongly the next US attorney general defended the Obama administration's 2012 order.

Less than two months later, the Democratic and Republican parties coalesced, if fitfully, around their candidates. While the GOP doubled down during its convention on its warnings about immigrants, the Democratic Party similarly tightened its message of acceptance and celebration of them, at times evoking an optimism about the country that seemed to ignore the reality of stagnant wages and job losses for many Americans. The prime-time lineups at the two conventions appeared like mirrored negatives of the same photograph, neither fully capturing the true image.

IN THE END, without DACA reinstated, Dario wasn't eligible for the Dumbarton fellowship, even though he tried in vain to use his expired work permit. He was too ashamed to tell his father. He would break the news when he returned to California. On his last night in Washington, he decided to go see the monuments. It was one thing on his Washington to-do list he might be able to accomplish before he left. He and a few friends took a cab from Georgetown to the Lincoln Memorial. They walked from there to the Korean War and World War II memorials, crossing Independence Avenue and continuing around the Tidal Basin to the Franklin Delano Roosevelt Memorial, and getting caught in a crowd of Pokémon GO players. Finally, when they could walk no more, they sat down beneath the rotunda at the Jefferson Memorial.

Dario found a bench apart from his friends. He looked across the marble at the four inscriptions on the towering walls, settling on the fourth. It was not one he remembered learning in school. But that night the carved letters etched into stone demanded his attention. "I am not an advocate for frequent changes in laws and constitutions, but laws and institutions must go hand in hand with the progress of the human mind. As that becomes more developed, more enlightened, as new discoveries are made, new truths discovered and manners and opinions change, with the change of circumstances, institutions must advance also to keep pace with the times," Thomas Jefferson had written some two hundred years before.

"I know there's a reason for all this," Dario said quietly. "I just don't know what it is right now."

HERE TO STAY

*United We Dream veteran leaders Alejandra Ruiz, Walter Barri-
entos, Cristina Jiménez, and Julieta Garibay at the Women's March
in Washington, DC, January 2017.* (COURTESY OF CRISTINA JIMÉNEZ)

Newton's Third Law, "For every action, there is an equal and opposite reaction," holds true in politics as well as physics. On

November 2, 2016, Donald J. Trump was elected president of the United States, overwhelmingly winning the nation's electoral college while losing the popular vote by nearly 3 million votes.

Trump's election was about more than immigration. Yet just as the young activists opened up space for all undocumented immigrants, their power also helped provoke a backlash that culminated in the election of a president who campaigned to drastically reduce immigration. For the first time, they found themselves living under an administration that seemed to struggle over how much to distance itself from its white supremacist supporters—and sometimes whether to distance itself at all.

Trump took the election as a mandate for his immigration plans. "From this day forward, a new vision will govern our land. From this day forward, it's going to be only America first, America first. Every decision on trade, on taxes, on immigration, on foreign affairs will be made to benefit American workers and American families. We must protect our borders," he said in his inaugural address.

He tapped Senator Jeff Sessions of Alabama, the man who had most consistently blocked both the DREAM Act and more comprehensive immigration reform, as attorney general. He made Stephen Miller, a campaign strategist and former Sessions staffer, who strongly supported stringent immigration controls, a top adviser. And he named Steve Bannon, who avowedly viewed Islam as a threat to the United States' Christian core, as one of his most senior advisers, though Bannon would leave just six months later.

Although deportations had increased drastically under Obama, the Trump administration ratcheted up the number of arrests and detentions. It ended the more selective prioritization outlined in the Morton memos, under which the Obama administration had specified which immigrants officials should focus their limited resources on. Now, once again, nearly everyone was a target. Immigration and Customs Enforcement officials conducted seemingly random, well-publicized raids, and Trump ordered DHS to hire 15,000 new agents to round up and process those in the country without authorization.[1] Meanwhile, the backlog in immigration courts continued to rise, and the actual number of deportations fell.[2]

Within months Trump tried to ban immigrants from half a dozen Muslim countries, only to be rebuffed by federal judges in several states. Still, a watered-down version of the ban slowly made its way to the Supreme Court. And the new administration successfully issued new rules to make it more difficult to prove asylum cases. DHS also quickly began seeking bids for the border wall, adding the estimated more than $2 billion into the proposed federal budget, despite having promised voters that Mexico would pay for it. He signaled he would not renew the temporary protected status (TPS), which for years had allowed millions of Haitians, Central Americans, and others who had fled natural and political disasters in their home countries to remain and work legally in the United States.[3] Trump also pardoned Arizona sheriff Joe Arpaio, who had been convicted over the summer in federal court of criminal contempt for continuing to target Latino drivers, despite a preliminary order to stop the practice.

The undocumented activists and their advocates responded quickly to the administration's actions. United We Dream leaders such as Cristina Jiménez and Julieta Garibay worked with their affiliates to set up massive chains of Twitter and texting networks whenever they learned of raids. They began to hold community meetings to teach immigrants their rights and worked with thousands of new allies whom UWD said had begun calling to help: lawyers who didn't specialize in immigration but wondered how they could be of use; community groups that wanted to know how to lobby against deportations, fill out basic immigrant paperwork, or even accompany immigrants to DHS appointments.

Mijente stepped up its organizing. For Tania Unzueta, watching young immigrants with DACA suddenly realize they might lose their cocoon of protection felt like déjà vu.

They are like us back in 2006, barely waking up, she thought.

Jose Antonio Vargas showed up at the president's inaugural speech before Congress and pushed forward with his film festival highlighting the lives of immigrants in America. Even if they couldn't succeed politically, he believed, they could continue to influence American hearts and minds by working with the producers of popular TV shows such as *Superstore* to better reflect the immigrant experience in pop culture.

In a handful of high-profile cases, DACA recipients were detained, but the activists remained outspoken, helping lead the fight to protect so-called sanctuary cities and enlisting the help of celebrities such as Lin-Manuel Miranda, who released a dark single entitled "Immigrants (We Get the Job Done)," which highlighted the struggles of the country's newly arrived workers.

Meanwhile, Colorado Republican representative Mike Coffman floated a bill in the House called the BRIDGE Act to enshrine DACA into law until a permanent immigration bill passed. Florida Republican representative Carlos Curbelo of Miami introduced a new version of the DREAM Act under the title Recognizing America's Children Act. Once more, the young leaders were conflicted over whether to support something that would exclude their parents, especially a bill they believed had so little chance of passing. They had developed new allies among Black Lives Matter activists, reproductive health advocates, Muslim Americans, and the LGBTQ community, all of whom also felt under threat.[4] They supported the Native American protests against the Dakota Access Pipeline.[5] They and the country had changed. They didn't want to be saved. They wanted to organize so they could save themselves and their communities.

In February, Isabel and Felipe moved back to Central Florida. New York had been expensive, and they missed the sunshine. But for Felipe, the 2016 mass shooting at the Pulse nightclub in Orlando, a place he'd frequented and that had welcomed both the LGBTQ and Latino immigrant communities, was a sign: he was needed in his old stomping grounds, and he was needed to bridge the world between the activists and the rest of America.

Felipe became the point person in the Orlando mayor's office heading up outreach to the victims and families of the Pulse massacre, his first government job. Isabel, too, was glad to be back. For so long, Isabel had yearned to be part of the intellectual rigor of academia. Only at the Graduate Center at City University of New York had they realized how much the action on the ground gave them purpose. Isabel went to work at the Florida Immigrant Coalition's Central Florida office, returning to the organization where they had gotten their political start. Now more than ever, Florida would serve as a bellwether state for immigrant rights, and Isabel would help lead that fight.

Before leaving New York for Orlando, Felipe visited his mother in Brazil once again, and for the first time she agreed to meet his husband. Isabel had caught a cold on the long flight, and when Felipe's mother saw them, it was as if a switch flipped. She began to fuss over Isabel, making them chicken soup and frequently checking in on them. Felipe and Isabel stayed with her for a few days, and Felipe later posted Facebook pictures of the three of them standing next to one another, awkwardly at times but finally together.

What has changed after so many years, he wondered, *for her to move from "You're a disgrace" to "I need to make soup for the person you married"?* He tried to ask her, but she never seemed to answer his question. Maybe his younger cousins and uncles had influenced her. Maybe she'd finally seen how happy they were together. Maybe it was just time.

Back in Los Angeles, Dario began helping his father on the administrative side of the business, picking up Andrea from school and overseeing her homework. He began driving for Uber. And in his spare time, he finished his thesis film about his mother's journey, sending it off to festivals in the hope that it might launch his career as a filmmaker. He tried not to think about what would happen if, under the new administration, his DACA application were not reauthorized.

On the other side of Los Angeles, as Alex awaited his final asylum hearing, he worked to implement an HIV-related research study through Children's Hospital Los Angeles, screening at-risk queer men of color. He had begun dating a fellow undocumented immigrant and DACA recipient from Mexico, and in December 2016, the two married. They spent the holidays with Alex's father. On Facebook, where he jokingly listed his profile as an "Exiled Political Whore," Alex shared posts asking for help to cover the nearly $465 fee for those seeking what could be their last DACA renewal. He sympathized with his husband and others who feared the loss of DACA. But he also continued to tweak activists over their focus on such a small segment of the nation's undocumented immigrant community.

Welcome back to our reality, he thought.

Hareth began helping with her father's business, too, ensuring the bookkeeping was up to date. At least for now, with her DACA protected status, she could secure credit cards with roughly half the interest rate her parents were given. Should anything happen to either of them under the new administration, she would be able to step in, and she would be able to care for Claudia and support Haziel. Betty and Mario increasingly feared leaving the house, but they had no choice. They needed to work. They weighed each trip to the grocery store, to a construction site, to one of Claudia's games. Was it necessary? After the election, they argued more. Fear over their future brought long-simmering tensions to the surface.

Hareth stayed out of it, but she wasn't shy about giving her mother advice. *You can't change the politics right now, but you can change you*, Hareth told her. Women older than Betty had taken classes with her at Trinity. Why shouldn't her mother go back to school?

Betty laughed at first but not for long. Slowly she began to map out her dream of finally earning her college degree. She returned to high school to study English and became a top student at her adult continuing education program. If she could pass her English exams, she could apply to community college. She didn't know how she would pay for it, but the family agreed they would find a way. Slowly, things improved between Betty and Mario. They adopted a puppy to fill their semi-empty nest. For the first time since they had left Bolivia, they were working closely together.

Still, by early 2017, Hareth could feel the stress returning, taking its toll on her mind, her throat, even her knees. Life had trained her to be an organizer, an activist, and a leader, yet sometimes she wondered just how all those skills would translate to the rest of her life. She'd found a place in the movement, but outside, she wasn't so sure. She took a part-time job with Vanessa, her father's immigration attorney, even as she again contemplated leaving all the politics and activism behind. She flirted with the idea of applying to interior design graduate programs, but in the end, she couldn't bring herself to fill out the applications. She thought about what she had told her mother. She couldn't control the outside world or her family's fate, but she did have a say over her own life. She began going to acupuncture, eating more healthfully. She joined a local Bolivian folkloric dance troupe, where for a few hours each week she could shimmy across the floor in a fitted top, bouncy sequin-dotted skirt, her heart beating in her ears. Finally she'd found a stage where she could move people, not with politics or policy or any words at all but with the pure joy of music, movement, and pizzazz.

After months of uncertainty, in July she received an offer to work on the gubernatorial campaign of Virginia Democrat Ralph Northam. She jumped at the chance. Soon after, she got word of a scholarship opportunity to get her master's in social work at the Catholic University of America, the same school where nearly two decades before Josh Bernstein had first learned about the plight of young unaccompanied immigrants. She applied to the program and was accepted. For the first time, she was studying the theory and history behind the social justice campaigns she had spent so many years working for.

EVEN AS the administration cracked down on undocumented immigrants, Trump remained conflicted when it came to the so-called DREAMers.

"We are gonna deal with DACA with heart," he told reporters during the first month of his presidency. ". . . It's one of the most difficult subjects I have because you have these incredible kids—in many cases, not in all cases," he said, carefully qualifying his words. "DACA is a very, very difficult subject for me, I will tell you . . . it's a very, very tough subject."[6]

Then the Lone Star State stepped up again. Texas attorney general Ken Paxton and attorneys general in nine other states (Tennessee would later pull out of the group citing the "human element") threatened to sue the Trump administration if it did not end DACA.[7] It was the lawsuit Cecilia Muñoz and other former Obama advisers had feared. Paxton gave the president a deadline of September 5. And unlike under the Obama administration, it was clear Jeff Sessions's Justice Department would not stand in Texas's way. On the morning of Tuesday, September 5, as the country struggled to recover from Hurricane Harvey's wrath and prepared for the imminent arrival of Hurricane Irma, Trump met Paxton and the other attorneys general's demands. But he had Jeff Sessions make the announcement. The administration would sunset DACA in six months, and the government would no longer accept new applications. Those whose DACA permits had expired before March could apply for one last extension that would protect them through 2019—but only if they applied by October 5. It would have been a short window under normal circumstances, but it was a nearly impossible time frame for the thousands of people displaced by the storms in south Texas, Florida, and parts of Georgia.

Once more, the administration sent mixed messages. Hours after his announcement, Trump followed up with the Tweet "Congress now has 6 months to legalize DACA (something the Obama Administration was unable to do). If they can't, I will revisit this issue!" Meanwhile, DHS issued a memo encouraging DACA recipients to make arrangements to prepare to leave the country.

Please, I just need to be alone for a while, Hareth told her parents when she heard the news. She went to her room, lay down, and contemplated her future. She would get her degree in social work in 2019, and she would promptly lose her DACA protection, along with her work permit. Haziel's DACA protection would end just after the March deadline, meaning she would be undocumented even sooner.

This time Hareth was more angry than scared. She got up and began calling her contacts in the governor's campaign and at the Virginia attorney general's office, urging them to make statements. She also joined Our Revolution, the organization founded by former Sanders presidential campaign staff, including Erika Andiola, to further his progressive agenda.

Like Hareth, activists nationwide began mobilizing even as they began mourning. Within hours, celebrities came out on social media to offer support. *Captain Marvel* actor Brie Larson, Cher, Mark Ruffalo, Gigi Hadid, Kristen Bell, and Sean "Diddy" Combs spoke up, as did tech leaders such as Mark Zuckerberg. *Time* revisited the immigrants it had featured on its cover in 2012 for a follow-up story. Companies such as Apple, Uber, Amazon, and Microsoft pledged to help provide legal and other support for their employees with DACA. Univision announced a lobbying and media campaign in support of those with DACA, as well as promising to help affected employees. Telemundo also went public with support for them. The University of California, led by its president, Janet Napolitano, the former head of DHS, filed a lawsuit to block the dismantling of the program. So, too, did at least fifteen state attorneys general. Microsoft and Apple filed statements in support of the lawsuit. The National Congress of American Indians also announced support for those with DACA.[*]

Over and over the young activists echoed similar words: *We will NOT go back into the dark closet. We will NOT go back into hiding.* In late September, DHS finally reinstated Dario's DACA protection, along with his two-year work permit.

In Congress, it began to look as though a stand-alone DREAM Act might once again have a chance. In July, Senator Lindsey Graham had offered a renewed version of the bill, cosponsored by fellow Republicans Jeff Flake and Dick Durbin, which quickly gained support.

---

[*] The support came in recognition of a shared history of discrimination in the United States but also following support from United We Dream and other immigrant and Latino groups of the oil pipeline protest.

The House was trickier. To pass, the bill needed 218 votes. Most of the 194 Democrats supported the proposal, and by the fall more than three dozen Republicans had signed on to some version of the bills, while dozens more had made favorable statements about them. Representative Gutiérrez knew they could easily lose both Democrats and Republicans if too much was tacked on to the bill, but if they could stave off any poison pills, and if Speaker Paul Ryan agreed to bring the bill to the floor, they might just have the votes.

Those were big *ifs*. Gutiérrez also understood how wary the young activists were of something that once again appeared to set them against their families. During a September 8 conference call, he addressed their ambivalence. "We need to focus on the DREAMers in a laser . . . way," he insisted. "You are the most beloved, the most cared for, the most recognized. If you aren't protected, then what chance do I have to protect your parents?"

United We Dream and other groups threw their support for the bill but urged it be a "clean" version, not one linked to the border wall or weighted down with numerous other security measures.

Everything comes with a price, Hareth thought as she followed the political debates, fearing her parents could find themselves in an even more precarious position under the latest version of the DREAM Act. But despite the uncertainty, despite her fear, she was buoyed by the support from Americans around the country, "people who are safe in their homes and have nothing to worry about, people in the top of their careers, and that matters. . . . These people have opted to speak up."

In a further sign of just how much support they now enjoyed, in October 2016, the John D. and Catherine T. MacArthur Foundation awarded one of its $625,000 "genius grants" to thirty-three-year-old Cristina Jiménez Moreta, the leader of United We Dram.

ALTHOUGH MANY Americans might still distinguish the DACA-protected immigrants from their parents and even their peers, the very recognition of their claim to the American dream, the recognition of their humanity, has changed the broader conversation. It has forced an unwilling nation toward a reckoning of the roles played by millions of other undocumented immigrants living in the shadows.

Regardless of whether they finally achieve a legislative victory, these young leaders have already claimed a cultural one, redefining not only the terms of the immigration debate in the United States but also the definition of what it means to be an American.

ACKNOWLEDGMENTS

On a sweltering November day in 2009, I sat in the back pew of a church in Miami's Little Haiti neighborhood, looking for a story. Someone had clued me in that a group of immigrants were planning a New Year's Day march from Miami to Washington. It was on my beat, and I was intrigued. When I arrived, my gaze fell almost immediately on Felipe and Isabel Sousa-Rodriguez, who along with their two young friends Gaby Pacheco and Carlos Roa, commanded the room with a mix of sincerity, determination, and bravado. I wrote a story about them, and then another, and eventually another. Nearly a decade later, I am deeply grateful to Felipe and Isabel for the countless hours they have spent with me, offering up their personal experiences, contacts, and political perspectives. I am also incredibly grateful to Hareth Andrade-Ayala, Marie Deel, Dario Guerrero, and Alex Aldana, and to their families, who, over the course of the last five years, fearlessly opened their lives to me, and along with Felipe and Isabel, are the heart and soul of this book.

Tania Unzueta, Erika Andiola, Gaby Pacheco, Cristina Jiménez Moreta, Julieta Garibay, and Ju Hong are chief among those who also spent significant time sharing personal experiences, as well as their vast, collective knowledge of the history and politics that have shaped the undocumented immigrant youth movement in America.

Countless other young immigrants, advocates, officials, and academic experts, many of whom are not explicitly mentioned in this book, contributed to my understanding of the modern immigrant movement in all its complexity, and to the broader political events that have propelled it forward and pushed it back.

Michele Rudy provided many initial contacts. Josh Bernstein emailed me a spreadsheet of key players early in my reporting. Douglas Rivlin provided lengthy legislative history and background. Eunsook Lee gave perspective on the early movement in California, and more broadly on Asian American undocumented immigrant organizing. Frank Sharry and Cecilia Muñoz were among those who provided crucial analysis of Washington political milestones and negotiations. Senators Dick Durbin and Harry Reid, Representatives Jim Kolbe, Luis Gutierrez, Lincoln and Mario Díaz-Balart, and former DHS secretary Janet Napolitano were also among the officials and former officials generous with their time and recollections.

In Miami, Maria Rodriguez served as a fountain of knowledge. I took to heart her frequent reminders that no one, two, or even six individuals make a movement. Cheryl Little, Esther Olavarria, and Ira Kurzban provided key legal expertise and historical perspectives.

This book might still be but a kernel of an idea were it not for my agent, Katherine Flynn, who nurtured me through this maiden voyage. She is, in fact, an amazing editor, with a passion for big ideas and well-told stories, and a commitment to her writers that shines through everything she does. Jessica Corbett's knowledge, thoroughness, and rainbow-colored note system put me in awe of fact-checkers.

It was a thrill to work with Luke Dempsey, Sarah Haugen, and the entire team at HarperCollins. Luke understood and valued the story I sought to tell at a time when many others in the publishing world did not, and he kept me focused on telling that story amid the rising political maelstrom. From the moment I saw the cover design, I knew Harper truly got it, and I was in good hands.

I am indebted to the Nieman Foundation for Journalism at Harvard, and most of all to Curator Ann Marie Lipinski, who provided me the mental space, tools, and unwavering support to seed this project.

The entire Nieman '13 family served as cheerleaders. In particular, Jane Spencer challenged me at the Grafton Street Pub & Grill to run with my dream of writing a book. Jeneen Interlandi reviewed my initial proposal in our tiny Dunster House apartment and provided nuanced editing of the manuscript. Mary Beth Sheridan also read the manuscript, offering excellent suggestions and even joining me on a midnight reporting run outside the Supreme Court of the United States. Paige Williams remained in my head long after her 2013 narrative nonfiction class ended, prodding me to do the brutal work of "killing the lovelies."

I am also ever grateful to Isaac Lee and to all my colleagues at Fusion and Univision who supported this project and gave me time to work on it. Lynn Medford read a rough early version, and her encouragement kept me going as my deadline loomed.

From her perch in Northern California, Jessica Garrison provided a crucial read on the revised manuscript and helped snip away loose threads.

The idea for this book was born over Thanksgiving 2012, during a conversation with Benjamin Wides. Ever since I can remember, he has challenged me to think more broadly about the world and about my role in it. He and Lori Chajet were constant sounding boards throughout this process, providing love, and at times lodging, during New York reporting trips. Also in New York, Barbara Demick shared the experience and wisdom earned from writing both award-winning and inspiring books and kept me going when I feared the story was coming apart.

Much of the broader narrative in this book evolved from more than a decade of reporting on immigration, mostly at the Associated Press. The AP is truly a fraternity, and there are too many brothers and sisters for me to name. You all know who you are. I am blessed to count among my AP mentors there: Sue Cross, Michelle Morgante, John Antczak, and the indomitable Kathleen Carroll.

I wouldn't be the writer I am were it not for Louise and Burton

Wides, who instilled in me a love of language and storytelling. They have always been there unconditionally, modeling what it means to be a citizen of the world.

And, finally, to Carlos Muñoz, without whose steadfast encouragement, tough love, wisdom, and patience this book might never have been born. As Mario Benedetti wrote: "My love my accomplice and my everything . . . your eyes are my spell against a cursed day."

A NOTE ON LANGUAGE

I am often asked about the terms Hispanic or Latino. Which is more respectful? Which is more accurate when referring to the more than 57 million people living in the United States? Both pop up in this book, as does the more recent term *Latinx*, so I thought I'd take a moment to unpack these terms. I chose to refer to anyone living in the United States of Latin American heritage as "Latino." That includes people regardless of whether, as with Hareth Andrade-Ayala, a family comes from a Spanish-speaking country like Bolivia, or, as in the case of Felipe Sousa-Rodriguez, from Portuguese-speaking Brazil. *Latino* covers those living in Puerto Rico, too, who, yes, are US citizens. To perhaps state the obvious, being Latino is not simply about race. There are black Guatemalans and white Mexicans. It is about a shared geopolitical history, cultural affinities, and, frequently but not always, language.

Hispanic is a term that has traditionally been used in states like Florida, New Mexico, and Texas by people of Spanish and Latin American descent. And it is still the preferred term of the US Census. But it is a word generally associated in the United States with Spanish language and culture, and thus often viewed as excluding those with heritage from Brazil, as well as Suriname or French Guiana. For some people, it also serves as an unwelcome reminder of Spain's brutal colonization across the Western Hemisphere.

Latinx is increasingly being used in lieu of the masculine word *Latino*. I support the idea that a group of people should not automatically be defined as masculine (under traditional grammar rules, a group of twenty women would be a group of Latinas, but add one man, and it becomes a group of Latinos). And *Latinx* also provides space for those like Isabel Sousa-Rodriguez, who eschew one specific gender altogether. Yet *Latinx* is a term that is still new and unfamiliar to many readers. It wouldn't have felt accurate to use it for events that occurred around the millennium, and it would have been confusing to switch midway through the book.

Add to all these nuances the fact that some Latin American immigrants eschew any of these terms, as in the case of my husband, who identifies more specifically as a Guatemalan immigrant or a Guatemalan American. Nevertheless, *Latino* is currently the most common word used to identify this diverse and dynamic group of people, and for ease of understanding, I went with it.

NOTES

CHAPTER 1: IN THE BEGINNING

1   William Finnegan, "Letters from Bolivia: Leasing the Rain," *New Yorker*, April 8, 2002. http://www.newyorker.com/magazine/2002/04/08/leasing-the-rain.

2   Clare M. Ribando, "Bolivia: Political and Economic Developments and Relations with the United States," Congressional Research Service, January 26, 2007. http://fas.org /sgp/crs/row/RL32580.pdf.

3   Jimmy Langman, "Bolivian Natives Draw Hope from Past," *Globe and Mail* (Toronto), September 4, 2001. https://beta.theglobeandmail.com/news/world/bolivian-natives-draw-hope-from-past/article4152579/?ref=http://www.theglobeandmail.com&.

4   "Occupy La Paz," *International Worker*, August 31, 2001, 12.

5   http://www.usadiversitylottery.com/green-card-lottery-dv2002-result.php.

6   "Cal Bernstein, Obituary," *New York Times*, August 13, 2003. http://www.legacy.com /obituaries/nytimes/obituary.aspx?n=cal-bernstein&pid=1294098.

7   The Illegal Immigration Reform and Immigrant Responsibility Act (IRIRA) was signed in 1996 but went into effect in April 1997.

8   *Rocio*, produced and directed by Dario Guerrero-Meneses, Carson, CA, 2016.

9   Liz Guillen, "Undocumented Immigrant Students: A Very Brief Overview of Access to Higher Education in California," Public Advocates, Inc. https://tcla.gseis.ucla.edu /reportcard/features/5-6/ab540/pdf/UndocImmigStud.pdf.

10 Chris Fuchs, "'Original Dreamer' Still Fights for Undocumented Immigrants 16 Years After First Dream Act," NBC News, March 30, 2017. http://www.nbcnews .com/news/asian-america/original-dreamer-still-fights-undocumented-immigrants -16-years-after-first-n740491.

11 Office of Senator Richard Durbin, "Durbin Statement on the Passage of Immigration Reform Bill," press release, June 27, 2013. https://www.durbin.senate.gov/news room/press-releases/durbin-statement-on-the-passage-of-immigration-reform-bill.

12 Children's Adjustment, Relief, and Education Act of 2001, S. 1265, 107th Congress, 2001. https://www.congress.gov/bill/107th-congress/senate-bill/1265.

13 "Education Spending per Student by State," Governing, 2014. http://www.governing .com/gov-data/education-data/state-education-spending-per-pupil-data.html.

14 Judiciary Committee Report: The Development, Relief, Education for Alien Minors Act of 2001, S. 1291, 107th Congresss, 2001. https://www.congress.gov/107/bills /s1291/BILLS-107s1291rs.pdf.

15 Eric Schmitt, "Bush Aides Weigh Legalizing Status of Mexicans in U.S." *New York Times*, July 15, 2001. http://www.nytimes.com/2001/07/15/us/bush-aides-weigh-le galizing-status-of-mexicans-in-us.html?pagewanted=all&_r=0.

16 Jonathan Peterson and Edwin Chen, "Immigration Reform Bid May Expand," *Chicago Tribune*, July 27, 2001. http://articles.chicagotribune.com/2001-07-27/news /0107270256_1_immigration-reform-american-immigration-lawyers-associa tion-deserving-immigrants.

17   U.S. Department of Commerce, Bureau of the Census, "Net Undercount and Undercount Rate for U.S. and States (1990). https://www.census.gov/dmd/www/pdf/understate.pdf, Table 1. "Population by Race and Hispanic or Latino Origin, for the United States, Regions, Divisions, and States, and for Puerto Rico: 2000," April 2001. https://www.census.gov/population/www/cen2000/briefs/phc-t6/tables/tab01.pdf.

18   FBI report, October 12, 2001, requested and held by Marie Deel through the Freedom of Information Act.

19   "Timeline: How the Anthrax Terror Unfolded," NPR, February 15, 2011. http://www.npr.org/2011/02/15/93170200/timeline-how-the-anthrax-terror-unfolded.

20   "Cholera spreading throughout Central America," Agent France Press, November 13, 1991.

CHAPTER 2: SEEDS PLANTED

1   Laura Wides, "Marine Killed in War Was Orphan Immigrant," *Midland Daily News*, March 24, 2003. http://www.ourmidland.com/news/article/Marine-Killed-in-War-Was-Orphan-Immigrant-7194603.php.

2   Samuel Gompers, "American Labor and Immigration—Gompers Letters (Reprint)," *Social Contract Journal* 15, no. 4 (Summer 2005). http://www.thesocialcontract.com/artman2/publish/tsc1504/article_1339.shtml.

3   Stone and Rodriguez, "Immigrant Rights."

4   Emily Eisenberg, "DREAM Warriors: Children of Illegal Immigrants Fight for Their Rights," April 21, 2004. http://www.mtv.com/news/1486499/dream-warriors-children-of-illegal-immigrants-fight-for-their-rights/.

5   Marie Gonzalez, untitled speech, draft version from the files of Josh Bernstein, April 20, 2004.

6   "Chapter 2: Religious Switching," *The Shifting Religious Identity of Latinos in the United States*, Pew Research Center, May 7, 2014. http://www.pewforum.org/2014/05/07/the-shifting-religious-identity-of-latinos-in-the-united-states/.

7   Naderet Pourat, Steven P. Wallace, Max W. Hadler, and Nina Ponce, "Assessing Health Care Services Used by California's Undocumented Immigrant Population in 2010," *Health Affairs* 33, no. 5 (May 2014): 840–47. http://content.healthaffairs.org/content/33/5/840.abstract.

8   Shannon McConville and Helen Lee, "Emergency Department Care in California: Who Uses It and Why?," *California Counts: Population Trends and Profiles* 10, no 1 (August 2008): 1–2. http://www.ppic.org/content/pubs/cacounts/CC_808SMCC.pdf.

9   U.S. Department of Commerce, Bureau of the Census, "Overview of Race and Hispanic Origin, 2010," March 2011. https://www.census.gov/prod/cen2010/briefs/c2010br-02.pdf.

10   Margaret Sands Orchowski, *The Law That Changed the Face of America: The immigration and Nationality Act of 1965* (Lanham, MD: Rowman & Littlefield, 2015), Kindle edition, location 658, "From States to Feds."

11   "No Country for Little Kids," *The Daily Show with Jon Stewart*, September 4, 2014. http://www.cc.com/video-clips/r7zfin/the-daily-show-with-jon-stewart-no-country-for-little-kids.

12   Megan Cassidy, "Ex-Minuteman Chris Simcox Sentenced to 19.5 Years in Child Sex-Abuse Case," *Arizona Republic*, July 11, 2016. http://www.azcentral.com/story/news/local/phoenix/2016/07/11/chris-simcox-sentenced-child-sex-abuse/86948200/.

13   Garance Burke and Laura Wides-Munoz, "Immigrants Prove Big Business for Prison Companies," *U.S. News & World Report*, August 2, 2012. https://www.usnews.com/news/us/articles/2012/08/02/immigrants-prove-big-business-for-prison-companies.

14 "Marie's Dream," directed and edited by Raimondo Di Egidio, 2012. https://vimeo.com/36886730.

15 Ibid.

16 Ibid.

CHAPTER 3: A WAKE-UP CRY

1 Edward Kennedy, "Senator Kennedy Rallies for Immigration," April 10, 2006. http://www.tedkennedy.org/ownwords/event/immigration_rally.html.

2 Oscar Avila and Antonio Olivo, "A Show of Strength," *Chicago Tribune*, March 11, 2006. articles.chicagotribune.com/2006-03-11/news/0603110130_1_immigration-debate-pro-immigrant-illegal-immigrants.

3 Mark Engler and Paul Engler, "Op-Ed: The Massive Immigrant Rights Protests of 2006 are Still Changing Politics," *Los Angeles Times*, March 4, 2016. http://www.latimes.com/opinion/op-ed/la-oe-0306-engler-immigration-protests-2006-20160306-story.html.

4 "Presidential Approval Ratings—George W. Bush," Gallup, 2001–2009. http://www.gallup.com/poll/116500/presidential-approval-ratings-george-bush.aspx.

5 Border Protection, Antiterrorism, and Illegal Immigration Control Act of 2005, H.R. 4437, 109th Congress, 2005. https://www.congress.gov/bill/109th-congress/house-bill/4437.

6 Teresa Watanabe and Hector Becerra, "How DJs Put 500,000 Marchers in Motion," *Los Angeles Times*, March 28, 2006. http://articles.latimes.com/2006/mar/28/local/me-march28.

7 U.S. Department of Commerce, Bureau of the Census, "Quick Facts: Florida," 2006. https://www.census.gov/quickfacts/table/PST045216/12.

8 Jens Manuel Krogstad, "In a Shift Away from New York, More Puerto Ricans Head to Florida," Pew Research Center, Oct. 30, 2015. http://www.pewresearch.org/fact-tank/2015/10/30/in-a-shift-away-from-new-york-more-puerto-ricans-head-to-florida/.

9 "Challenges Facing First Responders in Border Communities," Hearing Before the Subcommittee on Emergency Communications, Preparedness and Response, of the Committee on Homeland Security, House of Representatives, One Hundred Tenth Congress, First Session, July 12, 2007 (statement by Luis F. Sosa, Jr., Fire Chief, Laredo, Texas). https://www.gpo.gov/fdsys/pkg/CHRG-110hhrg48930/html/CHRG110hhrg48930.htm.

10 Michael Bonner, "Ten Years Later, Effects from Immigration Roundup at Michael Bianco Remain Fresh," *South Coast Today*, March 4, 2017. http://www.southcoasttoday.com/news/20170304/ten-years-later-effects-from-immigration-roundup-at-michael-bianco-remain-fresh.

11 Dan Adams, "Six Years Later, New Bedford Raid Still Stings," *Boston Globe*, March 10, 2013. https://www.bostonglobe.com/metro/2013/03/10/immigrants-commemorate-anniversary-new-bedford-raid/Bd2uvh9zjWDhpCgPGGrNoJ/story.html.

12 JJ Hensley, Craig Harris, Jim Walsh, and Michael Kiefer, "Fun-Park Raids Test Hiring Law," *Arizona Republic*, Jun. 10, 2008. http://archive.azcentral.com/community/mesa/articles/2008/06/10/20080610golfland-CP.html#comments.

13 Paul Rubin, "Arpaio's Busts of Immigrants at Popular Valley Water Parks Are All Wet," *Phoenix New Times*, July 9, 2009. http://www.phoenixnewtimes.com/news/arpaios-busts-of-illegals-at-popular-valley-water-parks-are-all-wet-6431410.

CHAPTER 4: DARK CLOUDS LEAD TO A TRAIL

1 United States Department of Labor, Bureau of Labor Statistics, "The Recession of 2007–2009," February 2012. https://www.bls.gov/spotlight/2012/recession/.

2   Chris McGreal, "Anti-Obama 'Birther Movement' Gathers Steam," *The Guardian,* July 28, 2009. http://www.theguardian.com/world/2009/jul/28/birther-movement-obama-citizenship.

3   Kerry Eleveld, "When Birther Queen Orly Taitz Needed an Anti-immigrant Judge, She Chose Judge Andrew Hanen," Daily Kos, February 25, 2015. http://www.dailykos.com/story/2015/2/25/1366778/-When-birther-queen-Orly-Taitz-needed-an-anti-immigrant-judge-she-chose-Judge-Andrew-Hanen.

4   Ibid.

5   Lukas Pleva, "No Big Push in First Year," PolitiFact, August 13, 2010. http://www.politifact.com/truth-o-meter/promises/obameter/promise/525/introduce-comprehensive-immigration-bill-first-yea/.

6   Megan O'Matz and John Maines, "Asylum Judge Known as Tough," *Sun-Sentinel,* January 7, 2013. http://articles.sun-sentinel.com/2013-01-07/news/fl-judge-immigration-jail-20130105_1_immigration-judges-immigration-review-immigration-laws.

7   "Letters to Barack Obama: Gaby Pacheco," DREAM Now Series: September 13, 2010. http://www.citizenorange.com/orange/2010/09/dream-now-letters-to-barack-ob-8.html.

8   "Maria Gabriela "Gaby" Pacheco," TheDream.US. http://www.thedream.us/about-us/staff/maria-gaby-pacheco/.

9   Casey Woods and Noah Bierman, "Family of Young Activist May Be Deported," *Miami Herald,* July 28, 2006. https://www.amren.com/news/2006/07/family_of_young/ From Laura: Also from Nexis, did not find original URL from Miami Herald, but did find story as reposted on another site with credit to Herald.

10   Laura Wides-Munoz, "Illegal Immigrants Argue Selective Deportation Before U.S. Board," *Florida Times-Union,* April 8, 2008. http://jacksonville.com/apnews/stories/040808/D8VTQG900.shtml.

11   Ward Sinclair and Herbert Denton, "Haitians Win Round on U.S. Asylum," *Washington Post,* July 3, 1980. https://www.washingtonpost.com/archive/politics/1980/07/03/haitians-win-round-on-us-asylum/d39e8741-a554-4b71-9819-27ded809746e/?utm_term=.858fc57eac87.

12   *Jean v. Nelson,* 472 U.S. 846, 1985. http://caselaw.findlaw.com/us-supreme-court/472/846.html.

13   Irwin P. Stotzky, "Ira J. Kurzban: Lawyer as Hero," *University of Miami Inter-American Law Review* 635 (1992): 637–41. http://repository.law.miami.edu/cgi/viewcontent.cgi?article=1441&context=umialr.

14   Abby Goodnough, "All in the Family, Brothers Wage War on Uncle Fidel," *New York Times,* March 8, 2006. http://www.nytimes.com/2006/03/08/national/08miami.html.

15   Laura Wides-Munoz, "Florida's New Speaker Brings a Passion for Politics," *St. Augustine Record,* November 21, 2006. http://staugustine.com/stories/112106/news_4226362.shtml#.Vsro8pMrKT8.

CHAPTER 5: A TRAIL OF TEARS AND DREAMS

1   Laura Wides-Munoz, "Youth Trek from Miami to DC for Immigrant Rights," *Newsday,* January 1, 2010. http://www.newsday.com/news/nation/youth-trek-from-miami-to-dc-for-immigrant-rights-1.1679772.

2   U.S. Department of the Interior, National Park Service, "Freedom Tower, Miami, Florida." https://www.nps.gov/nr/travel/american_latino_heritage/Freedom_Tower.html.

3   David Brooks, "Inicia marcha de estudiantes migrantes para la dignidad de esa comunidad en Estados Unidos," *La Jornada,* January 2, 2010, p. 19. http://www.jornada.unam.mx/2010/01/02/index.php?section=mundo&article=019n1mun.

4   United Farm Workers, "UFW Chronology." http://ufw.org/research/history/ufw
     -chronology/.

5   Felipe Matos, "I Think I'm Pregnant . . . ," Trail of Dreams, January 31, 2010. http://
     trail2010.org/blog/2010/jan/31/i-think-im-pregnant/.

6   Felipe Matos, "Moving Forward, Across, and Ahead," Trail of Dreams, January 18,
     2010. https://trailofdreams2010.wordpress.com/2010/01/page2/.

7   Taylor Branch, *Pillar of Fire: America in the King Years, 1963–1965* (New York: Simon
     & Schuster, 1999), 335.

8   Juan Rodriguez, "An Unjust Law Is No Law at All—St. Augustine," Trail of Dreams,
     January 18, 2010. http://trail2010.org/blog/2010/jan/18/unjust-law-no-law-all-st-au
     gustine/.

9   Mark Potok, "Led by the Antigovernment 'Patriot' Movement, the American Radi-
     cal Right Is Continuing to Expand Rapidly," *Intelligence Report*, February 23, 2011.
     https://www.splcenter.org/fighting-hate/intelligence-report/2011/year-hate-extrem
     ism-2010.

10   Juan Rodriguez, "Contradictions," Trail of Dreams, February 20, 2010. http://
     trail2010.org/blog/2010/feb/20/contradictions/.

11   Jacqueline Stevens, "America's Secret ICE Castles," *The Nation*, December 16, 2009.
     https://www.thenation.com/article/americas-secret-ice-castles/.

12   "Trail of Dreams Cary," April 8, 2010. https://www.youtube.com/watch?v=RfAzpt1xGP0.

13   Felipe Vargas "profe," "Testimonio 1: The Way of the DREAMURI," Trail of Dreams,
     January 29, 2010. http://trail2010.org/blog/2010/jan/29/DREAMURI/.

14   Felipe Matos, "Innocent Voices," Trail of Dreams, February 15, 2010. http://trail2010
     .org/blog/2010/feb/15/innocent-voices/.

15   Peter Wallsten, "President Obama Bristles When He Is the Target of Activist Tactics
     He Once Used," *Washington Post*, June 10, 2012. https://www.washingtonpost.com
     /politics/president-obama-bristles-when-he-is-the-target-of-activist-tactics-he-once-
     used/2012/06/09/gJQAoi7JRV_story.html?utm_term=.9f481139109f.

16   Ali Noorani, *There Goes the Neighborhood: How Communities Overcome Prejudice and
     Meet the Challenge of Immigration* (New York: Prometheus Books, 2016), 29.

17   Hillsborough County, Florida, police records.

18   Enrique Flor, "Detienen a estudiante en Tri-Rail," *Sun-Sentinal*, March 25, 2010. http://
     articles.sun-sentinel.com/2010-03-25/noticias/fl-elcomo327trirail-20100325_1_pa
     trulla-fronteriza-agentes-el-contrabando.

19   Felipe Matos, "Thoughts Running Through My Mind," Trail of Dreams, April 27, 2010.
     http://www.trail2010.org/blog/2010/apr/7/thoughts-running-through-my-mind/.

20   Isabel Rodriguez, personal emails. April 2010.

CHAPTER 6: ARRIVAL AND THE AFTERGLOW

1   Thomas Ferraro and Tim Gaynor, "Democrats Unveil Immigration Reform Plan,"
     Reuters, April 28, 2010. http://www.reuters.com/article/us-immigration-usa-ari
     zona/democrats-unveil-immigration-reform-plan-idUSTRE63R5HP20100429.

2   "Graham move imperils Obama agenda," *CNN Politics*, April 24, 2010. http://politi
     calticker.blogs.cnn.com/2010/04/24/graham-move-imperils-obama-push-for-immi
     gration-reform-climate-change/

3   Rafael Prieto, "Trail of DREAMs Walkers Arrive in Washington, D.C. to Deliver
     Message to President Obama," YouTube, April 28, 2010. https://www.youtube.com
     /watch?v=CQzOXSBVxD0.

4   Darren Samuelsohn, "Immigration May Be on Sidelines for a While—Obama," E&E
    News, April 29, 2010. https://www.eenews.net/stories/90368.

5   David Montgomery, "Trail of Dreams Students Walk 1,500 miles to Bring Immigra-
    tion Message to Washington," *Washington Post*, May 1, 2010. http://www.washington-
    post.com/wp-dyn/content/article/2010/04/30/AR2010043001384.html.

6   Marie Gonzalez blog, July 6, 2009. http://mariengonzalez.blogspot.com/2009/07/.

7   Julia Preston, "Immigration Advocates Rally for Change," *New York Times*, May 1,
    2010. http://www.nytimes.com/2010/05/02/us/02immig.html?_r=0.

8   Carlos QC, "Immigration Rally: Rep Luis Gutierrez Arrested at White House / May
    2010," YouTube. https://www.youtube.com/watch?v=AROZcIwoqio, May 2, 2010.

9   Anthony Cave, "Did John McCain Support the Dream Act, Then Vote Against It?,"
    PolitiFact Arizona, May 24, 2016. http://www.politifact.com/arizona/statements/2016/
    may/24/ann-kirkpatrick/did-john-mccain-support-dream-act-then-vote-agains/.

10 Julia Preston, "Illegal Immigrant Students Protest at McCain Office," *New York
    Times*, May 17, 2010. http://www.nytimes.com/2010/05/18/us/18dream.html.

11 thedreamiscoming, "Los McCain Cinco," YouTube, May 18, 2010. https://www.you-
    tube.com/watch?v=9WX2G3WooE8.

12 Jordan Fabian, "Gay Rights Protesters Interrupt Obama Speech at Fundraiser,"
    The Hill, April 20, 2010. http://thehill.com/blogs/blog-briefing-room/news/93193
    -obama-speech-interrupted-by-gay-rights-protesters.

13 Steven Portnoy and Sunlen Miller, "'Don't Ask, Don't Tell' Protesters Chain Them-
    selves to White House Fence," ABC News, March 18, 2010. http://abcnews.go.com
    /Politics/protestors-charged-chaining-front-white-house/story?id=10138564.

14 "Rep. Gutierrez talking down to youth and DREAM Act—Will CHC support
    DREAM?," youtoube video, posted by Mohammad Abdollahi, July 24, 2010. https://
    www.youtube.com/watch?v=GzW2IamxXlg.

15 Gutiérrez would eventually come around to supporting the DREAM Act. And in an
    ironic twist, half a decade later, students would come back to protest in his office
    because they felt he was too focused on the limited reach of the DREAM Act rather
    than on comprehensive reform. But some on his staff remained bitter about the sit-in
    and the leaked phone call. They saw it as a cheap attempt to shame one of the few law-
    makers who at the time was dedicated to helping and willing to engage with students.

16 Krissah Thompson, "Immigrant Rights Groups Adjust Focus to Passage of AgJobs,
    Dream Act," *Washington Post*, July 27, 2010. http://www.washingtonpost.com/wp-
    dyn/content/article/2010/07/27/AR2010072704307.html.

17 U.S. Census, "Hispanic Population, 2010," 2010 Census Briefs. https://www.census
    .gov/prod/cen2010/briefs/c2010br-04.pdf.

18 Roberto G. Gonzalez, "Wasted Talent and Broken Dreams: The Lost Potential of Un-
    documented Students," Immigration Policy Center, 2008. http://www.fosterglobal
    .com/policy_papers/WastedTalentAndBrokenDreams.pdf.

19 Vanessa Ho, "Dropout Rates Highest Among Mexican Immigrants, Study Says," *Se-
    attle Post-Intelligencer*, February 4, 2002. http://www.seattlepi.com/national/article
    /Dropout-rates-highest-among-Mexican-immigrants-1079333.php.

CHAPTER 7: A MARRIAGE, A DEATH, AND A VOTE

1   Marie Gonzalez, blog post, July 23, 2009. http://mariengonzalez.blogspot.com/2009
    /07/.

2   "As November Approaches," *Marie Gonzalez blog*, October 26, 2010 http://marien
    gonzalez.blogspot.com/2010/

3   Email correspondence among Marie Gonzalez, USCIS, and her attorneys. October 19 through October 28, 2010.

4   Cristina Jiménez and Peter Dreier, "How Undocumented Youth Moved the Immigrant Rights Movement," November 2015. http://www.peterdreier.com/wp-content /uploads/2016/01/Gettysburg-DREAM-case-Final-Nov-2015-clean.pdf, p. 8.

5   Carlos Saavedra, Facebook, December 17, 2010.

6   United States Senate, Roll Call Vote 111th Congress, Second Session, Vote 278, December 18, 2010. https://www.senate.gov/legislative/LIS/roll_call_lists/roll_call _vote_cfm.cfm?congress=111&session=2&vote=00278.

7   C-SPAN, December 18, 2010. https://www.c-span.org/video/?297168-4/senate-de bate-dont-ask-dont-tell-dream-act.

8   Ibid.

9   Ibid.

10   Ibid.

11   Ibid.

12   Elspeth Reeve, "What Happens When Mom Gets Stuck on Capitol Hill for Christmas," *The Atlantic*, December 5, 2012. https://www.theatlantic.com/politics/archive/2012/12 /when-mom-gets-stuck-capitol-hill-christmas/320790/.

13   Peter Wallsten, "President Obama Bristles When He Is the Target of Activist Tactics He Once Used," *Washington Post*, June 10, 2012. Wallsten described aides' recollection of Obama consoling staff who had sought to help the DREAMers. The president pointed to the "Don't ask, don't tell" vote, telling them "This is a journey, and we will get there," according to Wallsten.

CHAPTER 8: NEW PATHS

1   A 2014 Pew Research study found the average millennial college graduate making $46,032 per top graph in source cited in 2009, compared to $28,000 for a high school–only grad, a gap nearly double the difference in 1979. Richard Fry, "For Millennials, a Bachelor's Degree Continues to Pay Off, but a Master's Earns Even More," Pew Research Center, February 28, 2014. http://www.pewresearch.org /fact-tank/2014/02/28/for-millennials-a-bachelors-degree-continues-to-pay-off-but-a-masters-earns-even-more/.

2   Brendan O'Boyle, "Peru's LGBTQ Community Frustrated By Violence, Presidential Election," *Americas Quarterly*, March 3, 2016. http://www.americasquarterly.org /content/perus-lgbt-community-seeks-voice-presidential-election.

3   Dan Littauer, "Peru Gay Man Tortured, Dismembered and Burned to Death," Huffington Post, June 12, 2013. http://www.huffingtonpost.co.uk/dan-littauer/peru-gay-man-tortured-dis_b_4399107.html.

4   Jose Antonio Vargas, "My Life as an Undocumented Immigrant," *New York Times Magazine*, June 22, 2011. http://www.nytimes.com/2011/06/26/magazine/my-life-as-an -undocumented-immigrant.html.

5   U.S. Customs and Immigration Enforcement, "Secure Communities Monthly Statistics Through September 2012." https://www.ice.gov/doclib/foia/sc-stats/nation wide_interop_stats-fy2012.pdf

6   Burke and Wides-Munoz, "Immigrants Prove Big Business for Prison Companies."

7   Kevin Sieff, "Immigrant Detention Center in Va. Would Be Mid-Atlantic's Largest," *Washington Post*, July 18, 2010. http://www.washingtonpost.com/wp-dyn/content /article/2010/07/17/AR2010071701416.html.

8   Peter Galuszka, "Farmville's Gravy Train May Be Slowing," *Washington Post*, May 1, 2015.

https://www.washingtonpost.com/opinions/farmvilles-gravy-train-may-be-slow ing/2015/05/01/6ee059b6-edea-11e4-8abc-d6aa3bad79dd_story.html?utm _term=.dd3e23fcbf10.

9   ICE Office of Detention Oversight "Compliance Inspection for the Immigration Centers of America, Farmville, Farmville, Virginia," July 2015, p. 6. https://www.docu mentcloud.org/documents/2840181-2015FarmvilleVA.html.

10   produced by the American Civil Liberties Union, Detention Watch Network, and National Immigrant Justice Center, "Fatal Neglect: How ICE Ignores Deaths in Detention," February 2016. https://www.detentionwatchnetwork.org/sites/default/files /reports/Fatal%20Neglect%20ACLU-DWN-NIJC.pdf.

11   ICE Office of Detention Oversight Compliance Inspection, "Enforcement and Removal Operations Washington Field Office Immigration Centers of America-Farmville, Farmville, Virginia, https://www.documentcloud.org/documents/2644423-Farmville.html.

12   Ibid.

13   David Sherfinski, "Illegal Immigrant Pleads Guilty in Killing of Nun in Va.," *Washington Times*, October 31, 2011. http://www.washingtontimes.com/news/2011/oct/31 /trial-begins-illegal-immigrant-who-killed-nun-fata/.

CHAPTER 9: MOUNTING PRESSURE

1   "Secure Communities and ICE Deportation: A Failed Program?" TRAC Reports, April 8, 2014. http://trac.syr.edu/immigration/reports/349/.

2   U.S. Department of Justice, Bureau of Justice Statistics, "Immigration Offenders in the Federal Justice System, 2010," October 22, 2013. https://www.bjs.gov/content /pub/pdf/iofjs10.pdf, 17.

3   Laura Wides-Munoz, "AP Enterprise: States' Immigration Efforts Fizzle," *Victoria Advocate*, May 23, 2011. https://www.victoriaadvocate.com/news/2011/may/23 /bc-us-immigration-states/.

4   April Carter, Marie Lawrence, and Ann Morse, "2011 Immigration-Related Laws, Bills and Resolutions in the States: Jan. 1–March 31, 2011," National Conference of State Legislatures. http://www.ncsl.org/research/immigration/immigration-laws-and-bills-spring-2011.aspx.

5   "A Declaration of Five Principles to Guide Utah's Immigration Discussion," The Utah Compact, November 11, 2010. https://the-utah-compact.com/.

6   Devin Dwyer, "Kansas State Rep. Under Fire for Illegal Immigrant, Feral Hog Comparison," ABC News, March 25, 2011. http://abcnews.go.com/Politics/kan sas-rep-fire-comparing-illegal-immigrants-feral-hogs/story?id=13223497.

7   John Morton, Director, "Civil Immigration Enforcement: Priorities for the Apprehension, Detention, and Removal of Aliens," memorandum, March 2, 2011. https://www .ice.gov/doclib/news/releases/2011/110302washingtondc.pdf.

8   John Morton, Director, "Exercising Prosecutorial Discretion Consistent with the Civil Immigration Enforcement Priorities of the Agency for the Apprehension, Detention, and Removal of Aliens," memorandum, June 17, 2011. https://www.ice.gov /doclib/secure-communities/pdf/prosecutorial-discretion-memo.pdf.

9   Morton, "Civil Immigration Enforcement."

10   UnidosUS, "President Barack Obama Keynote Address at 2011 NCLR Annual Conference," July 29, 2011. https://www.youtube.com/watch?v=-udcY6ubfFw.

11   Ibid.

12   Alexandra Gratereaux, "Meet the DREAM Act Activist Who Cornered Mitt Romney at NYC Fundraiser," Fox News, January 18, 2012. http://www.foxnews.com/poli tics/2012/01/18/defying-mitt-romney-lucy-allain-fights-for-dreamers.html.

13   Laura Wides-Munoz, "Rubio: GOP Must Make Immigration a Priority," Beverly Hills Immigration Law, January 30, 2012. https://beverlyhillsimmigrationlaw.blogspot.com/2012/01/rubio-gop-must-make-immigration.html.

14   Ibid.

15   "impreMedia—Latino Decisions Tracking Poll Results—December 2011." http://www.latinodecisions.com/files/3013/4697/3823/Dec_2011_Tracking.pdf.

16   "American Dreamers," directed by Jenniffer Castillo and Saray Deiseil, Indigo Productions, 2015. https://www.facebook.com/AmericanDREAMersfilm.

17   Alex Aldana, "CAD Walk 2012: From the Desert of Nevada, Demanding Justice for Trayvon Martin," America's Voice blog, April 9, 2012. http://americasvoice.org/blog/cad-walk-2012-from-the-desert-of-nevada-demanding-justice-for-trayvon/.

18   U.S. Census, "The Hispanic Population: 2010," May 2011. https://www.census.gov/prod/cen2010/briefs/c2010br-04.pdf.

19   "American Dreamers," directed by Jenniffer Castillo and Saray Deiseil.

20   Barack Obama, "Remarks by the President on Immigration," The White House, Office of the Press Secretary, June 15, 2012. https://obamawhitehouse.archives.gov/the-press-office/2012/06/15/remarks-president-immigration.

21   Muzaffar Chishti and Faye Hipsman, "Key Factors, Unresolved Issues in New Deferred Action Program for Immigrant Youth Will Determine Its Success," Migration Policy Institute, August 16, 2012. http://www.migrationpolicy.org/article/key-factors-unresolved-issues-new-deferred-action-program-immigrant-youth-will-determine-its.

22   Obama, "Remarks by the President on Immigration."

23   Laura Wides-Munoz and Paul Wiseman, "Backlash Stirs Against Foreign Worker Visas," USA Today, July 6, 2014. https://www.usatoday.com/story/money/business/2014/07/06/backlash-stirs-in-us-against-foreign-worker-visas/12266783/.

CHAPTER 10: AFTER DACA
1   "About the 'No Papers, No Fear' Ride for Justice." http://nopapersnofear.org/.

2   Seth Motel and Eileen Patten, "Latinos in the 2012 Election: New Mexico," Pew Research Center, October 1, 2012. http://www.pewhispanic.org/2012/10/01/latinos-in-the-2012-election-new-mexico/.

3   Emily Deruy, "DREAMer Erika Andiola Will Work for Arizona Congresswoman," ABC News, January 16, 2013. http://abcnews.go.com/ABC_Univision/Politics/dreamer-erika-andiola-work-arizona-congresswoman/story?id=18228718.

4   Dan Nakaso, "Laurene Powell Jobs, Steve Jobs' Wife, Gives First Interview Since Husband's Death," Huffington Post, April 12, 2013. http://www.huffingtonpost.com/2013/04/12/laurene-powell-jobs_n_3071822.html.

5   AFL-CIO, "2013 Deliberated Resolutions." https://aflcio.org/about/leadership/conventions/resolutions-2013.

6   Frank Newport, "Americans Widely Support Immigration Reform Proposals," Gallup News, February 5, 2013. http://www.gallup.com/poll/160307/americans-widely-support-immigration-reform-proposals.aspx.

CHAPTER 11: THE NEXT BATTLE
1   Border Security, Economic Opportunity, and Immigration Modernization Act, S. 744, 113th Congress, 2013. https://www.congress.gov/bill/113th-congress/senate-bill/744/actions.

2   Alicia A. Caldwell, "Asylum Requests from Immigrants on the Rise in US" (corrected version), San Diego Union-Tribune, July 17, 2013. http://www.sandiegouniontribune.com/sdut-correction-asylum-requests-story-2013jul17-story.html.

3   89+ About. http://www.89plus.com/about/.

4   Elizabeth Llorente, "They're Back, en Masse: Dozens of 'Dreamers' Turn Themselves in at California Border," FOX News, March 10, 2014. http://www.foxnews.com/pol itics/2014/03/10/to-protest-us-immigration-laws-more-than-150-people-in-mexico-plan-to-approach.html.

5   "Judge-by-Judge Asylum Decisions in Immigration Courts, FY2011–2016," Trans-actional Records Access Clearinghouse, 2016. http://trac.syr.edu/immigration/re ports/447/include/denialrates.html.

6   Llorente, "They're Back, en Masse."

7   Cristina Constantini and Jorge Rivas, "Deported Dreamers Fleeing Violence Fight to Come Home," Splinter, March 10, 2014. http://fusion.net/deported-dreamers-flee ing-violence-fight-to-come-home-1793841002.

8   Kate Morrissey, "ACLU: End Private Contract for Otay Mesa Immigrant Detention," *San Diego Union-Tribune*, December 2, 2016. http://www.sandiegouniontribune .com/news/immigration/sd-me-aclu-ice-20161202-story.html.

9   *Rocio*, produced and directed by Dario Guerrero-Meneses, Carson, CA, 2016.

10 Ibid.

CHAPTER 12: NEW ALLIANCES

1   U.S. Department of Justice, Civil Rights Division, "Investigation of the Ferguson Police Department," March 4, 2015. http://apps.washingtonpost.com/g/documents /national/department-of-justice-report-on-the-ferguson-mo-police-department/1435/.

2   Barack Obama, "Remarks by the President on Immigration—Chicago, IL," White House Office of the Press Secretary, November 25, 2014. https://obamawhitehouse .archives.gov/the-press-office/2014/11/25/remarks-president-immigration-chicago-il.

3   Jean Chung, "Felony Disenfranchisement: A Primer," The Sentencing Project, Jan-uary 2017. www.sentencingproject.org/wp-content/uploads/2015/08/Felony-Disen franchisement-Primer.pdf.

4   *Mendez v. Westminster School District*, 64 F.Supp. 544 (S.D. Cal. 1946), *aff'd*, 161 F. 2d 774 (9th Cir., 1947). See *"Mendez v. Westminster* Case," October 3, 2007. http:// mendezwestminstercase.blogspot.com/2007/08/mendez-v-westminster-case.html.

5   *Mendez v. Westminster School District* was nearly forgotten by the broader public until Obama awarded the lead plaintiff's daughter the Presidential Medal of Freedom in 2011. Nicholas Dauphine, "Hispanics Are Forgotten in Civil Rights History," *Edu-cation Week*, May 13, 2014. http://www.edweek.org/ew/articles/2014/05/14/31dau phine.h33.html.

6   Laura Wides-Munoz and Peter Orsi, "Visa Granted to Harvard Junior Who Took Dying Mother to Mexico," *Boston Globe*, October 14, 2014. https://www.bostonglobe .com/news/nation/2014/10/14/harvard-junior-took-dying-mom-mexico-now-stuck /TDpoYfoHUat29KyToGpU6J/story.html.

7   Dan Roberts, "Two Families Watched Obama's Immigration Speech Together—but the President's Plan Only Helps One," *The Guardian*, November 21, 2014. https://www .theguardian.com/us-news/2014/nov/21/two-families-obama-immigration-speech.

8   Mike Blake, "U.S. Politics Takes Center Stage at Latin Grammys," Reuters, Novem-ber 20, 2014. http://www.reuters.com/article/us-music-latingrammys/u-s-politics-takes-center-stage-at-latin-grammys-idUSKCN0J506Q20141121.

9   Jeffrey S. Passel and D'Vera Cohn, "Chapter 1: State Unauthorized Immigrant Populations," Pew Research Center, November 18, 2014. http://www.pewhispanic .org/2014/11/18/chapter-1-state-unauthorized-immigrant-populations/.

10   Barack Obama, "President Obama Remarks in Nevada on Immigration," C-SPAN, November 21, 2014. https://www.c-span.org/video/?322888-1/president-obama-re marks-nevada-immigration.

11   "Obama Addresses Hecklers During Chicago Speech," NBC Chicago, November 25, 2014. http://www.nbcchicago.com/news/local/Obama-Addresses-Hecklers-During -Chicago-Speech-283908031.html.

12   Obama, "President Obama Remarks in Nevada on Immigration," C-Span, November 24, 2014, 00:06:52. https://www.c-span.org/video/?322888-1/president-obama-re marks-nevada-immigration.

13   Michael Kagan, "Immigration Law's Looming Fourth Amendment Problem," The Georgetown Law Journal, (Vol. 104:125) 2015, p. 126. http://scholars.law.unlv.edu /cgi/viewcontent.cgi?article=1936&context=facpub.

14   "Immigration Detainers Legal Update," Immigrant Legal Resource Center, July 2017. https://www.ilrc.org/sites/default/files/resources/ice_detainer_cases_july_2017.pdf.

15   Ibid.

16   Eric Gibble, "Bernie Sanders' Immigration Policy Track Record," *American Immigration Council:Immigration Impact*, May 1, 2015. http://immigrationimpact .com/2015/05/01/bernie-sanders-immigration-policy-track-record/

17   Ken Thomas, "Hillary Clinton Backs Obama Immigration Move," *Lexington Herald-Leader*, November 21, 2014. http://www.kentucky.com/news/politics-govern ment/article44525238.html.

18   Michael McCaul, "McCaul: President's Actions Tonight Threaten Our Democracy," press release, November 20, 2014. https://mccaul.house.gov/media-center/press-re leases/mccaul-president-s-actions-tonight-threaten-our-democracy.

19   Lindsey Graham, "Graham Opposes Obama's Executive Action on Immigration," press release, November 21, 2014. https://www.lgraham.senate.gov/public/index .cfm/press-releases?ID=170F274A-B8E6-59FA-9726-AC42F5FEC90D.

20   Molly Hennessy-Fiske, "What Happened to the President's Immigration Programs?," *Los Angeles Times*, October 19, 2015. http://www.latimes.com/nation/nationnow /la-na-nn-immigration-executive-action-20151019-story.html.

21   Mark Noferi, "When Reagan and GHW Bush Took Bold Executive Action on Immigration," The Hill, October 2, 2014. http://thehill.com/blogs/congress-blog/foreign-policy/219463-when-reagan-and-ghw-bush-took-bold-executive-action-on.

22   U.S. Citizenship and Immigration Services, "Interim Relief for Certain Foreign Academic Students Adversely Affected by Hurricane Katrina," press release, November 25, 2005. https://www.uscis.gov/sites/default/files/USCIS/Humanitarian/Special%20Situa tions/Previous%20Special%20Situations%20By%20Topic/faq-interim-student-re lief-hurricane-katrina.pdf.

23   Judge Andrew Hanen, opinion, *State of Texas, et al. v. United States of America, et al.*, 87 F. 3d. 733, 743 (5th Cir., 2015). https://www.documentcloud.org/documents/1668197 -hanen-opinion.html, 41.

24   Mila Koumpilova, "Hopes Fade for Would-Be Citizens: A Year After Obama's Action on Immigration, Millions Still in Limbo," *Star Tribune*, November 28, 2015. https:// www.highbeam.com/doc/1G1-436071392.html.

25   "Full Text: Donald Trump Announces a Presidential Bid," *Washington Post*, June 16, 2015. https://www.washingtonpost.com/news/post-politics/wp/2015/06/16/full-text-donald-trump-announces-a-presidential-bid/?utm_term=.62ec5014974c

26   Greg Sargent, "Opinion: Is This a 'Muslim Ban'? Look at the History—and at Trump's Own Words," *Washington Post*, January 31, 2017. https://www.washingtonpost.com

/blogs/plum-line/wp/2017/01/31/is-this-a-muslim-ban-look-at-the-history-and-at-trumps-own-words/?utm_term=.a7e4a86c066f.

27 Matt Vespa, "Clinton 2014: Children of Illegal Immigrants Have to Go Back as Soon as Possible," September 9, 2017. https://townhall.com/tipsheet/matt vespa/2017/09/09/clinton-2014-children-of-illegal-aliens-have-to-go-back-as-soon-as-possible-n2379046.

28 Jeh Johnson, "Statement by Secretary Jeh C. Johnson on Southwest Border Security," DHS Press Office, January 4, 2016. https://www.dhs.gov/news/2016/01/04/state ment-secretary-jeh-c-johnson-southwest-border-security.

CHAPTER 13: GRADUATION

1 Anna Bank, "The Fall and Rise of Trinity Washington University," *Georgetown Voice*, March 27, 2008. http://georgetownvoice.com/2008/03/27/the-fall-and-rise-of-trini ty-washington-university/.

2 Jena Johnson, "Trump Calls for 'Total and Complete Shutdown of Muslims Entering the United States,'" *Washington Post*, December 7, 2015. https://www.washington-post.com/news/post-politics/wp/2015/12/07/donald-trump-calls-for-total-and-com plete-shutdown-of-muslims-entering-the-united-states/?utm_term=.e8048497d7ca.

3 NAACP, "Criminal Justice Fact Sheet," 2017. http://www.naacp.org/criminal-justice -fact-sheet/.

4 https://mijente.net/.

CHAPTER 14: HERE TO STAY

1 Tina Nguyen, "Trump Contradicts D.H.S., Says Expanded Deportations Are a 'Mil-itary Operation' Now," *Vanity Fair*, February 23, 2017. http://www.vanityfair.com /news/2017/02/trump-deportation-military-operation.

2 Maria Sacchetti, "Trump Is Deporting Fewer Immigrants than Obama, Including Criminals," *Washington Post*, August 10, 2017. https://www.washingtonpost.com /local/immigration/trump-is-deporting-fewer-immigrants-than-obama-includ ing-criminals/2017/08/10/d8fa72e4-7e1d-11e7-9d08-b79f191668ed_story.html ?utm_term=.550684736b85.

3 Tal Kopan, "The next DACA? Trump administration turns to another class of im-migrants," CNN, September 11, 2017. http://www.cnn.com/2017/09/11/politics /next-daca-tps-temporary-protected-status/index.html.

4 Yamiche Alcindor, "Liberal Activists Join Forces Against a Common Foe: Trump," *New York Times*, February 14, 2017. https://www.nytimes.com/2017/02/14/us/poli tics/protesters-resist-trump.html?_r=1.

5 "United We Dream Stands in Loving Solidarity with the Protectors of Our Water & Land," United We Dream press release, January 24, 2017. https://unitedwedream .org/press-releases/united-we-dream-stands-in-loving-solidarity-with-the-protec tors-of-our-water-land/.

6 Nolan D. McCaskill, "Trump Says He Will Treat Dreamers 'with Heart,'" Politico, February 16, 2017. http://www.politico.com/story/2017/02/trump-press-conference -dreamers-heart-235103.

7 Adam Tamburin, "In Reversal, Tennessee AG Pulls Support from Effort to End DACA," *Tennessean*, September 1, 2017. http://www.tennessean.com/story/news/pol itics/2017/09/01/reversal-tennessee-ag-pulls-support-effort-end-daca/626221001/.

INDEX

Page numbers of photographs appear in italics.

ABOUT THE AUTHOR

Laura Wides-Muñoz is Vice President for Special Projects & Editorial Strategy at Fusion Network, where she serves as a senior editor for the digital and TV investigative teams. She was a staff writer at the Associated Press for more than a decade, has reported from Cuba and throughout Central America, and has written for the *Miami Herald* and the *Los Angeles Times*, among other outlets. She has won the Associated Press Managing Editors Award and multiple Society of Professional Journalists Awards. She conceived of this book during a 2013 Harvard University Nieman Foundation for Journalism fellowship. She lives in Miami with her family.